THE WADSWORTH ENGLISH FOR ACADEMIC PURPOSES SERIES

Series Editors:
Charles H. Blatchford, Fair Oaks, California
Jerry L. Messec, Florida State University

Academically Speaking
Janet Kayfetz, University of California, Santa Barbara
Randy Stice, Nova University, Florida

Academic Writing Workshop
Sarah Benesch, College of Staten Island, CUNY
Mia Rakijas, New York City, New York
Betsy Rorschach, City College, CUNY

Academic Writing Workshop II
Sarah Benesch, College of Staten Island, CUNY
Betsy Rorschach, City College, CUNY

English on Campus: A Listening Sampler
Sharon Bode, Bradenton, Florida
Charles G. Whitley, Chaminade University
Gary James, Honolulu Community College

Overheard and Understood
Sharon Bode, Bradenton, Florida
Sandra Moulding Lee, Linfield College

Improving the Grammar of Written English: The Handbook
Patricia Byrd, Georgia State University
Beverly Benson, DeKalb College

Improving the Grammar of Written English: The Editing Process
Beverly Benson, DeKalb College
Patricia Byrd, Georgia State University

Understanding Conversations
Catherine Tansey, Tokyo, Japan
Charles H. Blatchford, Fair Oaks, California

Improving the Grammar of Written English: The Handbook

Patricia Byrd
Georgia State University

Beverly Benson
DeKalb College

Heinle & Heinle Publishers
A Division of Wadsworth, Inc.
Boston, Massachusetts 02116

Series Editors: Charles H. Blatchford and Jerry L. Messec
English/ESL Editor: Angela Gantner
Production Editor: Jerilyn Emori
Cover and Interior Designer: Andrew H. Ogus
Print Buyer: Randy Hurst
Permissions Editor: Peggy Meehan
Copy Editor: Jennifer Gordon
Compositor: Graphic Typesetting Service
Cover: A detail of a "Sunshine and Shadow" quilt, courtesy of the Esprit Collection, San Francisco/Sharon Risedorph, photographer

Printed in the United States of America   48

3 4 5 6 7 8 9 10—93 92 91

Library of Congress Cataloging-in-Publication Data
Byrd, Patricia.
    Improving the grammar of written English : the handbook / Patricia Byrd, Beverly Benson.
        p.   cm.
    Includes index.
    ISBN 0-534-09660-3
    1. English language—Rhetoric—Handbooks, manuals, etc. 2. English language—Grammar—1950—Handbooks, manuals, etc. 3. English language—Textbooks for foreign speakers. I. Benson, Beverly. II. Title
PE1408.B92 1989   88-17239
808'.042—dc19   CIP

Contents

Chapter 1/The Sentence   1

Chapter 2/The Verb   21

Chapter 3/Passive Sentences   103

Chapter 4/Subjunctive Sentences   116

Chapter 5/Conditional and Hypothetical Sentences   120

Chapter 6/Causative Verbs   140

Chapter 7/Imperative Sentences   145

Chapter 8/Nouns, Noun Phrases, and Adjectives   148

Chapter 9/Determiners and Articles   176

Chapter 10/Pronouns   201

Chapter 11/Gerunds, Infinitives, and Participles   214

Chapter 12/Adverbs and Adverbials   239

Chapter 13/Prepositions and Prepositional Phrases   252

Chapter 14/Negation   266

Chapter 15/Question Formation and Embedded Questions   274

Chapter 16/Comparison   281

Chapter 17/Clauses   294

Chapter 18/Conciseness   319

Chapter 19/Using Grammatical Information in Paraphrasing and Summarizing   324

About the Wadsworth EAP Series

The Wadsworth English for Academic Purposes (EAP) series provides appropriate learning materials for university courses that focus on the academic uses of English. The EAP series has been planned to help ESL students communicate competently in all aspects of academic life in the United States. The materials support learning of academic-level skills in reading, writing, listening, and speaking. They can be used in intensive or nonintensive formats, in classroom, group, or individual study, and for courses of varying lengths.

The Wadsworth EAP series is based on three principles:

1. **Comprehensive Skills Development:** The series views language skills as integrated, so each book not only stands on its own but also builds on and relates to other texts in the series. Books targeted for all skill areas maintain a consistent yet nonrepetitive approach.

2. **Academic Community Context:** The series provides practice in the varied language uses that students will encounter in their academic careers. Teaching and learning activities are in the context of college or university classroom or campus life. This context-specific approach respects the learning skills and educational background of students at academic English centers.

3. **Student-Centered, Process-Oriented Materials:** The series places student learning activities at the heart of each lesson and requires stu-

dents to take responsibility for their active role in the learning process.

The components of the Wadsworth EAP series include:

—**A grammar reference guide and handbook** that encourages students to identify specific grammar problems and practice language appropriate to specific academic contexts.

—**Listening comprehension texts and tapes** that develop listening skills to the high level necessary for achievement in an academic program.

—**Reading skill development books** that provide opportunity to practice the skills needed to read authentic academic texts with purpose and understanding.

—**Progressive process-oriented writing texts** that develop academic writing skills from brief reports to rigorous research tasks.

—**Spoken language texts** that provide progressive communicative practice to the level demanded of international students in academic programs.

The authors of the Wadsworth EAP series are experienced teachers in academic programs and have developed their materials from their classroom experience. However, the series is not "teacher-proof." The books do not attempt to provide all the "correct" answers, nor do they set down a strict step-by-step approach. The ambiguity of language at this level and the importance of developing interpretative skills are emphasized by the authors.

Although no one book is ideal for all students (or for all teachers), these books will stimulate and encourage everyone who is willing to participate fully in student-centered classes. The authors have written books that they hope will broaden students' vision and empower them with the expanding possibilities of language.

Control and support must come not only from the books themselves but also from the teachers who work with students and from the students themselves who strive to become responsible for their learning. Just as students seek to make the language serve their needs, so teachers need to use materials to support their individual pedagogical styles and approaches to language-learning problems.

In sum, the Wadsworth EAP series seeks to do more than prepare students for an examination in language skills. It seeks to help international students master academic English in order to achieve their academic goals. The authors of these texts have shared their experiences in providing opportunities for students to fulfill their academic potential—and isn't that what each of us would like to achieve?

Charles H. Blatchford and Jerry L. Messec
Series Editors

To the Instructor

The Handbook serves both as a reference book and a textbook to enhance the ability of college- and university-bound ESL students to write more sophisticated and accurate English. *The Handbook* is a companion book for *The Editing Process*, a text that teaches an editing method developed to help ESL writers become more effective editors of their own work. Together these two books make up a grammar and writing course called *Improving the Grammar of Written English*. *The Handbook* provides grammatical explanations, illustrations, and exercises. *The Editing Process* teaches an editing strategy and provides materials to use in practicing that strategy. Field tested over a period of two years, *The Handbook* offers the following special features:

Grammatical Coverage

—All of the areas traditional in ESL grammars are included, but the material has been developed from the point of view of the ESL student who needs to learn to be a more effective writer and editor.

—In addition, *The Handbook* includes grammatical aspects of paraphrasing and summarizing.

—Punctuation is included as an important aspect of formal written English.

Format

—A detailed index guides the user to materials.

—The spiral binding was chosen so that students can easily lay *The Handbook* flat while using it.

—The "Focus on Editing" system quickly guides students to the sections they are seeking.

—Ready-reference appendixes at the back provide quick reference to alphabetized lists of often-used and/or confusing words and phrases.

Content

—*The Handbook* focuses on the grammar of written English.

—The need for grammatical accuracy is placed within the context of the writing process of prewriting, composing, revising, and editing.

—Grammar is explained and illustrated in the context of higher discourse levels.

—Emphasis is placed on aspects of written English grammar that are problems for high intermediate and advanced ESL students in their writing.

—*The Handbook* is organized so that students' attention can be directed to grammatical areas that may be new to them—or may be avoided by them—so that they can learn from this source of information as well as learning from their errors.

—Exercises are frequently based on written passages of significant content worthy of thought and discussion.

—Terminology and grammatical choices that are likely to be encountered in courses taught by English (rather than ESL) faculty are presented.

Teaching and Learning Strategies

—The materials in *The Handbook* are based on the realization that in the writing process students can use their learned knowledge (along with reference materials) to make grammatical corrections.

—*The Handbook* recognizes that students at this high proficiency level have knowledge about English grammar from prior study.

—Control is given to the instructor in the selection of grammatical areas to be covered with a particular group of students.

—Exercises include pair and small-group work as well as individual tasks.

—Exercises have students discover how particular features of English grammar are used in their own areas of interest and major fields of study.

—Exercises have students look outside the ESL classroom to see how grammar functions in other aspects of their lives.

Finally, it is our pleasure to thank the many people who helped in the development of *The Handbook*. Both of us are fortunate to work at institutions where faculty are encouraged to be creative in their teaching and in developing new materials to fit their students' educational needs. At Georgia State University, we would like especially to thank Dean Naomi Lynn of the College of Public and Urban Affairs; at DeKalb College, Dean Carol Copenhaver and Tom Chandler.

During the two years of the field testing, Grace Canseco gave innumerable hours to discussions with us about how the materials worked with her students in the advanced grammar course in the academic preparation ESL program at Georgia State University. We could not have lived up to our dreams for the materials without her advice, encouragement, and enthusiasm.

Additional thanks go to the other teachers at Georgia State who participated in the field testing: Stephanie Coffin, Beatric Divine, Phyllis Hurt, Wendy Newstetter, and Peggy Sweidler. Graduate students in Patricia Byrd's course on English grammar provided insightful research into several difficult areas: we thank Michel Kuchel, Mike Thomas, Karen Peterson, Laura Benson, and Mary Schmidt for the information they provided on the English article system, the modal auxiliary system, and the use of *no* in academic writing.

Janet C. Constantinides, assistant chair of the Department of English at the University of Wyoming, acted as our content editor; her recommendations led to significant improvements in the content and organization of *The Handbook*. We are also grateful to all of the reviewers who commented on the various versions of *The Handbook* as it was being written, revised, and edited. These reviewers include: Richard Appelbaum, Broward Community College; William Biddle, Harvard University; Gilbert D. Couts, The American University; David D. Dahnke, North Harris County College–South; Ronald Eckard, Western Kentucky University; and Bruce Leeds, Indiana University.

We thank the editors and staff members at Wadsworth Publishing Company who worked patiently and productively with us: John Strohmeier got us started; Steve Rutter helped in the final stages of revising the materials; Peggy Meehan advised on our many questions about permissions; and Jerilyn Emori, taking the raw manuscript and turning it into its printed form, taught us with kindness and humor about the realities of making books.

Special thanks are also offered Jerry Messec and Charles Blatchford for their encouragement in the development of the grammar track in Wadsworth's English for Academic Purposes series.

Most of all we thank the many ESL students who have used these materials and have helped us better understand the teaching and learning of grammar within the context of written English.

To the Student

The Handbook has been designed to help you in your study of written English grammar. As an advanced student, you no longer need to study the entire range of English but now should focus on particular areas. You and your instructor can identify special needs by analyzing the errors you make in your writing. You can also notice if you are not using grammatical forms that could make your writing better. For example, some students avoid the conditional because they are not sure how to use it correctly.

Each entry in *The Handbook* has explanations and examples. Most entries also have exercises and activities that can be done for practice. To find information, you can use the table of contents or the index. Also, within many sections you will find cross-references to lead you to related information.

It is not necessary to work through the entire *Handbook* from beginning to end. Because you already know a great deal of English, you do not need all of the information. Moreover, you need to learn English grammar in a different way now. That is, you may be able to make good scores on multiple-choice grammar tests but cannot use that knowledge of English grammar so effectively in your own writing.

The Handbook will help you learn about your own English and will teach you to be analytical about new structures. The major reason for learning about your own English grammar or for becoming analytical, however, is to improve the quality of your written English.

CHAPTER 1

The Sentence

1a Introduction to the Basic Sentence in English

Other terms used for the basic sentence are *simple sentence* and *independent clause.* This type of sentence is made up of

Subject + verb + (object) + (modifier).

This formula describes four possibilities for the simple English sentence.

1. Sometimes the sentence will have only subject and verb. Notice, however, that the sentence can be expanded by using compound phrases.

   The bomb exploded.

   The car exploded and burned.

   All the children and their parents escaped.

2. Some verbs must have objects, so the sentence has subject, verb, and object.

   Flemming discovered penicillin.

3. Some sentences have only subject, verb, and modifier. For example,

   He moved to New York.

4. Sometimes all four parts of the sentence are used. In this type of simple sentence, the parts are subject, verb, object, and modifier. It is also possible to have more than one modifier. Modifiers can often move to other positions in the basic sentence.

He turned on the computer at 5:30 p.m.

At 5:30 p.m., he turned on the computer in the laboratory.

It is also possible for some verbs to have two types of objects. These are usually called the *direct* (DO) and *indirect* object (IO). (See the Index for more information on indirect objects.)

```
              DO              IO
```
He gave the report to his professor.

```
              IO              DO
```
He gave his professor the report.

Why is the basic sentence so important? This combination of words is the fundamental unit out of which larger pieces of writing are made. Your ideas and information must be communicated through sentences. The things you know and believe can be communicated accurately to the reader only through well-formed sentences.

The basic sentence is also important in the study of English grammar because so many of the complexities can be explained only by referring to the basic sentence. For example, in Chapter 17, you will find relative clauses explained in terms of changes made to basic sentences.

The basic or simple sentence can be very short, or it can be quite long. For example, these are both simple sentences:

Economists study market forces.

The highly skilled and dedicated workers will have completed the installation project before December 31.

Sentences are made longer by having longer individual parts. In the first example, the subject has only one word while in the second example the subject has six words.

Basic sentences are often expanded by using prepositional phrases to modify nouns.

He will take two courses in number theory from ancient times to the present.

1b Problem Areas

Two major problems are possible with the basic sentence. First, the English sentence must always have a subject. Some languages do not have this requirement, so speakers of those languages can create ungrammatical English sentences by leaving out the subject.

Please note: A ▼ before a sentence means that the sentence is not grammatical.

▼ *Is important to make back-up copies of all diskettes.*

It is important to make back-up copies of all diskettes.

The second problem is the order of the parts. While English has some flexibility, the usual order of the parts is

Subject + verb + object + modifier.

Other languages have more flexibility or have different ordering for similar parts. Writers can make ungrammatical sentences by putting the modifier before the object.

▼ *The university should provide in the afternoon more sections of computer science.*

The university should provide more sections of computer science in the afternoon.

1c EXERCISES: The Basic Sentence

A. Divide these sentences* into the basic parts of subject, verb, object, and modifier. Underline the main subject once. Underline the main verb twice. Circle a direct object. Place brackets around an indirect object. Put parentheses around any modifiers. Numbers 1, 2, 6, and 21 have been done as examples.

1. The United States took ⟨its first census⟩ (in 1790.)

2. Few Americans lived (in urban areas) (then.)

3. Most Americans live in cities now.

4. Seventy percent of our people are living on about 1 percent of our land.

5. Our urban centers have huge problems.

6. These problems include ⟨congestion and pollution.⟩

7. Researchers study the emotional problems of city dwellers.

8. Life in the city can be extremely lonely.

9. Rural areas have tremendous problems now.

10. Farmers are leaving their farms for city jobs.

---

*Adapted from *Communities of Tomorrow* (U.S. Department of Agriculture, undated)

11. Many rural people live in poverty.

12. The U.S. must solve these problems in the 21st century.

13. We can revitalize the villages, towns, and cities in the countryside.

14. We can reverse the flow of population to the metropolitan centers.

15. Big cities can conquer their population problems.

16. We can preserve the maximum number of family-type farms in the country.

17. In rural areas, we can develop housing, community facilities, and good jobs.

18. Communities of tomorrow can hold their young people.

19. They can provide an excellent way of life.

20. Orderly and intelligent development of nonmetropolitan parts of the U.S. can ease congestion in our cities.

21. Such development can give every person good work and recreation opportunities outside the metropolitan areas.

22. Such development can give every person better chances in life.

B. Here are some basic sentences that are not grammatical. Each sentence has a problem that keeps it from being a complete simple sentence. Work with a small group of other students to find the problem and write a correct version of the sentence. Often it will be possible to have more than one acceptable correction. Many times you will need to provide additional information to make sense of the phrase; add whatever you think necessary to make a clear statement. Compare the edited sentences from your group to those prepared by other groups.

1. For example, seemed very cold in the classrooms.

   _____

2. In the beginning, the instructor began 15 minutes late the lectures.

   _____

3. Usually discussed too little the questions of the students.

   _____

4. Other students everyday talked too much in their languages.

_____

C. Here are some more complex editing problems. All of the following are fragments. Select any five and find ways to edit them so that they become complete sentences.

1. Because it gives me a chance to spend my money freely.

_____

2. Because there are cars, buses, and subways all over in the United States.

_____

3. Because failure is more traumatic and tragic for a foreigner than for an American student.

_____

4. Although relaxing is important to everyone and should not be forgotten.

_____

5. And to go back to the good memories of the past year.

_____

6. And to celebrate the New Year with my friends as well as partying the entire night.

_____

7. And to learn from mistakes that I made earlier in the year.

_____

8. Secondly, being updated on the important news and information that is announced each day.

_____

9. Many people begging in the streets and also many homeless.

   _____

10. The reason being that many musicians set the pattern for contemporary thinking.

    _____

11. Coming from North Providence, Rhode Island, to Atlanta, Georgia. For example, getting used to the language and new places.

    _____

12. People who do not go to schools because they do not have enough money to afford the price of a private school.

    _____

13. For example, the many cities in one state and the names of these cities, which are often complicated.

    _____

14. Secondly, a common form that all people use.

    _____

15. For example, people from China, Cuba, and Italy who don't speak the same language.

    _____

16. Second, the television because it gives us something to enjoy while sitting at home.

    _____

17. Especially those places that have large cities and big corporations.

    _____

18. The Arabic alphabet, the second most widely used alphabet writing system in the world.

    _____

19. In fact, a phrase sometimes longer than a short sentence.

_____

20. A thick moustache, thin cheeks, a broad nose that gives vivid testimony to every visitor.

_____

21. Especially from the outside with all the red and yellow flowers around the school.

_____

22. Finally, the photography that reinforces the written ad.

_____

2 Terminology of Grammar Study

In your English courses at an American university, you might be expected to be familiar with certain terminology. Not all English instructors will expect this knowledge, but many will. Usually the best definition for these terms is a good example rather than an abstract explanation. For example, "A _noun_ is a word like _book, car,_ or _man._ Usually it has a plural form, and it can be used as the subject of a sentence or as the object of a sentence or of a preposition."

Listed here are some important words that you might need to know. You can use the Index to _The Handbook_ to find the relevant sections where these terms are explained and illustrated.

adjective
adverb
article
appositive
clause
comma splice
complement
complex sentence
compound sentence
fragment
gerund
infinitive

interjection

modifier—time, place, manner, reason

noun—plural, singular, count, noncount, mass, definite, indefinite, abstract, concrete

object—direct, indirect

preposition

pronoun—personal, possessive, relative, demonstrative

run-on sentence

simple sentence

subject

tense

verb—regular, irregular

3a Parts of Speech

Your instructors in ESL, English, and even other academic subjects might use the term *parts of speech* in their explanations of English grammar in general and of your grammar mistakes in particular. The purpose of this section of *The Handbook* is to explain and illustrate a term that is often used but very difficult to define.

When an instructor or a textbook uses the term *parts of speech*, what is usually meant is the various categories of words such as *noun, pronoun, verb, preposition*. The best definition is a good example. For instance, a *noun* is a word like *book* in *The book is on the table*. Or, a *preposition* is a word like *on* in the same sentence. The traditional list of parts of speech includes these word groups: noun, verb, pronoun, adverb, adjective, article, preposition, conjunction, and interjection. (An *interjection* is a word like *oh* in the sentence *Oh, I lost my grammar book!*)

Grammarians have two major ways of analyzing English words. First, words can be grouped together on the basis of similarity in form—these are the *parts of speech*. For example, we talk about nouns as a group of words that have singular and plural forms. *Nouns* are words like *book, books, man, men*.

The second big category used by grammarians refers to the functions words have in sentences. For example, a sentence has a *subject* and possibly an *object*. This is relatively easy to understand for nouns and subjects. A noun is a part of speech that can work in several different ways in a sentence—subject, object, object of a preposition. *Book* is a noun that is the subject of the sentence *This book is about English grammar*. *Book* is a noun that is the object of the sentence *I lost my grammar book*. *Book* is a noun that is the object of the preposition in the sentence *Turn to page 21 in your book*.

The traditional terminology can be confusing, however, because sometimes a single word can have two different meanings. For example, a *verb* is a kind of word that functions as the *verb* in a sentence. A *verb* is also the kind of word that combines with *to* to make an *infinitive*.

Unless you are planning to be an English instructor, a linguist, or a grammarian, you do not need to worry about these details too much. The important skill is to recognize the big categories so that you can make English sentences that express your ideas and information as accurately as possible.

3b EXERCISE: Identifying Parts of Speech

Put each word from the following two quotations into the correct category on the chart. Notice that modifiers are frequently made up of a combination of preposition plus noun: *to the library* is made up of a preposition, an article, a noun. Notice also that a noun (part of speech) can be used as an adjective (sentence function): *computer store* is made up of two nouns. Do not identify function—just decide on the part of speech for each word. Talk with other students and your instructor to make decisions about difficult choices. Use your dictionaries only after you have made your own decisions. Then, check to see if you agree with the dictionary. The first sentence in the quotation from former President Eisenhower is done as an example.

"Nothing is easy in war. Mistakes are always paid for in casualties, and troops are quick to sense any blunder made by their commanders." (Eisenhower, 1953)

"Only one military organization can hold and gain ground in war—a ground army supported by tactical aviation with supply lines guarded by the navy." (Bradley, 1951)

Nouns: *war*	Prepositions: *in*	Articles:
Pronouns: *nothing*	Adverbs:	Conjunctions:
Verbs: *is*	Adjectives: *easy*	Interjections:

4a Coordination

Coordination is a method that English uses to combine words, phrases, and sentences. When coordination is used, the parts are considered equal and parallel. The two basic coordinating words are *and* and *or*. *But* is also frequently used for coordination.

Nouns can be combined:

The students and their instructor discussed the project.

Our company processes *coffee and tea*.

He bought books on *physics, chemistry, and mathematics*.

You can take *chemistry or biology* this term.

Verbs can be combined:

The musicians *sang and danced*.

An illiterate person cannot *read or write*.

Adjectives can be combined:

The book is *expensive but informative*.

The *expensive but informative* book is required for the course.

English can also combine phrases as well as single words:

A student must both *study seriously and have time for visits with family and friends*.

Simple sentences can be combined to make longer and more complicated sentences. There are several methods for making the combinations. One method involves combining two or more simple sentences so that each part is equal in importance. This method is called *coordination*. A sentence that is created by combining two or more sentences with coordination is called a *compound sentence*. (See Section 5a on p. 11 for more information.) An example of a compound sentence is

The student wrote a computer game, and IBM bought it for $100,000.

In addition to *and, or,* and *but*, numerous other joining words or phrases can be used when combining complete sentences. These are listed in Section 5a on p.11.

4b EXERCISES: Coordination

A. If you ride public transportation to school, find examples of coordination in the advertisements on or inside the buses or trains. Especially look for the coordinating conjunctions *and, or,* and *but*. Make a list of all the combinations of words, phrases, or sentences that you find in the ads. Write down the exact words that are in the ads.

B. If you do not ride public transportation, look for examples of coordination in advertisements in the local newspaper. Find several different types of coordination—some of words, of phrases, and of complete sentences.

C. Which of the combining words are more useful to know? Which of them are most commonly used by Americans? To find out, get from the library or from a friend a copy of a textbook in your major field of study. Read the "Introduction" to the textbook and mark all the combining words that you find. Count them to find out which ones are most frequently used. Compare your list to those of other students from other fields of study. What conclusions can you make about the relative importance of these words? (If the book does not have an "Introduction," then investigate the combining words used in the first chapter.)

5a Compound Sentences

Compound sentences are made by combining two or more simple sentences with an appropriate joining word. Look at the following sentence:

There are several types of exporting firms, and the manufacturer will have to decide on the best type to use.

This sentence combines two simple sentences by using a comma to show the end of the first sentence and the word *and* to add the second sentence. This combined sentence could be an improvement over having the two separate sentences. In formal written English, the writer frequently combines simple sentences to show relationships between ideas and information. It is considered poor writing style to write only or even primarily in simple sentences.

Coordination is done in one of three ways:

1. Comma with a joining word:

, and	, or	, so
, but	, nor	, yet
	, for	

2. Semicolon: ;

3. Semicolon with a joining word:

; also,	; first,	; indeed,
; furthermore,	; second,	; instead,
; however,		; on the other hand,
; in addition,		; then,
		; therefore,

Obviously, you select the joining word according to its meaning. *But,* grammatically they have the same work—they help combine two or more simpler sentences into one longer sentence.

5b Punctuation with Coordinating Conjunctions

If you are combining sentences with *and, but, or, nor, for, so,* or *yet,* punctuation requires a comma.

He tried to turn the computer on, but it did not seem to be functioning.

It is very important to recognize that *and* is used in many different kinds of combinations. When it is used to combine a list of single words, the typical punctuation can be in either of these styles—depending on the instructor for whom you are writing:

He knows Pascal, Basic, and several other computing languages. (usually preferred by English instructors)

He knows Pascal, Basic and several other computing languages. (sometimes preferred—especially in journalism)

When *and* is used to combine two sentences, a comma is required as a signal to the reader that a new sentence is coming after the *and.* If the words after *and* are not a new sentence, then no punctuation is used.

He knows Basic, and his friend will teach him Pascal this weekend.
He knows Pascal and Basic.
He knows Basic and will learn Pascal as soon as possible.

5c EXERCISES: Compounding

A. Select an appropriate joining word to go in the blank space.

1. My cold grew worse, _____ I decided to call the doctor.

2. The receptionist gave me an early appointment, _____ I went to the office immediately.

3. I got to the office in plenty of time; _____ I couldn't find a parking space.

4. I drove around the block six times; _____ I saw a man leaving a parking place.

5. The waiting room was full of sick people, _____ I decided to wait outside.

6. I waited two hours to see the doctor, _____ he told me to go home and take some aspirin.

7. This seemed expensive advice; _____ I was happy not to be seriously ill.

B. Select an appropriate joining word to go in the blank space. What punctuation should be used?*

1. Migrant farmworkers are a necessity for many farmers _____

   _____ these workers are a serious problem for U.S.

   society.

2. Their labor stabilizes and subsidizes the price of food _____

   _____ the price of this stabilization could be seen

   as human abuse.

3. The 5 million migrant farmworkers in the U.S. provide seasonal

   farm labor _____ they work in food processing
   plants.

4. They are employed an average of 6.5 months a year _____

   _____ they seldom work as long as 1 month for the

   same employer.

5. Our society needs migrant workers to perform unpleasant and some-

   times hazardous seasonal farm work _____ it

   expresses concern for the health and welfare of this same group.

6. We want the migrant workers to have a good and secure life _____

   _____ we don't want our food bills to rise as a

   result.

---

*Adapted from "Last and Still Least" (Larson, 1980)

C. In the following passages, all of the uses of <u>and</u> have been marked. Look at the sentences and decide in each case of the word <u>and</u> if you need to add a comma or if no punctuation is needed.

THE UNITED STATES COAST GUARD

Alexander Hamilton created the Coast Guard in 1790 to combat smugglers and it has been living up to its motto "Semper Paratus" (Always Ready) almost 200 years. Coast Guard personnel go out on 71,000 search and rescue missions each year and have become famous around the world for their lifesaving skills. But that is not the Coast Guard's only assignment. The Coast Guard also patrols for oil spills, inspects ships for safety defects, enforces fishing laws and operates the nation's only fleet of icebreakers. Coast Guard employees and volunteers conduct a nationwide boating safety program and in wartime the Coast Guard becomes an arm of the U.S. Navy.

Adapted from *Meeting America's Transportation Needs* (U.S. Department of Transportation, 1979)

THE REAL McCOY

The Industrial Revolution saw the creation of thousands of new machines to help manufacture new products, to change the way old products were made and to move both products and consumers from place to place. However, most of the marvelous new machines had to be shut down and oiled by hand at frequent intervals, wasting time, money and manpower. Elijah McCoy helped change this.

The son of slaves who had escaped from Kentucky, McCoy was born in Canada and trained as a mechanical engineer in Edinburgh, Scotland. He moved to the United States at the end of the Civil War, but could find employment only as a railroad fireman, not as an engineer.

At that time, steam engines had to be stopped periodically so that their crews could get out and oil the huge machines. McCoy created an "automatic locomotive lubricator" and received a patent for his invention in 1872. It soon became widely used throughout the world. Railroad workers, when setting out with a new locomotive, would check to make sure that it was equipped with "the real McCoy."

McCoy received a total of 57 patents during his lifetime and in 1915 he developed a graphite lubricator, which he considered his best invention. It used powdered, solid graphite rather than oil to lubricate certain complicated machines. He organized the Elijah McCoy Manufacturing

Company <u>and</u> this organization produced <u>and</u> sold his inventions until his death in 1929.

_____

Adapted from *Eureka!* (U.S. Small Business Administration, 1982)

_____

6a Embedding and Subordination

In addition to coordination, English uses another process called *embedding* to create sentences. Embedding is a process that uses one grammatical item as part of another grammatical item. For example, a noun phrase can be the object of a preposition:

She put the book [on *the long table*].

It is also possible for a complete sentence to be placed inside part of another sentence. Look at this example. The second sentence becomes a part of the subject of the first sentence:

1. *The book cost $45.*

2. *He bought the book for his calculus class.*

   The book that he bought for his calculus class cost $45.

This type of combination is discussed in detail in Section 4 on p. 10.

Another word that is used to discuss this type of process is *subordination*. Usually the meaning of *subordination* is limited to the combining of two or more clauses as in these examples:

He bought the textbook because it was required for the course.

Although he respected his instructor's intelligence, he disagreed with his political views.

Subordination is, thus, another way that English combines simple sentences to make complex sentences. In this method, one sentence is considered the more important—the main idea. One or more additional sentences are added to that basic sentence. *But,* these additional sentences are not considered of equal importance—they are subordinate. They become part of the basic sentence. The basic sentence is frequently called an *independent* clause. The other clause is called a *subordinate* or a *dependent* clause. The combination is called a *complex sentence.* Here is another example that uses the joining word *because*:

He is worried about the test because he has lost his notes.

6b Complex Sentences

A *complex sentence* is a combination of two or more sentences that use subordination or embedding to combine the sentences. These sentences are very useful in formal written English. Their use is considered educated style because it puts ideas and information into complex relationships. Writers must think about meaning to put their ideas and information into special relationships. They must first decide which material is most basic and important; then, they must decide on ways to indicate that the other material is part of and subordinate to the first material. Consider these statements from an article on advice for exporters.

1. *Pricing your product is very important.*

2. *The price must be high enough to return a suitable profit.*

3. *The price must be low enough to be competitive in foreign markets.*

The first sentence is the basic idea. The other ideas are added to it using *because* and *yet*.

Pricing your product is very important because the price must be high enough to return a suitable profit yet low enough to be competitive in foreign markets.

Here is a list of common joining words used for subordinating and embedding.

after	if, even if	when, whenever
although	in order that	where, wherever
as	since	whether
because	that, so that	which
before	unless	while
even though	until	who, whom
how	what, whatever	whose

6c EXERCISES: Embedding and Subordination

A. Compare these two versions of the same sentence.

1. *Because Tom missed the last lecture, he did poorly on the final exam.*

2. *Tom did poorly on the final exam because he missed the last lecture.*

In each sentence, which idea is more important? Which idea is subordinate?

Mark the main subject-verb combination.

Notice the subordinate subject-verb combination.

Is there any difference in meaning between the two sentences? What is the difference in punctuation? Write the punctuation rule for complex sentences here.

B. Analyze this example of written English. What joining words are used? Select one of the complex sentences to analyze. What sentences have been combined? Which is the most important? Which is subordinate?

THE TRANSPORTATION SYSTEM AND THE HANDICAPPED

Many of the nation's physically handicapped are unable to take advantage of the economic and social opportunities of their community, even though they may possess valuable vocational skills, an ability to learn, and a full human capacity for enjoyment of social and personal relationships. For the nation as a whole, this is a waste of its most valuable resource—people. For the individual, it can mean a life of loneliness and despair. Why?

Many handicapped people who have looked for employment have been discouraged by the attitudes of potential employers while others have found that their job skills are no longer marketable. Some have sought help from understaffed and underfunded agencies which have all too often failed them. Others have never asked for help because they feared embarrassment. Others have not sought help because of a simple lack of information.

A significant number of handicapped people have been frustrated in their attempts to find or hold jobs, obtain regular medical care, improve their education, shop in competitively priced markets or even to take part in everyday social activities because the transportation system did not fit their needs.

Estimates prepared by the National Center for Health Statistics indicate that there are approximately 6 million physically handicapped people whose mobility is limited as a result of a chronic or long-term medical condition. This group is of major national interest because improvements in the quality of public transportation are likely to result in the most significant changes in their lives.

The largest segment of the population that consistently experiences difficulty with public transportation is the aging. These 15 million citizens are unique among the handicapped because their disability results as much from the natural process of aging as from the effects of a chronic medical condition.

Adapted from *Travel Barriers* (U.S. Department of Health, Education, and Welfare, 1970)

C. Get a textbook that is being used in a course in your major field—from the library or from a friend. Bring the book to class and analyze any two pages of the text that interest you for joining words. How many are used? What kinds are they? Make a list of all the joining words and count the number of times each is used. What generalizations does this survey of usage suggest to you about the ways academic writers use coordination and subordination?

D. Work with another student to write a paragraph of about 15 sentences on any topic that interests both of you. Write only simple sentences. Do not use any coordination or subordination. Share your paragraph with the rest of the class. After reading all the paragraphs produced in the class, select the paragraph that interests the two of you most. Work together to improve the style of the paragraph by combining sentences where the meaning would be improved.

7a Parallelism

In formal written English, a writer is required to follow what is called *parallel structure*. This rule says that all of the coordinated words, phrases, or clauses must have the same grammatical structure. In this example, three infinitives are combined:

He prefers to eat breakfast, to exercise, and to shower before he goes to class.

a. to eat breakfast

b. to exercise

c. to shower

An error of parallel structure would be to use some other grammatical form for one of the three parts of the combination, as in this example:

▼ *He prefers to eat breakfast, exercising, and to shower before he goes to class.*

   a. to eat breakfast

   b. exercising

   c. to shower

Exercising is not grammatically parallel to *to eat breakfast* and *to shower.*

This error seems to occur more often in long strings of combined phrases or in very complex combinations. A general rule for a writer is to check the grammatical parallelism of any combination of words, phrases, or clauses.

7b EXERCISES: Parallel Structure

A. In the U.S., we frequently create sets with three members. Some thinkers have speculated that numbering of this kind is cultural—that some cultures prefer sets of two or four while ours likes to think of things coming in sets of three. Find advertisements in magazines for 10 to 15 products. Are any parallel structures used? What grammatical forms are made parallel? Do you find any errors of parallel structure? How many of the sets that you find include three members?

B. Analyze this passage. Point out any uses of coordination to create sets of items. What kinds of grammatical items are made parallel?

FOCUS ON USES OF WATER

What is it like to live in a community with polluted waters or with inadequate water supplies? If you live in such a community, it has probably been so long since you have even thought of swimming, fishing, or boating in nearby waters that you have forgotten it was once possible.

You have become accustomed to the strange taste in the water you drink. You do not worry about it because it does not make you sick, and you try to act unconcerned when visitors complain. If you read an article or see a TV documentary that says our increasing population may not have enough good quality water for drinking, agriculture, industry, recreation, and other useful purposes by 2000—well, that is a long time away and by that time "they" will have taken care of it.

We are learning that clean water may not always be there when we need it, and what there is will cost more. We are learning how wastes from our homes, factories, farms, boats, and numerous other sources are reducing our supplies of usable water. We are learning that many people are drinking "used" water—water that has gone through the water mains and sewers of upstream cities—and that this reuse, on an ever-greater scale, is inevitable. We are learning that the first step in making reuse possible is for our municipalities to construct, enlarge, and modernize their waste treatment facilities. And here are some other facts about water that we are learning.

Water is the No. 1 raw material of industry. It is a power source, a coolant, a transporting device, an ingredient, and a cleansing agent. Factories use water in astonishing amounts—1,400 gallons to produce a dollar's worth of steel, nearly 200 gallons for a dollar's worth of paper. But almost every use of water degrades its quality and makes it less useful for the same or different purposes. And our industries are growing at a tremendous rate.

Municipal use is increasing, too. As our population grows, so does the drain upon our water supplies. Higher standards of living and sanitation— multiple bathrooms, home laundries, garbage disposal units—mean greater consumption of water per capita. That is one reason why many cities are drawing their water from greater and greater distances.

Agriculture uses over seven times as much water for irrigation now as it did in 1900. While it uses less water than industry, it "consumes" more because almost all the water used by industry is recoverable whereas about 60 percent of water used in irrigation is "lost." In addition, much of the irrigation water returned to various watercourses is laden with salts, other minerals, and agricultural chemicals which are difficult to remove by conventional waste treatment methods.

Recreation is a water "use" which cannot be measured in gallons but is increasingly important nevertheless. Demand for water-oriented recreation is surging ahead of population growth. People have a natural desire to swim, fish, go boating, picnic, and camp beside water. They can fulfill these desires only if the water is of high quality esthetically and is free from health hazards.

Adapted from *Focus on Clean Water* (U.S. Department of Health, Education, and Welfare, 1964)

CHAPTER 2

The Verb

1 Introduction to the English Verb System

Grammarians frequently comment on the central importance of the verb in English sentences. The verb, they tell us, controls both meaning and structure.

The verb tells the reader about time and actions. It controls the objects—some verbs *must* have objects while other verbs *cannot* have objects. It is influenced by the subject; a singular noun as subject, for example, means that *-s* must be added for a present tense form of the verb. Some verbs can only have particular kinds of subjects. Verbs can be used to tell you how the writer feels about something. Here are some examples to illustrate these observations:

1. The verb tells time and action. Past time and movement are indicated by this verb.

   He walked to the library.

2. Some verbs must have objects.

   He bought a dictionary.

   ▼ *He bought.*

3. Some verbs cannot have objects.

   The sun rose.

   ▼ *The sun rose the book.*

4. Some verbs must have subjects that refer to human beings, or animals, or machines/forces capable of acting like either. Other verbs have other kinds of limits on their subjects and objects.

   The instructor opened the door.

   The dog opened the door.

   The electric eye opened the door.

   The wind opened the door.

   ▼ *The book opened the door.*

5. Some verbs can be selected to reveal the writer's feelings; for example, the selection of the modal shows how strongly the writer feels about the action in this sentence. (*Modal* is defined in Section 7a on p. 43.) *Must* is a much stronger choice than *should.*

   Traffic laws must be enforced in all situations.

Advanced writers often have particular problems with the English verb system. Some of these problems include:

—knowing which form of the verb to select for the right meaning, including understanding the systematic relations among the modal auxiliaries

—selecting the right verbs in sequence with each other in longer passages of writing

—spelling irregular verb forms

—spelling -*ing* and -*ed* forms of regular and irregular verbs

—recognizing when subject-verb agreement is needed

—knowing how to change verbs to create more complex sentence combinations

—knowing how to use the infinitive and gerund

—understanding when to use the passive

Individual writers might have other problems, but in general these are the major difficulties for most advanced writers. The rest of this chapter of *The Handbook* will deal with six of these eight areas. Passive voice is discussed in Chapter 3, and gerunds and infinitives are in Chapter 11. Since using the right verbs in extended passages of writing is your major problem, *The Handbook* first focuses on making verb choices. The individual verb forms are discussed only after you have thought about verbs in the context of academic writing. This organization is possible because, as advanced students, you already have basic knowledge about the different verb forms.

You already know a lot about English verbs. As a way to check your own knowledge, try answering these questions:

—How many forms does a regular verb have? (For example, how many different forms does the verb *walk* have?)

—How many forms does an irregular verb have? (For example, how many different forms does the verb *write* have? What about the verb *cut*?)

—How many forms does *be* have?

Obviously, *walk* has these four forms: *walk, walks, walked, walking*. You might also have listed the infinitive form with *to*— *to walk*. *Write* has *write, writes, wrote, written,* and *writing. Cut* has only three forms—*cut, cuts,* and *cutting.*

Be has the most forms of any English verb: *be, being, am, is, are, was, were, been.*

Note on grammatical terminology: There are some terms that we continue to use even though they are not exactly accurate. We use them because they are traditional. It is easier to use the words people are accustomed to than to make them learn new terms. This is true of the term *present tense.* You are aware that the present tense form of a verb has uses that are not exactly what we think of when we think "present time." The present tense form, for example, can be used to talk about things that are generally true.

The sun rises every morning.

The Sahara Desert is dangerous for the unprepared traveler.

2 The Forms of the English Verb

The most basic information about English verbs concerns the various forms that a verb can have. While this is beginning information, it is not necessarily simple or easy to remember and use correctly. For example, it is easy to remember that all verbs have *-ing* forms, but the spelling of the *-ing* form of a particular verb could be a problem.

English verbs can be divided into two large categories—regular and irregular verbs. Regular verbs form their past tense and past participle by adding the spelling *-ed.* (You will remember that *past participle* is the name of the form used to make the passive and perfect verb forms: *The text was* written *by our instructor. The project had* cost *$2,000,000. He has* studied *mathematics since he was two years old.*) Here are some examples of the forms of regular verbs:

The instructor talks.

The instructor talked.

The instructor has talked for 50 minutes.

The irregular verbs have several different patterns for forming the past and the past participle:

The student writes.

The student wrote.

The student has written.

The child hits the ball.

The child hit the ball.

The child has hit the ball.

In this *Handbook,* the grammatical term *tense* will be used for the present tense and the past tense. *Tense* means "a change in the form of the verb to reflect a change in the time meant by the verb." By this definition, English has only two tense forms—only two basic changes happen to the simple verb itself; it has a *present tense* form and a *past tense* form. Other time meanings are created by adding auxiliaries to the basic verb rather than by adding suffixes to the verb itself. For example, to talk about future time, the writer of English has many different choices:

She will attend the seminar this afternoon.

She is going to attend the seminar this afternoon.

She is to attend the seminar this afternoon.

She attends the seminar this afternoon.

She is attending the seminar later this afternoon.

3a Verbs in Academic Writing

As an advanced student, you understand the various meanings of the individual verb forms fairly well. You can give accurate definitions and usually make accurate choices on multiple choice tests. Your real problem is in making correct choices in your own writing. What verbs go together when you are writing more than one sentence at a time?

When you start to write on a topic, one of your first choices is about time. Is this a narrative set in the past? Is this a description of a general truth? Is the issue a matter of present time events? Is this a prediction about the future? Once you have made the basic choice of time orientation, then you have simplified your verb choices—only a limited range of verbs can be used.

While the following information might seem complicated at first, it can be helpful in understanding verb choices in English. The basic idea is that when you write you choose a time orientation. Then other times are put into relationship to that central time. This system does not always work, nor does it explain all of the possible choices. *But,* it does work well enough for you to benefit from studying it.

Past Time Focus   If you want to write about a past time event, you are focused on past time but you may want to include material that talks about things that happened *before* the past, or things that you anticipate after the central past time focus.

Central focus: past time using simple past tense

The investigation began on March 19, 1977.

Time before the central focus: past perfect

The police had become suspicious because of the suspect's purchase of a new Cadillac.

Time after the central focus: simple past tense

In the summer of that same year, the police found conclusive evidence of the suspect's guilt.

General Truth Focus   In your university work, you will frequently focus on general truths. The primary verb form will be the simple present tense. Past time events associated with the general truth focus will often be in the present perfect; events that occur after the present general truth focus can use any of the various future time choices.

Central time for general truth: simple present tense*

The U.S. maintains a close relationship with Great Britain.

Before the central time: present perfect

This relationship has developed for over 200 years.

After the present time: appropriate future form

It will certainly continue for many years into the future.

---

*Remember that various modals can also be used for general truth statements: *Oil will float on water. Expansion of the money supply may solve the economic crisis—or may create a worse situation.*

Present Time Focus In writing about present time events, your central focus will require either the present progressive or the simple present tense (for stative verbs). (See Section 9c on p. 60 for more information on stative verbs.) Past time events closely connected to the central focus will use the present perfect. Events that occur in the future after the central focus will use any of the future time forms.

Central focus:

John is studying in the library right now.

Before the central focus:

He has been there since 3:00 p.m.

After the central focus:

He will not leave until the library closes.

Future Time Focus You will find that you seldom write a long passage focused entirely on the future. But, you might—in writing a prediction about the future of your country, for example. When you are focused on the future, you use any of the possible future time forms for the right shade of meaning. For things that will happen before the future, use the modal + perfect combination (*will have happened, might have happened, should have happened,* for example). For things that happen after the central focus, just continue to use the future time forms.

Central time: future time using any of the appropriate forms such as *will* or *be going to*

The project will end in July.

Before the central time: future perfect

Before July, we will have gathered huge amounts of information. We should have analyzed most of it.

After the central time: either simple future form (for predictions about future) or future perfect (for completion by future date)

In the fall, we will prepare the final report on the project. The report will have been published by the end of December.

3b Charts to Use When Editing for Verbs in Academic Writing

Use the following charts to make decisions about verb forms in the exercises.

Present Time Actions		
before present activity	**Focus: Present Activity**	after present activity
present perfect	present progressive or simple present—stative	future forms

If you are writing about present time activities, you will primarily use present progressive verbs with some present perfect for past time connected to the present. For times after the central present focus, you use any of the possible future forms.

General Truth		
before general truth	**Focus: General Truth**	after general truth
present perfect	simple present tense*	future forms

*Remember that various modals can also be used for general truth statements: *Oil will not mix with water. The library will close at 12 o'clock midnight; books must be checked out by 11:00 p.m.*

If you are writing generalizations, you will primarily use the simple present tense with some present perfect for past time connected to the present. For time after the central present focus, you can use any of the various future time forms.

Past Time		
before past time	**Focus: Past Time**	after past time
past perfect	past forms	past forms

verb / _time_ (row labels on left side)

If your focus is on events completed in the past, you will primarily use simple past tense forms. To emphasize that an event was completed before the central past focus, you can use the past perfect form. For anything in the past (but after the central focus), you still use the simple past tense forms. Past progressive can be used for stylistic purposes when you want to emphasize that an action was in progress in the past. You should be aware, however, that past progressive is used sparingly in academic writing.

Future Time		
before future time	**Focus: Future Time**	after future time
future perfect	future forms	future forms

verb / _time_ (row labels on left side)

When you write about future time, you have many different choices for the verb. In academic writing, you will primarily use [_will_ + verb], although other forms are possible. For events completed before the future time focus, you use the combination of [modal + perfect]—often this is [_will_ + _have_ + past participle]. For events that occur in the future but after the central future focus, you still use the same future time forms.

3c Changing Time Focus

In writing long passages, you will sometimes change the time focus. Certain changes are found often in academic writing. For example, whole chapters of textbooks will primarily focus on general truth using the simple present tense, but examples and case studies will be given in the simple past tense.

Here are the common changes of *focus*:

present activity $\longrightarrow$	past time	(to give past time examples or historical background)
general truth $\longrightarrow$	past time	(to give examples or historical background; also the simple past tense is used to talk about examples or materials given earlier in the textbook)
past time $\longrightarrow$	general truth	(to give principles or currently true generalizations)

Writers usually warn their readers that a change of focus is going to occur. It is very confusing to be reading a passage and suddenly find the time focus has changed. Here are some of the phrases that writers use to indicate a time focus change:

To introduce a past time example:

On July 1, 1984 . . .
During the 60s and 70s . . .
Around 400 B.C. . . .
During the 1930s . . .

To refer to an example given previously in the text:

As discussed in Chapter 6 . . .
In Chapter 5 . . .
In the above example . . .
In Table 5.1 . . .
In our discussion of . . .
As pointed out earlier . . .

3d A Note on Use of the Present Perfect

Present perfect is often used to introduce a past time topic when the writer knows that the reader cannot know anything about the topic. That is, present perfect is much like *a* and *an* for the introduction of new topics. As soon as the topic is introduced, the focus changes to the past because the reader now shares the writer's definite past time knowledge. In this first version, the writer uses present perfect to introduce the topic and then switches to simple past to narrate the events.

I have gone to the library many times looking for information on my research topic, but I have never left as quickly as I did last night. I was there studying in the reference area when I realized that I had left my book bag on the floor beside the table in the cafeteria where I ate dinner. When I got to the cafeteria, my bag was gone. I lost my money, my driver's license, my classnotes, everything. The police told me that they did not think I would ever see my bag again. I did not return to the library because I was too upset to study.

Another version of this same information could be written totally in the past time framework. The writer uses past perfect for events before the central past time event. This version could be used when the writer is telling about past events that are not connected to the present time.

I had gone to the library many times looking for information on my research topic, but I had never left as quickly as I did last night. I was there studying in the reference area when I realized that I had left my book bag on the floor beside the table in the cafeteria where I ate dinner. When I got to the cafeteria, my bag was gone. I lost my money, my driver's license, my classnotes, everything. The police told me that they did not think I would ever see my bag again. I did not return to the library because I was too upset to study.

The choice between these versions depends on the larger context and the writer's purposes. Each is correct when put in the right context.

3e EXERCISES: Editing for Verbs

A. Answer the following questions about each passage given below.

1. What is the time frame?
   Present activity?
   General truth?

Future time?

Past time?

2. What verb forms do you expect for that time frame?

3. What verb forms did you find in the passage?

4. Is there a change in time orientation?

STOPPING SMOKING

It is not easy to stop smoking, but the moment you quit, your body begins to make repairs. If you make the choice to quit, you will not only feel better, but you will also improve your health.

Adapted from the *Drug Enforcement Administration: Physical Fitness Handbook* (U.S. Drug Enforcement Administration, undated)

STUDY OF CAR ACCIDENTS

In recent years, government scientists have studied motor vehicle collisions in an effort to reduce the severity of injuries. When a car strikes a solid object, it stops very abruptly. On impact, the car begins to crush and to slow down. The person inside the car has nothing to slow him down so he continues to move forward inside the car at 30 mph.

Adapted from *The Human Collision* (U.S. Department of Transportation, 1976)

In conclusion, I began studying Education Administration because of my individual needs, as a professional and leader of an educational institution. Fulfilling them, I will be able to improve my school, my university, and even my own country, Guatemala.

From the Conclusion of a Student Essay on Her Goals for Her Education

---

B. Use the charts in Section 3b on p. 26 to edit the passage that you are currently writing; answer these questions.

---

1. What is the time frame?

   Present activity?

   General truth?

   Future time?

   Past time?

2. What verb forms do you expect for that time frame?

3. What verb forms did you find in the passage?

4. Do any of the verbs need to be changed?

C. Read the following passages. Then discuss them with a group of other students. What is the time orientation? What verb forms are used?

THE EMOTIONAL IMPORTANCE OF FOOD TO HUMAN BEINGS

In the mid-1960s, a project was started in St. Petersburg, Florida, to carry food to elderly people. The project was based on the premise that the purchase, preparation, and/or consumption of food and beverage, in addition to having physiological meaning, has definite psychological and sociological significance. From birth, a person associates the taking of nourishment with physical and social contact. The newborn sucks and thus takes nourishment through contact with the mother. Family members come together at mealtime. Friends equate "having a good time" to sharing dinner or having a drink. These experiences reinforce the dependency of the individual on social relationships to motivate him to prepare and consume nutritious food. When these relationships are terminated, the associated motive is lost. Consider the woman who takes pride in preparing and serving meals to a large family, who is aware that the children, one by one, have left home, who finds herself 65 and suddenly widowed—and alone. From a practical point of view, she is uneducated as to how to purchase and prepare food for one person and, in most situations, has little sophistication regarding convenience foods. On a less identifiable level, she does not care. She does not "bother" to turn on the stove for herself alone. She is not accustomed to taking meals in cafeterias or restaurants. She is not hungry anyway—a cup of soup and some crackers is enough. Physiological deterioration is accompanied by confusion, disorientation, and withdrawal. In too many instances the result is institutional placement. The problem is no less, and in many cases greater, for the widower.

Adapted from *A Home Delivered Meals Program for the Elderly* (Buchholtz, 1971)

THE UPS AND DOWNS OF PEDAL POWER

"The discovery and progressive improvement of the bicycle," editorialized the New York *Tribune* in 1895, "is of more importance to mankind than all the victories and defeats of Napoleon, with the First and Second Punic Wars . . . thrown in." Some historians quibble over that statement, but there is no doubt that the bicycle was an important element of change. For the first time, people who could not afford a horse and carriage could enjoy wheeled transportation. In America, by the 1890s almost a million bicyclists organized in hundreds of cycle clubs were pressing for better roads. Women's skirts got shorter. Bicycle races and parades provided prime-time entertainment. Then came the automobile and the trolley. They moved people faster and with less physical effort. Gradually the bicycle boom faded. A bike was still every youngster's dream, but fewer adults used bicycles for everyday transportation.

But in the late 1960s, the bicycle came full cycle. Bicycling was the "in" thing, and another boom was on. By 1972 bicycle sales were outdistancing automobile sales—and about half of them were adult bicycles.

Why this return to the individualistic transportation so popular at the turn of the century? Primarily because the bicycle offers healthful exercise; reliability; low cost and upkeep; freedom of movement at one's own pace; quiet, nonpolluting transportation; cheap fuel supply; easy parking and storage—and fun. These are all qualities with growing appeal in today's complicated world. For many, the bicycle has become the most sensible and satisfactory means of short-haul transportation.

Teachers, as well as students, now ride it to school. Commuters pedal to work. Collegians on large campuses use their wheels between classes. Floridian retirees ride their three-wheelers to the beach. And in bicycle-oriented communities, many housewives ride their bikes to the supermarket.

Adapted from *Bicycling for Everyone* (U.S. Department of Transportation, 1974)

4a Alternative Ways of Writing about the Future

English has a number of different verb forms to use when referring to future time. Grammarians have not yet agreed that any one of these is *the* future tense. Some writers think of *will* as the future tense verb; others think of *be going to* as the future tense.

English expresses future time through the use of verbs and through the combination of verbs and adverbs of time.

Simple present tense (see Section 5a on p. 39) can be used to talk about scheduled events in the future—an exact time must be given. This verb has the strongest certainty.

The movie starts at 7:35 p.m.

Will is the most commonly used verb for future time meanings. (See Section 7a on p. 43 for information on the modals.) It is used for making predictions about the future. The meaning can involve the meaning "volition" or "willfulness."

The government will increase taxes next year.

"I will go if I decide that I want to. Otherwise I will not go."

Be going to is used more in conversations than in writing. It means something like "future completion of a current intention" or "future completion of a current cause." Usually it refers to events that are expected in the near future.*

"After class, I'm going to stop by the bookstore for a new pen."

The newspaper said that we are going to have bad weather all weekend.

---

*ESL students can seem strangely formal because of using *will* in conversations about plans when an American would be using *be going to*, especially if the ESL student uses the full form rather than the contracted form.

The present progressive (see Section 9a on p. 59) can be used for future time when the meaning involves a future achievement of a present time plan or arrangement. It cannot be used with stative verbs (see Section 9c on p. 60).

"I'm going home as soon as I get out of class."

The company is reopening for business next week.

The modal auxiliaries (see Section 7 on p. 43) can be used to refer to future time plus their other meanings of "ability," "probability," "obligation," or "necessity."

The company should reopen for business next week.

However, the most frequently used verbs for future time reference are *will* and the simple present tense. Remember that the simple present tense is used in dependent clauses as well as in complete sentences:

If she arrives at 8:45, we will have the meeting at 9:00.

For writers of formal academic English, a major issue is formality level. Some verb forms are felt to be more appropriate for speaking than for writing. For example, the periphrastic modal *ought to* is more appropriate for conversation (see Section 7f on p. 52); in formal written English you probably should use *should*. Generally, *will* is preferred in more formal written styles to the conversational *be going to*.

You should also notice that *be going to* will not be used repeatedly in a passage about future time. It will be used once or twice but not over and over. *Will* can be repeated sentence after sentence in extended discussions involving future time.

4b Present Tense in Future Time Clauses

One use of the simple present tense puzzles some students. Why does English use simple present tense when talking about future time? In the study of grammar it is difficult to answer "why" something happens. Languages are not so much logical as they are orderly. Grammar tells you "when" rather than "why."

Simple present tense can be used for future time meanings in two situations.

1. It can be used to talk about scheduled events in the future:

   The president arrives at the airport at 10:00 tomorrow morning.

2. It is used in clauses when the main verb is in the future, especially when the modal *will* is used.

When the president arrives, he will have a news conference. If the conference goes well, his popularity should increase. After his popularity increases, he may have better success in getting his program passed in Congress.

4c EXERCISES: Future Time

A. The following passage is from a publication called *Occupational Outlook Quarterly* (Winter 1986, Vol. 30, Number 4). As you would expect, a publication about *outlook* includes many predictions about the future. Read through the passage. How many different ways is future time indicated? (Remember to look for adverbs as well as verbs.)

Rarely do occupations flourish as the computer professions have. Since 1970, when the Census Bureau began tracking the number of programmers and systems analysts, employment has grown dramatically. Because of high demand, workers in these relatively new occupations could change jobs frequently as employers outbid each other for scarce talent. Many believed that things would only continue to improve. However, 1985 brought a rude awakening. That year, the computer industry experienced a serious and widespread slowdown in sales. This slump led to the first significant wave of layoffs ever for programmers and systems analysts.

This development raised questions in many people's minds about the future of these occupations:

What caused the events of 1985?

Will growth in these professions continue?

What education and training are now required?

Is an associate's degree still adequate preparation for some jobs?

How do people advance in these occupations?

What areas of the computer field are growing?

One important trend was clearly intensified by the slowdown in 1985: Graduates of junior college programs who learn COBOL will continue to find jobs, but employers will increasingly seek college graduates when they are filling positions for computer programmers and systems analysts.

Certain areas of computer application are expected to experience particularly strong growth in the coming decade, including services, defense, data communications, and artificial intelligence. People who wish to work as programmers or systems analysts would do well to pay particular attention to them.

Services. Nearly two out of every three new jobs for computer professionals through the mid-1990s will occur in the services industry. Software houses, computer consulting firms, and temporary help service firms will be especially important to computer programmers and systems analysts.

Defense. Government spending on military projects creates jobs for programmers and systems analysts. Modern weapons systems employ computers extensively and require the services of many computer professionals. For example, the Strategic Defense Initiative alone could require up to 100 million lines of programming.

Data Communications. One of the biggest challenges facing programmers and systems analysts is to link up all the computer systems within individual establishments, companies, or government agencies and to link these institutions' computers to the outside world.

The last two decades have witnessed many technological advancements in computers and communications equipment. For example, computer data now can be transmitted by telephone and telegraph lines, FM radio waves, micro waves, satellites, coaxial cable, and fiber optics. This development should have the effect of augmenting demand for programmers, because software will be needed to permit each kind of transmission. Similarly, demand for systems analysts should grow in response to the need to integrate these new forms of data transmission into systems.

Artificial Intelligence. A growing number of firms are specializing in artificial intelligence (AI), the effort to get computers to think like people. This goal will require a tremendous amount of creative research and analysis because the human brain is exceedingly complex. While scientists have not made a final breakthrough, they have made progress.

The field of AI does not currently employ many programmers and systems analysts, simply because it is so small. However, it is expected to grow rapidly in the coming decade and to provide an increasing number of jobs. One possible result, however, of successful developing AI is that the programs may be used in some cases rather than human programmers and systems analysts. This use would tend to hold down their employment.

Adapted from "The Outlook for Computer Professions: 1985 Rewrites the Program" (Drake, 1986)

B. Write a schedule of your plans for tomorrow (or some other day, if you prefer, for which you have lots of plans). Try out as many of the different future time forms as possible as long as your sentences are accurate. Compare plans with another student to see if you can learn any ideas from his/her writing for giving variety to your discussions of future time.

C. The conclusion to an essay often includes predictions based on the general content of the essay. Look back at any essays that you have written recently to see if you have used future time forms accurately. What changes might you make? Discuss these with your instructor.

D. In these sentences, find the main verbs and the verbs in the dependent clauses. What time orientation is used? How many different types of verbs are used? In the conditional sentences, what verbs are used? (See Chapter 5 for more information on the conditional.)

THE SEARCH FOR OTHER PLANETARY SYSTEMS: WHAT WILL WE LEARN?

An extensive search for other planetary systems, whatever the outcome, cannot help but have a major impact. If other planetary systems are found, then new directions will open up in both science and philosophy. Our own planetary system will become firmly established as only one specific instance of a general phenomenon.

On the other hand, if no other planetary systems are found after an exhaustive search, we will have to admit that planetary systems like ours are uncommon, and perhaps unique, in the universe. Our ideas about the formation of our solar system will have to be reexamined in the light of evidence that the system is a cosmic accident, some freak of nature, and not representative of anything general.

Whatever the outcome of such a search, the results will be electrifying, both from a scientific perspective and from a broader human perspective. The results will penetrate to the core of our perceptions about our place in the universe.

Adapted from *Planetary Exploration Through Year 2000* (U.S. National Aeronautics and Space Administration, 1986)

E. Using the passage in exercise D as a model, write a passage in which you discuss two possibilities for your future. For example, what two different results will occur if you enter/do not enter a university next term? Or what two different results will occur if you pay/do not pay your rent next month? Or what two different results will occur if you take/do not take a summer vacation? After you have revised the passage for content and style, then edit the sentences for verb forms. After you have edited the passage, ask another student to check it again to be sure that you have the correct verb forms.

5a Present Tense

The simple present tense form of the verb can be used to express a number of meanings:

1. Current time habits:
   He studies in the library.

2. General truths, customs, physical laws:
   Oil floats on water.

3. Present time (with verbs that cannot be used in the progressive—see Section 9c on p. 60):
   I have 30 minutes to prepare for the test.

4. Future time (for a scheduled event):
   The game starts at 3:30 tomorrow.

5. In the subordinate clause when the main verb is in future time:
   When he finishes this term, he will be a senior.

6. In the subordinate clause when the main clause is future conditional:
   If she drops the course, she will be out-of-status.

7. Some verbs are announcements of what the speaker intends to do:

I pledge $100 to the University. I promise to obey the rules of this group.

There are two other uses that you might encounter. Both are used more in spoken English than in writing.

8. In the immediate description of an event.

The announcer at a basketball game might say, *"Smith passes to Jackson. Jackson's shot is wild."*

9. The use of present tense forms to narrate a past time story. The speaker uses the present tense to make the story seem more immediate—as though it were happening right now. Sometimes you will read stories written in this style, but usually it is reserved for spoken story telling.

Registration yesterday was just terrible. First, I go to the department and talk with my adviser. Then, I walk over to the registration area.

Probably your major problems with simple present tense include:

Subject-verb agreement (see Section 15 on p. 88)

Knowing when to use present progressive rather than the simple present (see Section 3 on p. 24 and Section 9d on p. 61)

5b EXERCISES: The Simple Present Tense

A. Use a highlighter to mark the main verbs and the verbs used in clauses in these two passages. What time orientation is used in each passage? For what purpose is present tense used?

ISOLATION OF THE ELDERLY IN THE U.S.

Five million older Americans live alone. Many of them are active, well, and continue to take part in community life. But hundreds of thousands of them—even those who are mobile and could participate—live in virtual isolation. The phone does not ring; there are no visitors; there are no invitations; there are no easy, affordable ways to secure transportation to a senior center, a civic program, or even to market. There are no incentives to action.

And for the frailest, the truly physically homebound, life is lived in a kind of solitary confinement that is destructive to mental and physical health and to humanity.

Adapted from *Let's End Isolation* (U.S. Department of Health, Education, and Welfare, 1971)

REPORT ON U.S. PUBLIC EDUCATION IN 1976

The majority of the students in schools that reported racial/ethnic groups were white (70.1 percent), with a higher percentage attending public schools (72.8) than private schools (68.5 percent). Nearly 20 percent of the students were black and 8 percent were of Hispanic origin, representing in both cases a higher proportion than their representation in the general population 18 years and over. The following tabulation presents the percent distribution of racial/ethnic groups by public and private enrollments and by sex:

Racial/ethnic groups	Total	Total Public	Private
Total	100.0	100.0	100.0
American Indian	.7	.8	.7
Asian American	2.1	1.5	2.4
Hispanic	7.6	7.5	7.8
Black	19.5	17.4	20.5
White	70.1	72.8	68.6

Racial/ethnic groups	Men Total	Men Public	Men Private	Women Total	Women Public	Women Private
Total	100.0	100.0	100.0	100.0	100.0	100.0
American Indian	.8	.8	.7	.7	.7	.7
Asian American	1.8	2.1	1.8	2.4	1.0	3.0
Hispanic	7.6	6.3	8.5	7.7	8.7	7.3
Black	18.6	15.9	20.6	20.1	19.3	20.5
White	71.2	74.9	68.4	69.1	70.3	68.5

Adapted from *Occupational Education* (Kay, 1976)

B. Write 10 sentences using simple present tense to make general truth statements about any topic that interests you—yourself, your university, the room you are sitting in, your field of study, and so on.

C. Write 10 statements of scientific truth or fact. For example, *Oil floats on water.*

D. In a journal in your field of study, find an article of interest to you. As you read it, look for any uses of simple present tense. If possible, work with another student with the same major. What time meanings are used?

E. Academic writing is often focused on general truth statements—using simple present tense. When an example is added, the example is often a past time event that is given in the simple past tense. (See "Synthetic Light Polarizer" in Section 8c on p. 56 for an example.) To see how this combination works in your academic speciality, select a textbook used in a course in your major field and find a section that gives general truths, especially definitions. Then, see what verbs are used in the examples. Report on your research to your class and show examples of the uses of present tense to make general truth statements.

F. Many academic disciplines (including law, medicine, business, anthropology, and the social sciences) use *case studies* to teach important concepts and processes. Your instructor will bring a textbook from one of these fields to show you how case studies are used. Compare the general truth sections of the text to the case study. How are the verbs different? Analyze the questions that are given with the case study, too. Decide on the best answers.

G. Write a case study to illustrate one of the following situations. First, write a general truth discussion of the principles and processes that will be illustrated in the case study. Then, write a case study that shows the principles and processes. If possible write the case with other students who are majoring in your field of study. Share the case study with the rest of your class. Possible topics include: (1) the various forces in a person's life that lead to the selection of a major field of study, (2) communication/miscommunication across cultures, (3) the importance of laboratory experimentation in the hard sciences, or (4) some other topic that is of interest to you.

6 Past Tense

The basic verb in English can be changed to make a form that is traditionally called *past tense.* As you learned long ago, regular verbs form the past by adding *-ed* while irregular verbs form the past by some internal change of spelling and/or pronunciation.

While past tense forms are primarily used to express past time, other uses are also possible. For example, past tense is used in the subjunctive (see Chapter 4):

I wish I had a computer at home. (current time wish)

Moreover, other verb forms also have past time meanings—past perfect, present perfect, and some of the modals (*I could speak German when I was a child.*).

Simple past tense is used for these meanings:

1. An event/action completed at a definite time in the past:

   I took calculus last term.

2. Past time habits or events repeated in the past:

   She went to the computer lab every weekend last term.

3. An action or event that lasted over a period of time but is over:

   He lived in Switzerland for about five years.

4. Unreal or imaginative events (see Chapter 5 for more on the hypothetical):

   If you had a terminal at home, you wouldn't need to be in the lab so much.

   He wishes he had a better background in calculus.

Probably your major difficulties with the simple past tense include these problems:

Spelling (see Section 14 on p. 85)

Knowing when to use the present perfect rather than the simple past (see Section 3 on p. 24 and Section 8b on p. 54)

Using the various forms of conditional and hypothetical sentences (see Chapter 5)

For practice in these three areas, turn to the relevant sections of *The Handbook* as indicated in the Index.

7a Modals

The English verb phrase can be a single verb—the simple present or the simple past. It can also be made up of two or more verbs combined into one unit. The modal auxiliary verbs combine with a simple form of a verb—modal + verb. The modals include *will, would, can, could, shall, should, may, might,* and *must.* Verbs with similar meanings and grammar are *have to, ought to, be able to,* and other periphrastic modals (see Section 7f on p. 52).

You have probably memorized some definitions for each of the modal auxiliaries similar to these:

1a. *will* future time

The research project will be completed next term.

1b. *will* determination, volition

I will pass this test if it kills me.

1c. *will* scientific fact, general truth

Oil will float on water.

2. *would* hypothetical

We would report more exact measurements if we had more modern equipment.

3. *can* ability, informal permission, possibility

He can use several different computer languages.

4. *could* hypothetical ability, past time ability

If we had better equipment, we could complete the research project more efficiently.

When I was younger, I could learn new information much faster than I can now.

5. *shall* formal version of *will*

In this chapter, I shall explain the historical development of current beliefs.

6. *should* obligation, expectation

Many instructors think that good students should be on time to class, do their homework, and be polite.

Other instructors think that good students should think deeply and ask difficult questions.

We should have the results of the project by the end of this week.

7. *may* permission, possibility

Student to librarian: "May I check out this issue of The New York Times?"

8. *might* possibility

We might need an additional two weeks to complete the report, but we might finish it sooner than that. It is difficult to predict how fast the data can be analyzed.

9. *must*   necessity, logical probability

When working in this lab, all students must wear safety glasses because of possibile damage to the eyes.

John has a scholarship; he must have made good grades in high school.

7b EXERCISE: Review the Meanings of Modals

Before continuing with this section, write one sentence to illustate the meaning of each of the modals. Compare those examples with those written by other students to see which you think best illustrate the basic meanings of the modals. Write your favorite examples here in *The Handbook* for later reference.

_____

_____

_____

_____

_____

_____

_____

_____

_____

7c Modals as a System

You have probably noticed that the modals interact as a system. Grammarians suggest that the system has two major parts:

1. Modals can be used to talk about social relationships—the making of requests or the giving of advice. Some examples are:

   Advice: *You should attend all of the lectures.*

   Requests: *May I turn in the research paper two days late?*

   Demand/Rules: *You must turn the paper in exactly on time.*

2. Modals can be used to make guesses about things, events, people. This function is sometimes called the "logical probability" use of modals.

The new computer should make the computations more exact and easier to do.

He must be an excellent instructor—he won the teaching award last year. But, I've never had a class with him myself.

How are the following four requests different from each other?

Will
Would
Can
Could
} *you tell me where the chemistry lecture hall is?*

What about these four?

Can
Could
May
Might
} *I close the door?*

Generally, *would, could,* and *might* are felt to be more polite and less abrupt when making requests. *May* is thought to be the most formal way of asking permission—and thus best used when talking to someone of higher rank or status. When talking with friends or peers, Americans tend to use *can* to ask permission.

These are important issues in the effective speaking of English. Since this *Handbook* is focused on written English, no additional information will be given about the asking of questions with modals. You will find, however, that the social relationship uses of the modals do occur in written English. Think about the changes in meaning in these sentences as the modal changes:

You might/could obey the university's regulations.

You should obey the university's regulations.

You must obey the university's regulations.

You will obey the university's regulations.

Each change makes the statement stronger. The writer is giving you less freedom of choice as the modals change from *might* or *could* to *should* to *must* to *will*.

The logical probability system has much the same structure. The modals interact to suggest the certainty of the writer that the statement is correct. Think about the changes in meaning in these sentences as the modal changes:

That might/could be the answer.	*She might/could graduate this term.*
That may be the answer.	*She may graduate this term.*
That should be the answer.	*She should graduate this term.*
That must be the answer.	*She must graduate this term.*
That will be the answer.	*She will graduate this term.*

The speaker expresses stronger and stronger certainty with the change from *might* or *could* to *may* to *should* to *must* to *will*.

When you select a modal, you are making a decision about how strongly you feel or about how certain you are of your information. Native speakers of English are aware of slight but important differences in meanings of the modals. In answer to an invitation or a request, they say things like

"I would if I could . . . but I can't."

In answer to commands, they may ask

"Is that a 'must' or a 'should'?"

However, be careful to notice that the meaning of *should* or *might* can really be *must* if the speaker is a polite person of great power in your life. Because the status of the speaker can influence the strength of the modals, it is possible for modals to take on meanings different from their basic definitions. For example, if a professor in a course politely says, "You should read this material for the test," he or she is really making a very strong statement—a *must*! Or, if an instructor says, "You might want to get here a little early for this test," the wise student knows that a command has been given.

7d A Note on Use of *Shall*

While Americans do not generally use *shall* much in speaking, this modal does occur frequently in formal academic writing. The traditional rule for *shall* and *will* says for future time meanings to use *shall* with *we* and *I* and to use *will* with other subjects. That same traditional rule tells us to reverse the use for emphasis—*will* with *I* and *we*; *shall* with other subjects.

A more modern rule (based on observation of what educated Americans actually do) reports that *will* is used for future time meanings and that *shall* is more emphatic.

Another rule says that Americans use *shall* with *we* or *I* when they are being very formal.

Look at this example from a textbook used in undergraduate physics courses. Use a highlighter to mark the modals. What does *shall* seem to mean? Does it refer to future time? Does it seem emphatic? Are the writers being formal?

Isaac Newton is considered by many to be the most brilliant scientist who ever lived. His genius came into full bloom in his early twenties when, during one 18-month period, he formulated the laws of gravitation, invented calculus, and proposed theories of light and color. On his tomb in Westminster Abbey is the following epitaph: "Mortals, congratulate yourselves that so great a man lived for the honor of the human race." Newton's contributions to several branches of physics are truly remarkable. In this chapter we shall investigate only a few of the contributions he made to the field of mechanics. It is in this area that Newton is most widely known today, primarily because of his three laws of motion and his theory of universal gravitation.

As background to this chapter, recall that in our previous work we described the motion of objects based on the definitions of displacement, velocity, and acceleration. However, we have not yet been able to answer specific questions related to the nature of motion, questions such as "What mechanism causes motion?" and "Why do some objects accelerate at a greater rate than others?" In this chapter, we shall use the concepts of force and mass to describe the change in motion of objects. We shall see that it is possible to describe the acceleration of an object in terms of its mass and the resultant external force acting on it. The mass of an object is a measure of the object's inertia, that is, the tendency of the object to resist an acceleration when a force acts on it.

We shall also discuss *force laws,* which describe how to calculate such quantities as the force on an object or its acceleration. We shall see that although the force laws are rather simple in form, they successfully explain a wide variety of phenomena and experimental observations. These force laws, together with the laws of motion, are the foundations of classical mechanics.

The purpose of classical mechanics is to provide a connection between the acceleration of a body and the external forces acting on it. Keep in mind that classical mechanics deals with objects that (a) are large compared with the dimensions of atoms $(\approx 10^{-10}\text{m})$ and (b) move at speeds that are much less than the speed of light $(3 \times 10^8$ m/s). If either criterion is violated, the equations and results of this chapter do not apply.

Our study of relativity and quantum mechanics in later chapters will enable us to cover the complete range of speeds and sizes.

Adapted from "Introduction to Classical Mechanics" (Serway and Fraughn, 1985)

7e EXERCISES: Modals

A. Since social judgments are based on cultural values, things that are optional or required change from place to place. For example, in the U.S. most of us would tend to think that *"Children should obey their parents . . . unless the parents request some harmful thing."* In many other countries, people believe that *"Children must obey their parents."*

First, gather information about *should*s and *must*s in your culture by working with another student from your own country. Make a list of five things that are absolutely required—the *musts*. Make a second list of five things that are valued but not required—the *shoulds*.

Second, use this information as evidence in a composition about cultural values and cultural differences. Before writing gather more information by comparing lists with students from other countries. Can they substitute *should* for your *must*? Do these differences reveal anything to you about your own values? All of this information can be used as evidence for generalizations about cultural values and differences.

After you have written the composition, read it aloud to another student. This process frequently helps writers to find out where their work needs improvement. Ask the other student to make suggestions about the organization and the content of the composition—not about the grammar or spelling. When you have finished with revision, carefully edit the composition for verbs, especially for correct use of the modals.

B. Read the following passage and find all the modals. Decide on the meanings of the modals. What do you think is happening in this conversation?

Neville said, "I'll ask you again. Are you ready to tell me that the Pump *will* destroy us? Never mind 'might,' never mind 'could'; never mind anything but 'will.'"

Selene shook her head angrily. "I can't. It's so marginal. I can't say it will. But isn't a simple 'might' sufficient in such a case?"

From *The Gods Themselves* by Isaac Asimov

C. In this report, select the most appropriate modals to go in the blanks. Work with another student to decide on which modal is most appropriate in the context. Be prepared to explain your choices.

NOISE POLLUTION AND THE TRANSPORTATION SYSTEM

Noise, defined as unwanted or excessive sound, is now broadly recognized as a form of environmental degradation. Noise _____ _____ be annoying, _____ interfere with sleep, work or recreation and, in extremes, _____ cause physical and psychological damage. Until recently, both industrial and transportation noise problems were largely excused as part of the cost of progress.

Highway vehicular noise is clearly the most pervasive transportation noise source in our society today. All states _____ consider the benefits that their residents _____ obtain from effective regulation. Industry, and the Federal and State Governments, _____ increase the tempo of research on vehicular noise reduction. Federal, state and local highway and city planners _____ design new highways and establish land-use zoning to avert future noise problems. And responsible authorities _____ take corrective steps to improve present high noise situations.

D. Select a topic of concern at your college or university. Plan a survey of American students on the topic. For example, you could ask "Should physical education courses be required of all students?" Write down the exact response of the students to that question. What modals do they use? Write a report based on the survey in which you use the modal system to explain the attitudes of the American students.

E. Editorials are expressions of opinion by the writer and the newspaper. Check the editorials in a recent issue of your student newspaper to see what modals are being used. Are there any *musts*?

F. Look at the introductory paragraphs at the beginnings of chapters in textbooks you are using for your courses (other than English). What verbs are used to state the purpose of the chapter?

G. In formal written English, *should* and *must* are often found in passages that focus on moral or ethical issues. For example, a management textbook might have many uses of *should* and *must* in a discussion of employee/employer relationships. *The Chronicle of Higher Education,* a weekly newspaper read by most faculty members and administrators in U.S. colleges and universities, is very influential because so many educators read it. It published an article in its January 20, 1988, issue by Dr. Mark Reisler from the University of Virginia's Graduate School of Business in which he called for greater activity by colleges and universities to achieve racial integration. What modals does he use? What do these modals tell us about his feelings on this issue?

If genuine integration is to be achieved, the academic community must acknowledge the problem and establish aggressive and inspiring leadership to deal with it. Faculty members, administrators, students, and alumni must recognize the unfinished business of their particular institution, join together to eliminate the injustices of the past, and assume the responsibility for integrating their campus.

Each institution must examine its unique racial history and its efforts, or lack thereof, to enhance the opportunities for blacks. The product of such examination should be a comprehensive strategy, including specific policies, programs, and resources, to promote a welcoming atmosphere for blacks.

The responsibility for implementing the strategy must be clearly allocated to specific individuals and groups. They, in turn, must be held accountable through a formal and continuing monitoring system. Integration is an ongoing, highly active process. It requires continual hard work.

We must recognize that effective integration will greatly enrich higher education. Failure to achieve it will pose an incalculable threat to the growth of the minds and souls of all students, white as well as black. Without the presence and influence of blacks at all levels on the campus, the university itself will be deficient and the education it offers sadly narrow.

From "Colleges Need Aggressive, Inspiring Leadership If They Are to Achieve Genuine Integration" (Reisler, 1988)

H. "The situation of foreign and foreign-born students is similar to that of black students." Review the passage given in exercise G. Then, discuss the statement at the beginning of this exercise. Write a passage in which you state your ideas on what the university should or must do to improve the situation of foreign and foreign-born students.

7f Periphrastic Modals

Grammarians have different names for these verbs. Sometimes they are called *semi-modals* or *quasi-modals.* Whatever the term, these verbs are synonyms for some of the meanings of certain modals.

Modal	*Periphrastic Modal*
must	*have to, have got to*
should	*be supposed to, ought to*
will	*be going to, be about to*
would	*used to*
can	*be able to*
may	*be allowed to*

The periphrastic modals are grammatically different from the true modals.

1. Subject-verb agreement must be followed (except with *used to,* which is always past tense).

   John has to go to the lab; then, we have to meet Jose.

2. They use *to* while the true modals do not.

   John has to go to the lab.

   ▼ *John must to go to the lab.*

3. *Have to* adds *do/does* to form negatives and questions.

   Do you have to take the test?

   He doesn't have to give his report today.

4. *Ought to* is like the regular modals in that it does not use an auxiliary or *to* for its negative.

   You ought not miss so many lectures.

Usually the periphrastic modals are felt to be less formal than the regular modals, especially when the contracted forms are used in speech. Compare these sets of sentences:

1a. *All students should attend the reception.*

2a. Instructor: *"You oughta go to the reception."*

1b. *The U.S. must attend to the interests of its allies.*

2b. *The U.S. has to take care of its friends.*

7g EXERCISES: Periphrastic Modals

A. Revise each of these informal statements into more formal written English.

1. Student: "The university is gonna raise tuition next year."

2. Instructor: "You guys have gotta get here on time."

3. Student: "Instructors oughta be nice to their students."

4. Politician: "The president is gonna get us in a war if he doesn't watch out."

B. Which, if any, of the periphrastic modals are found in academic writing? Select three articles from journals in your field of study. Analyze the introductions and conclusions of those articles. Modals or periphrastic modals are more likely to be found in introductions and conclusions than in the body of the paper since the body usually is descriptive rather than evaluative. What periphrastic modals occur? Compare your survey to that of other students. Discuss the implications of the survey.

8a Perfect

The present and past perfect forms combine the correct form of *have* with the past participle of the verb:

The computer industry has developed a dazzling array of software.

He had studied calculus before he entered the university.

Both present and past perfect involve time relationships. The past perfect means that one past event was completed prior to a second past event:

First, he studied calculus. Second, he entered the university.

He had studied calculus before he entered the university.

The present perfect relates a past time to the present:

The development of software began in the past. It continues to the present.

The computer industry has developed a dazzling array of software.

The verb form that seems to cause most problems for advanced students is the present perfect. This verb is used to talk about events that occurred in a time period that started in the past and continues to the present. These are the essential features of present perfect: the time is past, the time started in the past and continues to now, and the time is not specific. The speaker is taking the point of view that what he/she is talking about occurred "before now." Events can have happened only once, many times, a long time ago, or recently.

Only one time:

I have been to New York only once in my life.

Many times:

I have been to the beach more times than I can count.

A long time ago:

I have visited New York only once and that was in 1944.

The U.S. has been independent from England for over 200 years.

The earth has revolved around the sun since time began.

Recently:

You have just read sentence 1.

Sentences with present perfect verbs frequently use the connectors *for* and *since* because the purpose of these two words is to define periods of time. As you know, *for* gives the total amount of time while *since* gives the starting point.

He has studied mathematics since he was a child.

He has studied mathematics for almost 20 years.

8b Simple Past Tense vs. Present Perfect

The sections on time orientation have already introduced the contrast between the simple past tense and present perfect (see Section 3 on p. 24). Because of the difficulty advanced students have in choosing between the simple past tense and the present perfect verb form, the topic will be discussed again in this section. To native speakers of English, the various verb forms are not isolated from each other, but rather exist as parts of an interrelated system. This interrelatedness is the basis upon which decisions are made about which forms to select. Grammarians have suggested that you consider the following relationships.

If the speaker is focused on present time, use simple present tense or present progressive as appropriate. Events that occurred before the present time are talked about with present perfect. Events that occur after the present time are talked about using a future time form.

Present time:

He is writing a research paper.

Before the present:

He has already been to the library.

After the present:

He will finish the paper next weekend.

If the speaker is focused on the past, use simple past tense. For events that happened before the past, use the past perfect. For events that happen after the past, the simple past is also used.

Past time:

He wrote a research paper last term.

Before the past:

He had done hours of reading before he wrote the paper.

After the past:

After he wrote the paper, he typed it on his computer.

Grammarians have also pointed out another contrast between the simple past tense and the present perfect based on the difference between "definite" and "indefinite." Just as *a* differs from *the*, so the present perfect differs from the simple past. Remember that *a* is used for first reference to something when the speaker does not think that his/her audience knows what is being talked about. After the noun has been identified and made definite, the speaker changes to *the*.

Once long ago, an *old woman lived in a small town. Bad children laughed at* the *old woman.*

English has a similar definite-indefinite contrast with past and present perfect. When the speaker is not definite about the past time, the present perfect is used. When he/she makes the time definite, then the switch is made to the simple past tense form. Many times a topic is introduced with the present perfect because the speaker cannot be sure that the listener knows what is being talked about.

Tom: "*Have* you ever *taken* Business Law?"

Mary: "Yes, last summer."

Tom: "Who *was* the instructor?"

8c EXERCISES: The Perfect

A. Use a highlighter to mark the main verbs in this example of time orientation in written English. Then study the explanation.

SYNTHETIC LIGHT POLARIZER

Ordinary light waves are made up of helter-skelter vibrations, moving in all directions. If the vibrations in one direction are made to predominate over the others, the light becomes "polarized."

As a freshman at Harvard in 1929, Edwin Land was preoccupied with the problem of producing a practical material that could be used to polarize light. Experiments had gone on for over a hundred years, but natural crystals that could polarize light were small and costly. In 1852, an English doctor had discovered a synthetic crystalline material that worked, but the crystals were difficult to grow to suitable size, and they shattered into powder on the slightest impact.

Land approached the problem from a different point of view: instead of trying to construct one large polarizing crystal, he proposed that a transparent layer could contain innumerable submicroscopic crystals oriented to provide the optical equivalent of a large crystal. He took a leave of absence from his courses at Harvard College and experimented with making such a polarizer in his own laboratory for one year and a half. Land returned to Harvard with a successful polarizer, which he described in a 1932 presentation to the Harvard Physics Department: "A New Polarizer for Light in the Form of an Extensive Synthetic Sheet." Soon afterward Land left Harvard to devote his time fully to further research on polarizers and polarized light.

Applications for the new, convenient light polarizer were varied. Polarizing sunglasses and camera filters were among the earliest commercial products utilizing sheet polarizers. The polarizers were first manufactured by the Land-Wheelright Laboratories, the predecessor to Polaroid Corporation established in 1932 by Edwin Land and George Wheelright.

In 1937, Land formed Polaroid Corporation, which continued to produce polarizers for scientific, industrial, and consumer use. Although he has served as the company's president, chairman, and chief executive, as well as its director of research, business activities have not kept Land away from the laboratory. His continuous research has yielded many innovations, including specialized polarizers and optical elements for use in World War II, and, of course, the Polaroid instant films and cameras, first introduced in 1948. In more than 50 years of research, Land has been issued 524 U.S. patents.

Adapted from *Eureka!* (U.S. Small Business Administration, 1982)

The passage begins with a general truth orientation—using present tense—to give two sentences of scientific fact. Then, the writer changes to a past time orientation to tell the history of the development by Edwin Land of a practical method for polarizing light. The second sentence of the final paragraph changes to a present time orientation—which continues for the rest of the passage. Notice that in the past time orientation these verb forms are used:

past tense for specific events in the past

past perfect for events that occurred in the past before the past time of the passage

In the final paragraph, the present time orientation uses present perfect because Land is still alive. The passage is focusing on a time period that started in 1937 and continues to the present.

B. Find the verbs in these passages. What is the basic time orientation of the passage? Why is the present perfect used? If the present perfects were changed to simple past, how would the meaning be changed?

UNDERSTANDING HUMAN LANGUAGE

During the past two decades, major advances have been made in our understanding of human language. Moreover, these advances in knowledge have occurred in virtually all facets of language and communication behavior. . . . My own concern with human language has centered almost exclusively on the perception and processing of speech at the phonetic level. . . . As I will attempt to demonstrate, studies concerned with the perception and processing of speech have an equally important significance for those investigators who are attempting to unravel the mysteries of why some children fail to develop full linguistic competence.

Adapted from "On the Processing of Speech" (Eimas, 1979)

INTERNATIONAL COOPERATION FOR SOCIAL DEVELOPMENT

Social Welfare has become an indispensable element in country development programs in every geographical area of the modern world. The swift progress made in recent years in translating general objectives for human betterment into practical community services of value to families and children is directly due to exchange of ideas across national boundaries.

The United Nations has provided the major leadership in recent years in international exchange in the social welfare field. Opportunities have also been available on a regional basis through the Organization of American States and the individual country technical assistance programs and voluntary agencies and foundations. The United States and other member governments have cooperated in countless ways to share new knowledge and methods. These productive programs have come into being because many countries have worked together through governmental and voluntary organizations to promote social development and to create avenues for exchange of learning.

Adapted from *International Cooperation: The Contribution of the Welfare Administration* (U.S. Department of Health, Education, and Welfare, undated)

C. The following passage has a present time orientation. What forms of the verb fit best in the blanks?

THE EXPLORATION OF SPACE

The exploration of space _____ (be) one of the great adventures of humanity. Our generation _____ (make) its permanent mark on history by pushing back the frontiers of knowledge and human experience to include the Earth's neighbors in the solar system. The manned space program _____ (be) an achievement almost in the realm of fantasy. The exploration of distant planets using robotic spacecraft _____ (be) no dream; it _____ (be) an extraordinary technical and scientific adventure. For the past two decades, the United States

_____ (lead) the way in this enterprise.

_____

Adapted from *Planetary Exploration Through Year 2000* (U.S. National Aeronautics and Space Administration, 1986)

D. A report on English grammar stated that the perfect forms are found in only 10 percent of verb phrases. Select two pages from a textbook in some field of study that interests you. Look through it to find the perfect forms of the verb. How many do you find? Compare the number that you find with the number of verbs in the passage. Find out what other students discover in other textbooks. Does your research support the percentage given in the report? What does this research suggest about the perfect? What does it suggest about your study of grammar?

9a Progressive

The rule that describes the formation of the progressive (or *continuous*) verb phrase is tense + *be* + verb*ing*. This description means that the progressive must begin with either a present tense or past tense form of *be*. (For information on complex verbs that include the progressive, see Section 10 on p. 65.)

She is *studying calculus this term.*

She was *leaving the library when she ran into her professor.*

This list of the possible uses of the present progressive is given as a review:

1. An action in progress:

   You are reading this sentence now.

2. A temporary action in the present:

   You are studying English this term.

3. A repeated action in the present:

   He is tapping his pencil on the desk.

4. An action in the future:

   He is picking up his new computer tomorrow.

The past progressive is used to communicate about past time actions that are viewed as having been in progress in the past rather than completed. Generally, you will use the past progressive in these situations:

Two past actions occurred at the same time. One was in process when the other happened:

He was typing his final report when he realized that he did not have correct references for two quotations.

A past action occurred at a particular time:

He was watching the news on TV at 6:30 p.m.

The past action was repeated many times:

My neighbor's dog was barking all night.

9b Progressive to Mean Repeated Actions

The meaning of a sentence is a result of the meaning of the particular verb when combined with a particular verb form. That is, if the verb refers to something that can be done repeatedly, then the progressive suggests that the action was done over and over rather than just once. Compare these sets of sentences.

He was knocking on the door. *She is bouncing the ball.*

He was locking the car.   *She is taking the test.*

Knocking and *bouncing* involve repeated actions while *locking* and *taking* are thought of as single actions.

9c Stative Verbs

The adjective *stative* refers to "states of being" in contrast to actions. The difference in meaning between stative and nonstative can be illustrated with the difference between the verbs *love* (a state of being) and *walk* (an action).

Stative verbs use simple present tense to mean present time. Nonstative verbs use present progressive to mean present time.

This hamburger seems expensive. (The hamburger is not doing anything.)

You are reading this example. (You are doing the action of reading.)

Grammarians divide stative verbs into five major categories

1. Verbs of **sensory perception**: *taste, hear, see, smell, feel, appear, look* (When it means "appear," *She appears tired* means *She looks tired.*)

2. Verbs of **mental and intellectual states**: *know, believe, understand, remember, doubt, think, wonder, suppose, imagine, recognize, mean* (When it refers to definitions rather than plans: "Walk" means to *move around using your feet.*)

3. Verbs of **emotional states**: *want, desire, love, hate, like, dislike, prefer, need, appreciate, seem*

4. Verbs of **ownership**, **possession**, **or relationship**: *have, own, contain, entail, belong*

5. Verbs of **measurement**: *weigh, measure, cost, equal.* These verbs are very close to general truth in meaning, so the use of simple present tense may not seem as strange as it does for other stative meanings. For example:

The text I bought for business law weighs 3 pounds.

In conclusion, it is probably more accurate to think of *stative* as a kind of meaning that a verb can have. For example, *taste* has two different meanings:

The soup tastes good. (This is a state-of-being meaning.)

The cook is tasting the soup. (This is an action meaning.)

Have can also be used for either an active or a stative meaning:

He has a computer. (Ownership is seen as complete and not in process.)

He is having a lot of trouble learning Basic. (The trouble is not complete, but is continuing over a period of time.)

When selecting the verb form, you must consider whether the meaning refers to an action or to a state of being. The list of *stative verbs* can serve as a guide in making your choice, but it cannot be used without thought. Appendix L of Ready Reference provides an alphabetized list of the stative verbs given in this section.

9d Present Progressive vs. Simple Present Tense

The major problem in using the progressive is the contrast between simple present tense and the present progressive.

First, if the verb has a stative meaning, then present tense means "present time." (Stative verbs are reviewed in Section 9c on p. 60.)

This hamburger tastes too salty.

The baby loves his mother.

Second, if the verb is not stative but has an active meaning (especially one that emphasizes process and change from one form to another), then present progressive means "present time." Notice that the "present" time can cover greatly varying periods of time. Also, notice that verbs that are usually "stative" can sometimes be given "active" meaning.

You are reading this sentence right now.

You are studying English grammar this term.

You are living in the U.S. currently.

The earth is beginning to experience the "Hot House" effect.

The U.S. is becoming an urban, nonagricultural society.

The postal worker is weighing the package.

The mother is looking at the baby and loving it with her eyes.

Third, if the verb has a general truth meaning, the simple present tense is used.

The earth rotates on its axis.

Organic chemistry studies carbon compounds.

9e EXERCISES: The Present Progressive

A. Even advanced students sometimes have trouble deciding whether to use the simple present tense or the present progressive. Before doing any of the other exercises in this section, review the rules that control your choices by explaining why the underlined verb in each of these sentences is correct.

1. The president <u>believes</u> that his policy will end the war.

2. This flower <u>smells</u> good.

3. Children <u>love</u> their parents.

4. The cook <u>is smelling</u> the soup.

5. The Beatles sang a popular song with the words "I <u>Am Loving</u> You."

6. We <u>are leaving</u> at noon for the picnic.

7. We <u>leave</u> at noon for the picnic.

8. Different people <u>breathe</u> at different rates.

9. You <u>are breathing</u> right now—or something is terribly wrong.

Rule for 1, 2, and 3:

_____

_____

Rule for 4 and 5:

_____

_____

Rule for 6 and 7:

_____

_____

Rule for 8:

_____

_____

Rule for 9:

_____

_____

B. Because academic writing is often about the past, the present progressive that means "present time" is not often found in textbooks or journal articles. It is more likely to be used in writing that has a present time focus, for example, newspapers or popular weekly magazines. Get a copy of _Time, Newsweek,_ or some similar weekly magazine. With another student, scan the magazine for uses of the present progressive verb form. Then, decide if each verb is being used for "present time" or "future time" meanings. Share your most interesting examples with the rest of the class.

C. In writing, you are much more likely to use the simple present tense than to use the present progressive because you will write more about the general truth than about the present. Remember, the simple present is used:

to mean present time with verbs frequently used in academic writing (_think, know, believe, understand,_ for example) to give generalizations

to mean present time when *be* is the main verb

Anál\ze each of the sentences in the following passages. Use a highlighter to mark each of the main verbs. What verb form is used for the main verb? What time is meant? If the verb is simple present tense, can a present progressive be substituted?

THE RICHES OF SPACE

Use of near-Earth space for profit-making activities is no longer a subject for the distant future. The space environment is being used now for economic activities. Communications satellites are an important part of our industrial growth. Commercial sales of the first space-fabricated commodity (latex microspheres) have started. The processing of pharmaceuticals and biological compounds in microgravity is on the verge of becoming another commercial activity.

Adapted from *Planetary Exploration Through Year 2000* (U.S. National Aeronautics and Space Administration, 1986)

NEW WORLD, NEW QUESTIONS

The brief encounters of the *Voyager* spacecraft with the Jupiter and Saturn systems dramatically demonstrated that the outer solar system contains a dazzling array of potential targets for future planetary exploration. Beyond the asteroid belt lie four giant ringed planets (Jupiter, Saturn, Uranus, and Neptune), more than 50 moons (two of which—Titan and Ganymede—are larger than the planet Mercury), at least two planetary magnetospheres larger than the Sun itself, and the curiously small world Pluto. The center of gravity of our planetary system is here; these worlds (chiefly Jupiter and Saturn) account for more than 99 percent of the mass of the solar system, including the Sun.

Exploration of the outer planets, especially Jupiter, can provide unique insights into the formation of the solar system and the universe itself. Because of their large masses, powerful gravitational fields, and low temperatures, these giant planets retain the hydrogen and helium that they collected from the primordial solar nebula. The abundance and composition of these elements in the atmosphere of Jupiter, for example, can provide fundamental clues to the formation of the solar system 4.5 million years ago.

In addition to information about the past, these giant planets will certainly provide other clues to help us unravel the history of the solar system. Chemical reactions are now taking place in the atmospheres of the giant planets and of Saturn's moon Titan. These reactions may resemble some of the early history of the Earth and may therefore help us to study some of the pathways to our own beginnings.

Adapted from *Planetary Exploration Through Year 2000* (U.S. National Aeronautics and Space Administration, 1986)

D. In writing personal essays (especially in freshman composition courses), you might use more of the present progressive because you will talk about yourself in the present. Here are some topics that have been used in essay-writing tests. Decide if you could use present progressive to write on the topic. Give an example to support your analysis. Share your examples with other students in the class.

Why did you come to this university to study your major?

What characteristics do you regard as important in a person you would choose as a friend?

Explain what it means to be poor. Be specific.

To what extent, and in what ways, does television affect you?

How have your eating habits changed since you've been in college? Discuss.

E. Write a composition on one of the topics given in exercise D. After revising the essay, edit it carefully for verb forms. Share any of the examples that you have written of appropriately used present progressive verbs with the rest of the class.

10a Combinations

The organization of the English verb phrase can be described by this formula:

(tense) or (modal) + (perfect) + (progressive) + verb

This formula does not say anything about the meaning of the verb, but it is a complete description of all the choices (except the passive). *Tense* can be either *present* or *past*. The parentheses mean that the part is optional. *Perfect* is *have* + the past participle. *Progressive* is *be* + the *-ing* form of the verb. The simplest verb must always contain either tense and the verb or a modal and the verb. Here are all the choices:

1. tense + verb

   He walks home. He walked home.

2. tense + perfect + verb [tense + *have* + past participle of the verb]

   He has walked home. He had walked home.

3. tense + progressive + verb [tense + *be* + *-ing* of the verb]

   He is walking home. He was walking home.

4. tense + perfect + progressive + verb

   He has been walking home. He had been walking home.

5. modal + verb

   He will walk home.

6. modal + perfect + verb

   He will have walked home.

7. modal + progressive + verb

   He will be walking home.

8. modal + perfect + progressive + verb

   He will have been walking home.

1 describes the simple present tense or the simple past tense. It just means that a verb phrase can be the simple present tense form or the simple past tense form. 2 describes the perfect forms—present or past. The perfect is made of the present or past of *have* followed by the past participle of the verb. 3 describes the progressive forms—present or past. The progressive is made of the present or past tense of *be* followed by the *-ing* form of the verb. 4 describes the combination of all the possibilities.

5 describes the combination of modal and verb. In this rule, any of the various forms of the modal can be used. 6 describes the combination of the modal with the perfect; 7 is the modal combined with the progressive. 8 combines all the possible forms.

While 4 and 8 are not the most common forms of the verb, they certainly are the most complicated.

The combinations are discussed in this order:

modal + perfect

modal + progressive

tense + perfect + progressive

model + perfect + progressive

10b Modal + Perfect

Traditional discussions of the modal auxiliaries divide them into present and past tense forms. But, few of the modals actually have a past time meaning; usually they refer to the present, to general truth, or to the future. Only *would* and *could* have past time meanings in the simple modal + verb combination. *Had to* can be used for the past time meaning of *must*.

He would write all night until he was exhausted.

She could speak French when she was younger.

He had to take the test last week even though he was quite ill.

The major function of the perfect when combined with a modal is to add past time meaning. In the following example, the speaker is talking about a past time event: John was sick. John did not take the test.

John would have taken the test if he had not been sick.

Section 7c on p. 45 divides the meanings of the modals into two large categories labeled *logical probability* and *social interaction*. The use of modal + perfect for social interaction meaning is limited to the giving of advice or to talking about obligations. The implication is that some past time obligation was *not* carried out:

He should have studied for the test. (He did not study.)

You could at least have said "Hello." (You did not speak.)

Modal + perfect is used primarily for logical probability meanings. The writer is making a guess about the past. Each change of modal makes the guess stronger:

John may have made a mistake.
John might have made a mistake.
    May and *might* are approximately the same in meaning.

John could have made a mistake.

John must have made a mistake.

Can is rarely used with the perfect—except in negative sentences such as:

He can't have arrived already; he wasn't expected so soon.

The combination of modal + perfect can also be used for present and future time predictions; they predict that something is finished now or will be completed by a future time. This is sometimes called the *future perfect.*

The package should have arrived by the time you reach the office.

You will have been here three years before you leave next summer.

10c EXERCISE: Modal + Perfect

Read and think about the following situation. Then, write an evaluation of the actions of the participants that includes information about how you might have behaved differently. Was there anything that anyone could or should have done that would have changed the outcome? The people involved include the farmer, his wife, his children, some doctors, the owners of a lumber company, and the man who was the agent for the lumber company. You might also think about the agencies that should have been involved—the hospital, the government, and so forth. You might need to review the uses of the hypothetical before writing your composition (see Chapter 5).

THE DEATH OF A BLACK FARMER IN ALABAMA IN 1956

On May 4, 1956, while plowing in his corn field, my father* felt pains in his chest as he often had. Making his way to the house where my mother was, he asked for baking soda (he thought it was indigestion again), but the pain did not let up. At the hospital, 18 miles away in Butler, the county seat, the doctors diagnosed a heart attack and said they would perform surgery if he would pay the $250 for admission to the hospital. Because they were general practitioners and because he felt he was dying anyway, my father refused to allow my mother to pay. He chose instead to go to a hospital in York, Alabama, another 32 miles distant, where he died the next day.

1955 had been a good year for my father. After harvest and having paid off his farm operating debts, he purchased a 21-cubic-foot deep freezer for my mother so that she would not have to spend so much time in the hot kitchen canning over the wood stove. It was our first electrical appliance. And, after sending away to the mail order store as usual for the children's winter school clothes and shoes, there had been money left over—$450. In the emergency room, he proclaimed that it would not be touched, that he was dying and would do so with or without the surgery, and that the money was for his wife and children. He could leave that much.

On the morning after my father was buried, my 13-year-old brother donned a pair of overalls and a blue chambray shirt he had worn so often, turned in the doorway, and said to all of us assembled there: "Daddy is dead now, and from now on, I'm in charge. From now on, I'm the man of this family and don't nobody ever forget it," and he picked up the milk buckets and went out to milk the cows. He set about the task my father had taught him so well, harvesting a bumper crop of corn that year.

But things soon began to change radically. Within two weeks, my mother was notified by an agent of the lumber company that the owners did not think she and the children could handle what my father had been doing, that it would be necessary for us to move, and that she should begin looking around for somewhere else to go by fall. We harvested the crops and left.

---

*The farmer was a 71-year-old man with a family of seven children, who ranged in age from 2 to 20. Their farm was rented from a lumber company. By the way, $450 was a very large amount of money in 1956, especially for a poor farmer.

Adapted from "Naheola, Alabama: A Remembrance of a Black Farming Community" (Young, 1980)

10d Modal + Progressive

If you look back at the formula given at the beginning of Section 10a on p. 65, you can see that it is possible to combine modals with the progressive:

He will be working on the research project for five years.

This verb phrase combines the meaning of the modal with the meaning of the progressive.

Sometimes this is called the *future progressive*. That name is somewhat misleading if you think of *will* as the only auxiliary for the future. (See Section 4a on p. 34 for more information on writing about future time.) All of the modals can be combined with the progressive:

He can be studying . . .	*He shall be studying . . .*
He could be studying . . .	*He should be studying . . .*
He will be studying . . .	*He may be studying . . .*
He would be studying . . .	*He might be studying . . .*
He must be studying . . .	

Some of these are more common than others. You are more likely to encounter combinations of *could, will, must, should, may,* and *might* with the progressive than any of the others.

Should + progressive has a social interactive meaning—obligation or advice—in sentences such as:

You should not be at this party. You should be studying for your examinations.

Should + progressive also has a logical probability meaning in sentences such as:

His calculus exam was supposed to end at 10:00. He should be finishing it about now.

All of the other combinations of modal + progressive are used for logical probability meanings of various degrees of certainty. The progressive adds the meaning of the action being in process rather than completed.

Question: *Where is the chairman of the department?*

Possible Answers:

She might be meeting with the faculty.	I'm not sure.
She may be meeting with the faculty.	
She could be meeting with the faculty.	It's possible.
She should be meeting with the faculty.	She's supposed to, so I expect it is happening.
She must be meeting with the faculty.	The meeting was scheduled. The door to her office is closed. No faculty are in their offices. I'm very sure this is happening. *But* life is full of uncertainty. There is a small chance that I'm wrong.
She will be meeting with the faculty at 10:00.	This is a statement of complete certainty about a scheduled future time event.

10e EXERCISE: Modal + Progressive

Think about some member of your family or about a good friend. What time of day is it where that person is? What is that person doing? Write a description that includes statements about things that you are sure about but also include some other guesses. After revising the passage for content and organization, edit it carefully for verb forms. You might find it helpful to share that passage with another student and with your instructor for additional suggestions for editing.

10f Tense + Perfect + Progressive

If you look again at the formula given at the beginning of Section 10a on p. 65, you will see that it is possible to combine perfect with progressive:

You have been studying English for a long time.

The verb phrase combines the indefinite past time meaning of the perfect with the in-progress, ongoing meaning of the progressive. The example sentence means that your study of English started at an unspecified time in the past and continues to the present. There is little difference between the first example and this sentence:

You have studied English for a long time.

The use of the progressive emphasizes that the action is something that has been in progress. The difference is more one of style and emphasis than of significant difference in meaning.

10g Modal + Perfect + Progressive

This combination uses all the possibilities—(a) the social interaction or logical probability meaning of the modal, (b) the indefinite, past time meaning of the perfect, and (c) the in-progress, ongoing meaning of the progressive. You might have learned to call this the "future perfect progressive." However, other modals can also be used in this combination:

What was John doing last night?

He might/may have been working . . .

He could have been working . . .

He should have been working . . .

He must have been working . . .

Should has two possible meanings—either the social interaction meaning of "obligation/advice" or the logical probability meaning of "expectation." The other modals have logical probability meanings of various degrees of certainty.

When *will* is used in this combination, the meaning is complete certainty about something ongoing until finished at a given future time.

You will have been studying English for 10 years by the end of this term.

John will have been living in New York for five months on his birthday.

You will have been paying on the car for four years before you own it.

10h EXERCISE: Modal + Perfect + Progressive

The combinations described in Sections 10f and 10g are possible but not very common. See what examples you and the other students in your class can find. Look at these sources; then, share the examples you find.

the first article in the most recent *Time* magazine

the third chapter in a textbook that you are using this term in a class other than English

the front page of the local newspaper

the editorial page of the student newspaper at your college or university

the description and history of your college or university given at the beginning of its undergraduate catalog

11a *Be*

Be is probably the first English verb that you studied. Many ESL books start with it because it is the most commonly used verb in English. As you might recall from those early days of English study, *be* is also the most complex verb in English and has more forms than other verbs. It can be used in more ways and has more possibilities for its object. The word *complement* is frequently used for these forms that "complete" the meaning of *be*.

As an advanced student, you certainly know all the forms of *be*. To focus on the subject of this section and to remind yourself of the forms, please fill in this chart.

```
┌─────────────────────────────────────────────────────────────┐
│                      Forms of Be                            │
├─────────────────────────────────────────────────────────────┤
│                                                             │
│   1. Present tense                                          │
│                                                             │
│        I _____        We _____        │
│                                                             │
│        You _____                                 │
│                                                             │
│        It _____        They _____     │
│                                                             │
│   2. Past tense                                            │
│                                                             │
│        I _____        We _____        │
│                                                             │
│        You _____                                 │
│                                                             │
│        It _____        They _____     │
│                                                             │
│   3. Past participle _____                       │
│                                                             │
│   4. -ing form/present participle _____          │
│                                                             │
│   5. Infinitive __to_____                              │
│                                                             │
└─────────────────────────────────────────────────────────────┘
```

Be can be the main verb in a sentence, or it can be the auxiliary for a progressive or passive verb phrase:

The dictionary is on the top shelf. (main verb)

He is looking for the dictionary. (auxiliary in progressive)

The dictionary was misplaced or stolen. (auxiliary in passive)

Be as a main verb can have three different types of object:

He is a student. (noun phrase)

He is tall. (adjective)

He is in the library. (prepositional phrase)

Advanced students seldom have problems with the forms of *be* except for subject-verb agreement in complicated sentences. (See Section 15 on "Subject-Verb Agreement" on p. 88.)

11b EXERCISE: *Be*

To review the uses of *be* read the following passages. Mark all uses of *be*. Analyze these into two categories—*be* as main verb or *be* as auxiliary verb.

THE HUMAN COLLISION

It has become clear that there are really two kinds of collisions within a single automobile accident. The first is the car's accident in which the car hits something, buckles and bends, and then comes to a stop. The second and more important collision is the "human collision" which happens when a person hits some part of the car. It is the human collision that causes injury.

In a 30-mile-per-hour crash into a barrier, a car is crushed and comes to a stop about one-tenth of a second after hitting the barrier. Slow-motion film would show that the people are moving forward at their original speed when they slam into the steering wheel, windshield, or some other part of the car. This is the human collision.

Adapted from *The Human Collision—How Injuries Occur . . . How Seat Belts Prevent Them* (U.S. Department of Transportation, 1976)

OCCUPATIONAL SAFETY LAW

Early safety laws were few in number and limited in scope. Those that existed were for the most part related to sanitation and ventilation or to requirements for fire escapes and means of extinguishing fires. Some applied to safety in connection with certain machines. However, new machines and new methods were being developed rapidly, and the legislatures, usually meeting every two years, were unable to keep pace with changing industrial processes. To deal with this problem, states established industrial commissions that were given wide power to develop and issue rules and regulations in the field of occupational safety and health.

Adapted from *Summary of State Occupational Safety and Health Legislation* (U.S. Department of Labor, 1968)

12a Indirect Speech: Dealing with Verbs in Quotations

In writing research papers and other types of compositions in your academic work, you will need to know how to deal with quotations. One important aspect of quotations is using correct punctuation and giving references so that you cannot be accused of plagiarism. However, cheating and plagiarism are more properly topics for a composition course, so they will not be dealt with here.

In giving a quotation, you have three basic choices: (1) you can give the exact words and mark them with quotation marks; (2) you can change the wording in the style called "indirect quotation" or "indirect speech"; (3) you can paraphrase (see Chapter 19).

Before going through the rules of indirect quotation, first look at this example. The president of MIMDEX Corporation is quoted in a newspaper as saying, *"I plan to improve our productivity as well as our profits by better use of our human resources."* You want to use this quotation in a research paper on the relationship between productivity and profit, but you already have used a lot of direct quotation and decide that you want to blend this statement into your paper without quotation marks. How do you change it to make it into an indirect quotation? Write the sentence here. Then compare your answer to that of another student to see if you forgot anything in making the change.

In making the change to indirect quotation, you must deal with several grammatical changes. First, because the point of view is changing from first person (*I*) to third person (*he, she, it, they*), most of the pronouns will need to be changed.

Second, because of the lack of quotation marks, some type of wording will be necessary to indicate that this is a quotation—not your own words but a version of someone else's words. These phrases include *he said that . . ., she remarked that . . ., they indicated that . . ., he suggested that . . .,* and many others.

Third, in very formal writing, it might be necessary to change the verbs of the quotation in a pattern that is sometimes called "sequence of tense." (Even in very formal situations, the rules are not as exact as you might have been taught. Changes are not made that would make significant changes in the meaning of the original quotation. See the box on p. 77 for exceptions to the rule.)

Finally, depending on the dates and time involved, you may need to make changes in the time words used in the quotation. To review how these changes affect a quotation, consider this quotation:

At a news conference this morning the president of the university said, "Although I deeply regret the change, I have today asked the Board of Regents to increase tuition next fall by 10 percent."

The first change will be to select a quotation-marking phrase. In this case, *the president of the University announced. . . .* The second change will be to consider any necessary changes from *I* to *he*—two *I*'s will become *he*'s. The third set of changes will influence the two verbs—*regret* and *have asked.* These verb changes are controlled by the sequence-of-tense rule explained below.

Sequence-of-Tense Rule

1. Simple present tense becomes simple past tense.

2. Present perfect becomes past perfect.

3. Present progressive becomes past progressive.

4. Modals are changed in the following pattern:
   may becomes either *might* (for possibility)
   could (for permission)

   can becomes *could*

   will becomes *would*

   must becomes *had to*

   shall becomes either *would* (purely for future time)
   should (to give advice)

One possible sentence is:

At a news conference this morning, the president of the university announced that although he deeply regretted the change, he had today asked the Board of Regents to increase tuition next fall by 10 percent.

This sentence still has some problems because of the time adverbs— *this morning, today,* and *next fall.* This version of it would be adequate if it were used soon after the president's news conference. But the time adverbs are misleading if they are used much later. For example, what would you do if you were using the quotation two years later in a paper about changes in tuition over the history of the university? You would need to know the exact date of the news conference; then you could make the statement more accurate. For example,

At a news conference on March 10, 1986, the president of the university announced that although he deeply regretted the change, he had that day asked the Board of Regents to increase tuition the next fall by 10 percent.

While these changes are sometimes followed in formal written English, there are many exceptions to the rule because nothing can be done that will distort the meaning of the original statement.

Exceptions to the Sequence-of-Tense Rule

1. General truth statements using simple present tense are frequently left in present rather than changed to past. You have the choice.

   The chemistry instructor reminded his students that oil and water do not easily mix.

   The chemistry instructor reminded his students that oil and water did not easily mix.

2. If the change from simple past to past perfect would change the meaning of the quotation, the change is not made.

   The politician said, "I signed the treaty because I wanted to provide food and shelter for all our people."

   ▼ *The politician said that he* had signed *the treaty because he* had wanted *to provide food and shelter for all his people.* (The first change is no problem because *had signed* is accurate—past time prior to the past time of his statement. The *had wanted* is a problem because it can mean that he failed in his plan—or that he changed his mind.)

   The politician said that he signed the treaty because he wanted to provide food and shelter for all his people. (Neither is changed to past perfect.)

   The politician said that he had signed the treaty because he wanted to provide food and shelter for all his people. (Only *signed* becomes *had signed.*)

---

3. If the event talked about in the quotation is still in the future, the quotation will probably not change from *will* to *would*. You have a choice unless the use of *would* makes the statement too conditional.

The law student said, "I will be elected president soon after the beginning of the 21st century."

The law student said that he will be elected president soon after the beginning of the 21st century.

The law student said that he would be elected president soon after the beginning of the 21st century.

4. Hypotheticals do not change to past forms because their meaning would be changed.

The labor leader said, "If I had my way, all laborers would have full-time work."

The labor leader said that if he had his way, all laborers would have full-time work.

▼ *The labor leader said that if he had had his way, all laborers would have had full-time work.*

(If you changed to a past tense version, you would change his meaning; this is a statement about past time failure rather than his original statement about future intentions.)

Another grammatical difficulty with indirect quotation involves pronouns that cannot easily be exchanged for other pronouns. In some cases it is necessary to add different words by using brackets—[ ]—to show that you are changing the quotation. Try this version of the last example:

The union leader said, "If I had my way, all of our members would have full-time work."

What can be done about "all of our members"? You cannot substitute *his* because that would change the meaning—the members of the union are not *his*. You cannot use *its* because there is no word for it to refer back to.

The union leader said that if he had his way, all of [the union's] members would have full-time work.

The brackets mean that these are not his exact words but are a necessary substitute for the exact meaning of the quotation.

12b EXERCISES: Quotations in Indirect Speech

A. Here are some quotations along with additional information about the speaker and the context. Make them into indirect quotations that do not change the meaning of the original. Compare your versions with those of other students in the class.

1. At a news conference this morning. The president of your university. "Starting next term, all classes will last 75 minutes."

2. In an interview last week. The vice president of the U.S. "I will run for the presidency if the members of the party support me."

3. Franklin Delano Roosevelt. U.S. President. 1911 interview. "There is nothing I love as much as a good fight."

4. Abraham Lincoln. U.S. President. 1858 letter. "As I would not be a slave, so I would not be a master."

B. Look in today's newspaper for interesting quotations. Select three and turn them into indirect quotations. Share these with another student and your instructor to be sure that you handled all the details correctly.

13a Irregular Verb Classes

The irregular verbs of English demand much of the ESL student. You must learn the meanings as well as many different forms, pronunciations, and spellings. When you are memorizing a large amount of material, the most efficient method is usually to divide it into a number of smaller groups. The irregular verbs are much easier to deal with when they are put into groups on the basis of similarities of formation.

The following division is based on one given in *A Comprehensive Grammar of the English Language* (Randolph Quirk, Sidney Greenbaum, Geoffrey Leech, and Jan Svartvik. 1985. London: Longman).

The irregular verbs are divided into these seven classes on the basis of pronunciation. This list includes the more common irregular verbs and does not claim to be a complete listing of all the irregular verbs of English. An alphabetized version of these verbs is given in Appendix A. A space within a class indicates a subclassification within the larger class.

Class 1 The past tense is formed with *-t* or *-d*. The past tense and the past participle are the same. The vowel is the same in all forms. *Smelled* and *burned* are more common in the U.S. than *smelt* or *burnt*—so these two verbs are better considered regular verbs in American English.

Base Form	Simple Past and Past Participle
burn	burned/burnt
bend	bent
build	built
lend	lent
send	sent
spend	spent
have	had
make	made
smell	smelled/smelt

Class 2 The past tense is formed with *-ed*. There are two forms of the past participle—one with *-ed* and the other with *-n*. Usually the vowels remain the same in all forms. The past participle with *-n* is most typically used as an adjective in front of a noun:

He fell down; his ankle swelled up quickly; his swollen ankle hurts.

Base Form	Simple Past	Past Participle
mow	mowed	mowed/mown
saw	sawed	sawed/sawn
sew	sewed	sewed/sewn
show	showed	showed/shown
sow	sowed	sowed/sown
shear	sheared	sheared/shorn
swell	swelled	swelled/swollen
prove	proved	proved/proven
shave	shaved	shaved/shaven

Class 3 The vowel changes from the base form to make the past. The past tense and the past participle are the same. A suffix is added—*-t* or *-d*.

Base Form	Simple Past and Past Participle
creep	crept
deal	dealt
feel	felt
keep	kept
kneel	knelt
leap	leapt
leave	left
mean	meant

Base Form	Simple Past and Past Participle
sleep	slept
sweep	swept
weep	wept
bring	brought
buy	bought
catch	caught
seek	sought
teach	taught
think	thought
lose	lost
flee	fled
sell	sold
tell	told
hear	heard
say	said

Class 4 This group has a large number of subgroups because so many different vowel sounds are involved. However, all subgroups have these characteristics in common: the past tense and the past participle are different, the vowel of the base is not used in the past tense, and just about always the past participle is formed with -n. Notice that in some of the subgroups the vowel of the past participle is the same as that of the past tense—*broke/broken*—while in other subgroups the vowel of the past participle is the same as that of the base form—*eat/eaten*.

Base Form	Simple Past	Part Participle
break	broke	broken
choose	chose	chosen
freeze	froze	frozen
speak	spoke	spoken
steal	stole	stolen
awake	awoke	awoken
wake	woke	woken
weave	wove	woven
bear	bore	born
swear	swore	sworn
tear	tore	torn
wear	wore	worn
bite	bit	bitten
hide	hid	hidden
forget	forgot	forgotten

Base Form	Simple Past	Part Participle
lie	lay	lain
blow	blew	blown
grow	grew	grown
know	knew	known
throw	threw	thrown
forsake	forsook	forsaken
shake	shook	shaken
take	took	taken
give	gave	given
draw	drew	drawn
fall	fell	fallen
eat	ate	eaten
see	saw	seen
drive	drove	driven
ride	rode	ridden
rise	rose	risen
write	wrote	written
fly	flew	flown
do	did	done
dive	dived/dove	dived
thrive	thrived/throve	thrived

Class 5   All parts are identical.

bet

bid

cast

cost

fit

hit

hurt

knit

let

put

quit

rid

set

shut

split
spread
thrust

Class 6 No suffix is added. A vowel change marks the difference between the base and the other forms. The past tense and the past participle are the same.

Base Form	*Simple Past and Past Participle*
bleed	*bled*
breed	*bred*
feed	*fed*
hold	*held*
lead	*led*
meet	*met*
speed	*sped*
read	*read*
cling	*clung*
dig	*dug*
fling	*flung*
hang	*hung*
spin	*spun*
stick	*stuck*
string	*strung*
swing	*swung*
win	*won*
wring	*wrung*
bind	*bound*
find	*found*
grind	*ground*
light	*lit*
slide	*slid*
sit	*sat*
get	*got**
shoot	*shot*
fight	*fought*
stand	*stood*

---

*American English distinguishes between *got* and *gotten* as past participles for two different meanings. When "have" or "possess" is the meaning, Americans use *got*: *He's got a really old car.* When Americans mean "buy," "acquire," "cause," or "become," *gotten* is used: *She's gotten the books for the course already.* Or, *The students have gotten the instructor to agree to postpone the test.* Or, *He has gotten old before his time.*

Class 7 No suffix is added. All of the vowels are different. Notice that the vowel change in *begin* is in the stressed syllable; the first vowel remains the same in all forms.

Base Form	Simple Past	Past Participle
begin	began	begun
drink	drank	drunk
ring	rang	rung
shrink	shrank	shrunk
sing	sang	sung
sink	sank	sunk
spring	sprang	sprung
swim	swam	swum
come	came	come
run	ran	run
go	went	gone

13b EXERCISES: Irregular Verbs

A. Discuss with other students methods that they use to memorize new vocabulary, especially the forms of irregular verbs. Different students have found different methods to use, and you might discover something more effective than the method you are currently trying. List the various memorization techniques in the space given below. Try different methods to see which is most effective for you.

_____

_____

_____

_____

_____

_____

B. While you probably already know most of the common irregular verbs, give yourself a test to find out what you do not know. For example, place a strip of paper over the past participle column and see if you can write (not just say, but also spell!) the past participles for each of the seven classes of irregular verbs. Write in the space given here the words that you still have trouble with. Select a method from exercise A for learning and using the words that you do not yet know.

_____

_____

_____

_____

_____

_____

14a Spelling of Verb Forms

The spelling of English can be confusing. However, in the case of the spelling of the *-ing*, past tense, and past participle forms of the verbs, the rules are relatively simple and consistently applied. Both regular and irregular verbs spell their *-ing* forms in the same ways. Most regular verbs follow the same rules for forming their past tense/past participle form.

Group 1 If the verb ends in *-e*: drop the *-e* and add *-ing* or *-ed*.

vote	*voting*	*voted*
create	*creating*	*created*

Group 2 If the verb ends with two vowels + a consonant: just add *-ing* or *-ed*.

wait	*waiting*	*waited*
appear	*appearing*	*appeared*
repeat	*repeating*	*repeated*

Group 3 If the verb ends in a vowel + a consonant: for one syllable verbs

1 Vowel → 2 Consonants

beg	*begging*	*begged*

If the verb ends in a vowel + a consonant: for two-syllable verbs

First Syllable Stressed → 1 Consonant

label	*labeling**
visit	*visiting*
travel	*traveling*

Second Syllable Stressed → 2 Consonants

occur	*occurring*	*occurred*
prefer	*preferring*	*preferred*

Group 4 If the verb ends in -*y*, keep the -*y* for the -*ing* form.

obey	*obeying*
pry	*prying*
try	*trying*

If the verb ends in -*y*, keep the -*y* for the -*ed* form, if the -*y* is preceded by a vowel.

obey	*obeyed*

If the verb ends in -*y*, change the -*y* to -*i* for the -*ed* form, if the -*y* is preceded by a consonant.

try	*tried*
pry	*pried*

Group 5 If the verb ends in -*ie*, change the -*ie* to -*y* for the -*ing* form, but just add -*d* for the -*ed* form.

die	*dying*	*died*

Group 6 If the verb ends in two consonants, simply add -*ed* or -*ing*.

call	*calling*	*called*

Group 7 If the verb ends in vowel + -*c*, a -*k* is added before -*ed* or -*ing*.

picnic	*picnicking*	*picnicked*
panic	*panicking*	*panicked*

---

*This form is preferred in the U.S.

14b EXERCISE: Spelling Verb Forms

If you are having trouble with the spelling of these words, use the following list for practice. Put each word on a piece of paper with the base form on one side and the -*ing* and past tense/past participle forms on the other. Practice with these using this method: First keep all the words with similar spelling together as a group. By going over many examples of the same rule, you can learn the rule more effectively. After you have practiced the groups of similar words for a while and feel confident about them, then mix all of the pieces of paper randomly and test yourself to see if you can do the words this way. If you have trouble with a word, put it back in the stack only 10 or 12 slips from the top so that you will see it again soon. When you have learned the word and feel that you know it very well, then put its slip of paper farther down in the stack to see if you can remember it when you have not seen it for a while.

Group 1—these end in -*e*:

acquire, bake, believe, change, date, describe, hope, injure, raise, reinforce, use

Group 2—these end with 2 vowels + 1 consonant: *wait, look, rain, shout, need*

Group 3—these end with a vowel + consonant combination:

a. one-syllable words that end with a vowel and a consonant—*stop, top, mop, tap, plan*

b. two-syllable words with the first syllable stressed—*channel, happen, listen, open*

c. two-syllable words with the second syllable stressed—*control, occur, prefer*

Group 4—these end in -*y*:

a. the -*y* is preceded by a vowel—*play*

b. the -*y* is preceded by a consonant—*cry, try, worry, marry*

Group 5—these end in -*ie*:

die, tie

Group 6—these end in 2 consonants:

help, learn, present, start, work

Group 7—these end in -*c*:

panic, picnic

15a Subject-Verb Agreement

The basic rule of subject-verb agreement is simple to explain and to memorize.

If the subject of the sentence is a singular noun, a proper noun, a noncount noun (see Section 2c on p. 149), or *he, she,* or *it,* a present tense verb adds -*s*.

The textbook costs $45.

John walks to the bus.

Mathematics seems orderly in comparison to economics.

It feels hot today.

She plans to be a medical doctor.

Only *be* has subject-verb agreement in past tense:

The course is part of the required core for the Ph.D.

The test was long and difficult.

She is the instructor for the biology lab.

She was a student at Continental University.

Only *be* has a special form for when the subject is *I*:

I am the instructor for this biology lab.

While much of what a university student writes is in the past tense, present tense forms are common, too, especially in reports of general truth and scientific fact.

The earth rotates on its axis and revolves around the sun.

For reasons that cannot yet be explained, subject-verb agreement is one of the last things mastered by most students of ESL. That is, while most students memorize the rule fairly early in their study of English, they do not begin following that rule automatically until the later stages of learning English.

Generally, there are five types of problems with subject-verb agreement:

First, a student is still at a low proficiency level in English and just has not yet learned to recognize the need for subject-verb agreement—even in simple cases. Your friends who are beginners or intermediates have this problem.

Second, a student is not consistent in use of the rule. Sometimes he/she remembers. Sometimes the rule is forgotten. This student can benefit from learning to be a good editor, so that he/she checks all of his/her writing to be sure that subject-verb agreement is included.

Third, there are complex sentences in which even native speakers of English make mistakes by misjudging the grammar of the sentence. In this example, the writer was in a hurry and had the verb agree with the wrong noun. What seems to happen is that the writer makes a choice for the verb while thinking about the last noun that he/she has written. Here the writer is thinking about the noun *party* while writing a passive verb *was misspent.*

▼ *The funds that were budgeted for the party was misspent.*

The funds that were budgeted for the party were misspent.

The writer who is a good editor would realize that the subject is the plural *funds,* so the verb needs to be changed to *were.*

Fourth, English has a large number of nouns and pronouns that are controlled by special rules. For example, you could be tricked by nouns that end in *-s* but are not plural:

Economics studies the relationship between supply and demand.

Fifth, English has many nouns and pronouns that cause difficulty in deciding on the correct form of the verb. Even native speakers do not agree on preferred usage in some of these cases. You will find that certain instructors have very strong feelings about these forms. It would probably be wise to conform to the usage that each instructor advocates. The simplest method for discovering an instructor's feelings is to show a sample sentence and ask for help in writing it correctly. Another method is to take careful note of the corrections made on papers and texts. The following discussion lists the various choices that you have in these troublesome cases. For example, educated native speakers of English do not agree about the choice of verb when the subject is *none.* Some would use the first version of the sentence while others would use the second version.

None of the students was late for the test.

None of the students were late for the test.

We will first review the aspects of the rule that native speakers generally agree about. Then, we will discuss a number of complexities and difficulties.

15b Subrules of Subject-Verb Agreement

1. Collective nouns (see Section 2f on p. 154) take either the singular or the plural verb depending on meaning. Americans tend to use the singular with these collective nouns.

   The committee has reported to the president. (committee acts as a unit)

   The committee have disagreed violently about their report to the president. (committee members act as individuals)

2. There is a group of nouns that end in -s that are not plurals. These "false plurals" are words such as *news, mathematics,* and *physics.*

No news is good news.

Mathematics is very difficult for him.

This news makes me very happy.

You already know many of these nouns. Fill this chart with as many of these nouns as you can think of. Then compare lists with other students to get as complete a list as possible.

economics

_____

_____

_____

_____

_____

_____

---

3. Titles of books, plays, movies, and TV shows are always singular—even if the words in the title are in the plural.

"The Snows of Kilamanjaro" is a powerful story.

4. The word *pair* is singular. What confuses some people is the change when that word is *not* used. Look at these sentences:

The new pair of shoes hurts my feet.

The new shoes hurt my feet.

5. *Each* and *every* are not problems when they modify a singular noun—a singular verb is used.

   Each car has a tape player as well as a radio.

   Every car has a tape player as well as a radio.

The problem arises for some students when *each* or *every* is followed by a plural noun in sentences such as

Each of the students . . .   *Every one of the problems . . .*

Most educated writers of English use the singular with such subjects— they seem to agree that the actual subject of the sentence is *each* or *every*.

Each of the students has a dictionary and a notebook.

Every one of the problems is easily solved.

15c Subject-Verb Agreement
in Mathematics

Two similar phrases are easily confused: *A number* is plural. *The number* is singular. The confusion is made worse because both are usually followed by a prepositional phrase using *of* plus a plural noun.

A number of doctors have learned the new procedure.

The number of foreign students in the U.S. has increased dramatically since the Second World War.

   Fractions and percentages take the singular or plural verb depending on the type of noun they modify. If a plural noun is modified, a plural verb is used. If a noncount noun is modified, the singular verb (with -*s*) is used. If a collective noun is modified, either the singular verb or the plural verb can be used. If a singular noun is modified, a singular verb is used.

Plural:

Twenty-five percent of the new buildings have structural defects.

Half of the children are suffering from malnutrition.

Noncount:

Ten percent of the crop was damaged by the frost.

Collective:

Ninety percent of the faculty have doctorates.

Ninety percent of the faculty has doctorates.

Singular:

Twenty-five percent of the building was damaged by the bomb.

15d Complexities and Difficulties

Educated native speakers of English do not agree on the correct form of the verb when the subject is *none, majority/minority, either . . . or/neither . . . nor, either of/neither of* or involves a relative clause.

Our best advice is to find out the preference of your composition and grammar instructors—and do it their way. Also, try to be as consistent as possible, especially within any one paper or essay.

1. Some traditional grammarians and composition teachers say that *none* is always singular because it means "not one." However, educated native speakers of English do not consistently follow this rule. If *none* modifies a plural noun, the tendency is to use a plural verb. If *none* modifies a noncount noun, the tendency is to use a singular verb. *But,* you will find that some writers always use the singular, some writers switch back and forth, and some writers avoid using *none* because they are not sure what to do.

   Noncount:

   None of the stolen furniture has been recovered.

   Plural:

   None of the students have passed the test.

   None of the students has passed the test.

   None of the cars have adequate safety devices.

   None of the cars has adequate safety devices.

2. Educated writers of English seem to switch from singular to plural when using *minority* or *majority* depending on different meanings given the words. No completely convincing explanation has yet been made by grammarians. However, the following meanings have been suggested: (a) *Majority/minority* can be an abstract principle having to do with numbers and counting; for such meanings, the singular is used.

   a. *The majority rules in this club.*

   (b) *Majority/minority* can also be used to refer to the people who make up the group; in that case, it is a collective and either verb form can be used.

   b. *At the political meeting, the majority was/were able to control the results.*

   (c) When a plural noun phrase is modified, educated writers seem to prefer the plural verb.

   c. *The majority of the students were against the change.*

Since native speakers have trouble with these words, we suggest two alternatives for you: First, do whatever your instructor prefers. Second, find some way to rewrite the sentence. For example, you might use a passive to rewrite example b:

At the political meeting, the results were controlled by the majority.

3. When using *either . . . or/neither . . . nor*, the writer will sooner or later be brought to a halt to consider what form of the verb to use. Which verb should be used in this sentence?

Either the books or the instructor is/are in error.

The rule that is followed in most cases is called the "proximity rule." That is, the noun that is closest to the verb controls the form of the verb. The sentence would read:

Either the books or the instructor is in error.

Thus, if you changed the order of the nouns, the verb would be changed:

Either the instructor or the books are in error.

The most serious difficulty comes when the writer wants to use a personal pronoun in this combination. What would you do in this sentence?

Either my assistant or I is/am/are going to write up the lab report.

Some educated writers would insist on using *am* because of the proximity rule. Many other educated writers of English would choose *are*—just as it is used in tag questions (*I'm stating this correctly, aren't I?*). No one would choose *is*. Many other writers would rewrite the sentence to avoid the problem altogether.

4. The following sentence illustrates another difficulty in subject-verb agreement. When one or more prepositional phrases come between the subject and its verb, the choice is sometimes difficult.

The basic reason for most of the accidents on the state's highways is/are drunk driving.

Most writers think that the subject of this sentence, *reason*, should control the choice of verb. They would write

The basic reason . . . is drunk driving.

An important editing skill is being able to find the basic subject and have it agree with its verb.

5. If the subject of the sentence is *either of/neither of*, educated writers do not completely agree on the verb choice. While the traditional rule is that the singular should be used, educated writers sometimes choose the plural.

Neither of them is/are correct.

Neither of the answers seems/seem accurate.

Either of the books is/are going to provide the information.

6. Traditional grammar tells us that *leaders* is the subject of the verb in the relative clause in this sentence.

The president is one of those leaders who control through charm.

The plural verb goes with the plural subject. However, in the examples given below, many educated writers feel that the subject is *one*.

His research is one of those rare projects that leads/lead to changes in how we understand economic processes.

She is one of those influential thinkers who makes/make us reconsider our basic ideas.

You must make a decision about how to write such sentences. In the formal writing of the university, your best choice may be to follow the traditional rule—the subject of the embedded sentence is the noun immediately in front of the relative pronoun. You will, however, find many examples in your academic reading in which writers decide that *one* is the subject, rather than the noun.

7. Another difficult subject-verb agreement choice involves noun clauses (see Section 2 on p. 295) as subjects of sentences. For example,

That an educated work force is necessary for high-tech industries seems undeniable.

The traditional rule is that these subjects are always singular. For example, what past tense form of *be* should be used in this sentence?

What the instructor gave his students . . . a solid foundation in mathematics and a love of learning.

If you are not careful with these sentences, you will look back and see *students* and make the verb plural to agree with that noun. The sentence should read

What the instructor gave his students was a solid foundation in mathematics and a love of learning.

15e EXERCISES: Subject-Verb Agreement

A. To remember what you already know and to discover some of the things that you still have trouble with, find the main subject of each sentence. *Do not fill in the blanks—just mark the main subject.* The first step to successful editing for subject-verb agreement is always to be sure which words are the main subject.

1. The news from the cities damaged by the earthquakes _____ _____ (continue) to be bad.

2. Each student _____ (pay for) health insurance.

3. John, the student with 10 sisters, _____ (live) at home.

4. A number of books _____ (be) missing from the library.

5. The number of books missing from the library _____ (increase) every term.

6. The student committee _____ (be) made up of representatives of 20 different countries.

7. The members of the committee _____ (be) unhappy about the food in the cafeteria.

8. John is one of those students who _____ (like) to study in the library.

9. Studying in the library reading areas _____ (give) me a headache.

10. *Familiar Quotations* _____ (be) a famous book of quotations collected by John Bartlett.

B. Now fill in the blanks in the sentences in exercise A with the present tense form of the verb in parentheses.

C. Write sentences using the following subjects. Use the present tense.

1. Each of the students in this class . . .

2. Every student in this university . . .

3. None of my relatives . . .

4. Neither the United States nor the Soviet Union . . .

5. Either the instructor or the students . . .

6. Either the students or the instructor . . .

7. A number of my friends . . .

8. The number of students . . .

9. Neither my classmates nor I . . .

D. Select a topic that you know quite a lot about—your major field, your work, your family, yourself, and so on. Complete these sentences by writing about that topic using only present tense verbs. Use the given word in the subject of the sentence.

1. Each of . . .

2. Every . . .

3. None of . . .

4. The majority . . .

5. Either . . . or . . .

6. Neither . . . nor . . .

E. Fill in these blanks to remind yourself of what you already know about using fractions and percentages.

1. Fifty percent of all marriages _____ (end) in divorce.

2. One hundred percent of the furniture _____ (be) on sale.

3. Almost half of the coffee crop _____ (be) destroyed in the storm.

4. About one-third of the members of the committee _____ (agree) with each other.

5. About one-third of the banana I brought for lunch _____ (be) rotten.

6. A number of my courses _____ (require) research papers.

7. The number of students majoring in mathematics _____ (have) decreased in the past 10 years.

F. The verbs have been removed from these passages. First, use a highlighter to mark the main subject of each sentence. Then, fill in the blank with the correct form of the verb given in parentheses.

ELECTRICAL DANGERS

Household electricity _____ (be) a great

convenience. Nevertheless, misuse of electricity and electrical appliances

_____ (cause) shocks, bodily injuries, and death.

Adapted from *Protect Someone You Love from Burns* (U.S. Consumer Product
Safety Commission, undated)

INDIAN LANDS AND FARMING

The ownership and control of land _____ (be) the

most important issue facing American Indians. Indians _____

(hold) title to vast tracts of agricultural land, but most of this land

_____ (be, not) farmed by Indians. Also, the rate

of profit on the land that is being farmed by Indians _____

(be) nearly half what it _____ (be) for non-Indian

farmers.

The statistics tell the story: nearly 2.5 million acres of Indian land

_____ (be) classified as agricultural. Of this, 29

percent _____ (be) irrigated. However, 73 percent

of the money made off this land _____ (go) to

non-Indian farmers who _____ (lease) the land from

the Indians.

Adapted from *Indian Tribes: A Continuing Quest for Survival* (U.S. Commission
on Civil Rights, 1961)

G. Edit a paper that you wrote earlier this term. Check for subject-verb
agreement errors. Do you seem to have a continuing problem with this
feature of English? If the answer is "yes," then be sure to edit all of your
writing for subject-verb agreement.

H. Use the information from the graph and chart to write sentences using percentages and fractions as the subject. The information is about the percentage of people who survive a stroke, depending on their age. First complete the statement below the chart by filling in the blanks. Then add five statements of your own.

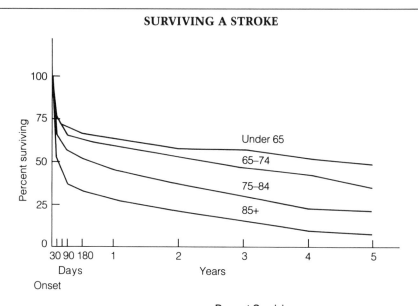

SURVIVING A STROKE

	Percent Surviving							
Age Group		Days				Years		
	Onset	30	60	90	180	1	2	3	4
Under 65	100.0	73.7	71.1	69.4	65.9	63.2	57.6	57.6	52.0
65–74	100.0	75.6	69.5	65.2	63.1	59.4	52.9	46.1	42.7
75–84	100.0	68.1	62.1	57.6	52.4	45.7	37.2	30.0	23.1
85 +	100.0	52.4	45.8	37.2	33.0	27.8	20.7	15.1	9.2

Approximately half (49 percent) of the persons under 65 years of age

who _____ (be) hospitalized for acute stroke

_____ (survive) five years. The survival rate

_____ (be) lower for each older age group. Only 7.4

percent of those 85 and older _____ (reach) the fifth

anniversary of their stroke.

_____

_____

_____

_____

_____

_____

_____

_____

_____

_____

_____

_____

Adapted from *National Survey of Stroke* (U.S. Department of Health, Education, and Welfare, 1980)

16a Phrasal Verbs

Phrasal verb refers to those two- and three-word combinations like *look up* and *look forward to* that are sometimes called *two-word verbs.* The verb is combined with an additional word (or two) that is sometimes considered a preposition or an adverb. In this text, the additional word will be called a "particle." When combined, the two- and three-word phrase works as a unit—in a sense, the words are combined into one larger "word."

These combinations are *idioms* because you cannot predict the meaning of the combination from the meaning of the individual words. That is, *look* plus *up* should mean something about the direction of the eyes but really means to "seek information in a reference book" or "find or contact a person." While many phrasal verbs are considered informal, they can be used in formal writing for stylistic variation.

Phrasal verbs are often used metaphorically, so that the idiom becomes even more difficult to interpret. Consider this statement about John's performance on the test. *Tear it up* is used to mean "did really well."

"John did really well on the test. He really tore it up."

In learning to use phrasal verbs, ESL students have several problems: They have to learn the right meanings for the right word combinations, and they have to deal with the word order when the phrasal verb has a direct object.

Like other verbs, phrasal verbs can be divided into two large categories—those that can take direct objects (transitive phrasal verbs) and those that cannot take direct objects (intransitive phrasal verbs).

16b Transitive Phrasal Verbs

Most phrasal verbs must have direct objects: *turn on, turn out, do over, look over, look up, fill out,* and *find out.* (See Appendix G for a more complete list.)

These transitive phrasal verbs can be subdivided into four categories:

Category One   For verbs like *look up,* a pronoun as the direct object must be placed between the verb and the particle. This category has the largest number of commonly used phrasal verbs, including *turn out* (the lights), *turn on* (the TV), *call off* (the meeting, the party), *throw away* (the old magazine, the broken clock), *look up* (the information, the new word). (See Appendix G for a more complete list.)

He looked it up in the dictionary.

Category Two   For verbs like *come across,* it is never possible to separate the verb from the particle. (See Appendix G for a more complete list.)

▼ *He found the information easily, coming it across in the first article he read.*

He found the information easily, coming across it in the first article he read.

Category Three   For verbs like *get through* and *see through,* the direct object is always between the verb and the particle. There are very few verbs in this category.

The messenger must get the information through to the army.

The country's economic problems are severe. The leaders must get the message through to the public about the need for reduced spending at all levels.

He is not especially interested in this research project, but he will see the work through until it is completed.

Category Four   Some phrasal verbs need prepositions to connect their direct objects. These verb combinations cannot be separated. (A more complete list of these verbs with their prepositions is given in Appendix G.)

Many scientists look down on people who put feeling ahead of thinking.

16c Intransitive Phrasal Verbs

The following phrasal verbs cannot take direct objects for certain meanings: *break down, burn down, come in.* (See a more complete list in Appendix G.)

My car broke down.
The house burned down.
Please, come in.

Some of them have related forms that do have direct objects.

The fireman broke down the door.
The soldiers burned down the house.

16d EXERCISES: Phrasal Verbs

A. Change the direct objects to pronouns as appropriate. Make any word order changes that are necessary.

1. The students in Business Law decided to ask their instructor to cancel the final examination. After he heard their reasons, the instructor agreed to call off the final examination.

2. The students handed in their term project on May 22, and the instructor handed back their term projects on June 22.

3. Because John's term project received the highest grade, the instructor called on John to go over his term project with the rest of the class.

4. John was very embarrassed because he was afraid his friends would think he was showing off, but he gave in to the instructor's request.

5. He picked up his term project and looked over his term project quickly to figure out what to say.

6. He picked out three major points and pointed out three major points as the most important parts of his project.

B. Grammarians say that phrasal verbs are more common in informal, conversational English than in academic writing. To check the accuracy of this statement, analyze a chapter in a textbook in your field or an article in a professional journal. Can you find any phrasal verbs? Make a list of any that seem to be used a lot.

C. Talk with other students about ways that they learn synonyms. What methods can be used to learn that *call on* means *"ask to recite or answer"* or *"visit"*?

D. It is generally a good idea to know what you do not know. Then, you can make a plan to study and learn those things that you decide you need to know. Go over the list of phrasal verbs in Appendix G of Ready Reference. Give yourself an informal test to see which ones you do not know. Talk with other students and your instructor about a plan for learning these important words. Write in the space below the phrasal verbs that you decide to add to your vocabulary.

_____

_____

_____

CHAPTER 3

Passive Sentences

1 Introduction to Passive Sentences

Correct use of passive sentences is an important part of academic writing that even educated Americans can have trouble with. Like most advanced ESL students, these educated writers do not usually have trouble with the formation of the passive. Their difficulties lie in knowing when to use the passive rather than the active.

This chapter will first provide a brief review of the ways in which passive sentences are formed. Then a longer section will discuss the effective use of passive sentences in formal writing.

2 Formation of Passive Sentences

To review what you have already learned, compare these two sentences.

Sir Alexander Fleming discovered penicillin in 1928.

Penicillin was discovered in 1928 by Sir Alexander Fleming.

List here the four ways in which the second sentence differs from the first:

1. _____

2. _____

3. _____

4. _____

The usual descriptions tell us that the differences include (1) the direct object of the first sentence is the subject of the second; (2) the passive verb uses *be* + the past participle of the verb; (3) the noun phrase in the subject position of the first sentence can be used as an adverb/modifier at the end of the second sentence if it is (4) combined with *by*. (Note that the *by* + noun phrase will be referred to as *by* + agent because this preposition phrase tells the agent (or actor) who performed the action.)

3 Forms of the Verb in the Passive Sentence

Only verbs that can have direct objects can have passive forms, for example, *lose* as in *lose a book, lose your money, lose his life.* So, an example of a passive sentence would be

The book was lost by the student.

But, intransitive verbs do not usually have a passive version.

He lived in New York.

▼ *In New York was lived by him.*

The passive verb is *be* + past participle of the verb: *to be used, to be discovered, to be lost, to be written, to be taught.* This passive verb can be used in any of the forms possible for English verbs—from simple present tense to the complete combination of tense or modal + perfective + progressive.

The computer was bought by the university.

The computer will have been being used for six years by the end of this term.

Below the possibilities for *to be used* are illustrated:

1. *The process is used to test drugs in the blood system.* (simple present tense)

2. *The process was used to test drugs.* (simple past tense)

3. *The process will be used to test drugs.* (modal + verb)

4. *The process would be used if it were cheaper.* (modal + verb)

5. *The process has been used to test drugs since 1985.* (present perfect)

6. *The process had been used for 10 years when a better method was invented.* (past perfect; simple past)

7. *The process is being used to test for drug addiction.* (present progressive)

8. *The process was being used to test for drugs before it was made illegal.* (past progressive; simple past)

9. *The process will have been used to test for side effects before the drugs can be produced.* (modal + perfective; modal + verb)

10. *The process will be being used during the next Olympics to test athletes for drug addiction.* (modal + progressive)

11. *The process has been being used for five years to test new drugs for harmful side effects.* (perfective + progressive)

12. *The process will have been being used for two years by the end of the test period.* (modal + perfective + progressive)

4 Use of the *By* Phrase

The addition of the *by* + agent in the passive sentence is frequently optional. Sometimes it is good to include it if the information is important. Sometimes it is unnecessary to include it because the information is obvious. Sometimes it is impossible to include it because the information is not known. In scientific and technical writing, the *by* phrase is not often used.

The new law will be supported by the president. (necessary information)

This text was written to help students learn business calculus. (unnecessary to say *"by the author"*—who else?—unless the author is a famous person and then it might be important information)

The wheel was invented thousands of years ago. (inventor unknown or not important for this statement)

One of the earliest writing systems was devised by the Sumerians. (important information)

5 Use of the Passive Sentence

The passive sentence should be selected carefully for particular uses. In scientific and technical writing, the passive is frequently found because of the emphasis on the process rather than the person who does the process.

The passive can be selected when the actor/agent is not as important as the action/process.

Your article is about use of the computer in manufacturing: *Computerized robots are now being used by General Motors in a new experimental factory.* The passive is more appropriate than the active because it keeps the focus on your topic.

Your article is about General Motors and its ability to use new technology: *General Motors is now using computerized robots in a new experimental factory.* The active is more appropriate than the passive because it keeps the focus on your topic.

You can use the passive when you do not know the actor/agent or when the actor/agent is extremely obvious.

Numerous animals were domesticated long before paper was invented or the wheel was discovered.

Peaches are harvested all during the summer.

Select the passive when you want to hide the actor/agent—for ethical or unethical reasons.

You might not want to give the name of the actor/agent as a way of protecting a person's privacy. *I was told that you were the person who poured coffee on the computer keyboard.* (I am protecting the person who gave me the information.)

You might not want to give the name of the actor/agent as a way of avoiding a confrontation with another person. *The report was poorly designed and even more poorly researched.*

An unethical salesman might say, *"This product has been tested repeatedly for safety."* Who did the testing? His boss? His mother? A reliable laboratory?

The passive sentence provides an effective connector to the end of the previous sentence. This happens sometimes in conversations when one person raises a topic and the second person responds to that particular topic.

John: "Hey, a portable computer! Where'd you get **it**?"

Maria: "**It** was given to me by my grandfather as a graduation present."

Maria uses the passive because she wants *it* (the computer) as the subject of her reply.

The research and development division of the corporation worked for 10 years on a better paper napkin. These napkins were then produced in small quantities in a field test by their San Antonio factory. This combination ties the two sentences together tightly and cleverly.

The research and development division of the corporation worked for 10 years on a better paper napkin. Their San Antonio factory then produced these napkins in small quantities in a field test. The active version of the sentence is perfectly grammatical, but it separates the two mentions of *napkin.* In fact, this might be the preferred version if the whole paragraph is really about the San Antonio factory.

6 Modals with the Passive

As shown in examples 3, 4, 9, 10, and 12 in Section 3 on p. 104, the passive verb can include any of the modals. The modal + passive combination can take either of the two possibilities for modal meaning—the social or the logical.

This medicine must be taken only with milk. (social—strong advice/ requirement)

This medicine must be very effective because it is so expensive. (logical—high level of expectation)

Research has shown that scientific and technical writing can be expected to use no more than 7 percent of modal + passive sentences. When this combination does occur, *can, will, may,* and *would* are the most commonly used modals with their ability, logical, inferential meanings. However, in discussions of ethical issues and other matters of social responsibility, *should* and *must* are often used with the passive.

Here are some examples of logical-inferential meanings from academic textbooks:

Therefore, under the accrual basis, adjusting entries are needed to bring the accounts up to date for economic activity that has taken place but has not yet been recorded. Accurate financial statements can then *be prepared.* (accounting)

Each type of adjusting entry will *be illustrated in this chapter.* (accounting)

The next step is to survey a set of key financial ratios that can *be used to assess the firm's financial condition.* (finance)

The following list includes some of the more important pitfalls that may *be encountered in computing and interpreting financial ratios.* (finance)

If you pull on a coiled spring, the spring stretches. If the spring is calibrated, the distance that it stretches can *be used to measure the strength of the force.* (physics)

Several decades earlier, in his publication The New Sciences, *Galileo wrote, "Any velocity once imparted to a moving body* will be *rigidly* maintained *as long as the external causes of retardation are removed."* (physics)

Social meanings from academic textbooks include the following:

Labor has certain rights that must be recognized. (ethics in management)

Codes of ethics should be formalized *in writing and* communicated *to all employees.* (ethics in management)

7 EXERCISES: Passive Sentences

A. To review the possible forms of the passive, try changing sentence 1 to use all of the various verb forms. Check your answers with your instructor. Only if you have a problem should you practice forming the verb again using sentence 2.

1. *The letter (be) written by her lawyer.*

2. *A new discovery method (be) selected by the research group.*

B. Look over these sentences to decide if the *by* phrase is necessary. What happens if it is removed?

The child was bitten by a coral snake.

This book was written by Mohammad Ali to teach his boxing methods.

After the store was opened by the clerk, we bought our textbooks for the term.

After the new store was opened by the President of the University, a reception was held.

Paper was invented by someone early in the history of civilization.

Paper was invented by the Chinese early in the history of their civilization.

C. The verbs have been removed from this passage. Add the passive form of the verb in parenthesis. Compare your answers to those of another student. If you disagree, talk over your reasoning with your instructor. Notice how frequently the passive of *call* is used in giving definitions of terms.

WHAT CAUSES STROKE?

Blood _____ (carry) from the pumping heart to the brain and other parts of the body through a network of blood vessels that _____ (call) arteries. In the most common form of stroke, the flow of blood _____ (disturb) as an artery serving the brain gradually _____ (clog). Eventually the artery _____ (may with close) entirely by the formation of a clot.

The mass that forms within the artery _____ (call) a *thrombus*, the Greek word for *clot* or *lump*. A stroke that _____ (produce) when the blood supply to the brain _____ (block) because of such a clot _____ (call) a *thrombotic stroke*.

A brain artery _____ (can with block) or _____ (plug) by a clot that _____ (perfective with *form*) elsewhere in the body, usually in the heart or the arteries of the neck, and _____ (carry) in the body's bloodstream to the brain. This kind of traveling clot _____ (call) an *embolus* (a Greek word for *plug*).

Stroke patients _____ (diagnose and treat) by neurologists, physicians who specialize in disorders of the brain. Stroke is a neurological problem because part of the brain _____ (damage). The destroyed nerve cells _____ (may with never and with replace).

Adapted from *Stroke: Hope Through Research* (U.S. Department of Health and Human Services, 1983)

MUSIC SYNTHESIZER

Recent innovations in the art world _____ (sometimes with perfective of *greet*) with allegations that they are not "natural." Responds Robert Moog, inventor of the electronic music synthesizer: "No music is natural. It _____ (produce) only after people invest strenuous and extended efforts to gain intimate control over a vibrating system—be it vocal chords, a violin, or a synthesizer."

Robert Moog began making electronic instruments commercially in 1964. Since then, synthesizers _____ (perfect of *use*) by many musicians—from rock stars to classical composers—to create a new musical vocabulary with electronic sounds.

Adapted from *Eureka!* (U.S. Small Business Administration, 1982)

D. Research has shown that passive sentences are used frequently in technical and scientific writing because such writing focuses on what happened in a research project—rather than on the technicians or scientists. The following sentences would be better in the passive. Rewrite them, and then edit them with another student before sharing them with the rest of the class.

DETECTION OF CANCER-CAUSING SUBSTANCES IN COOKED FOODS

We used standardized procedures for preparing and cooking foods. *We approximated* the common practices in American households. *We purchased* food locally. *We cooked* food in such a way that *we did not burn* it but in some cases it was well done. When normal cooking required oil, *we used* corn oil. *We pan-fried, oven-broiled, baked, boiled, stewed, braised, and left raw* food in various experiments.

We made ground beef into hamburger-sized patties *and cooked* them for a few minutes per side on electric stainless-steel grills. *We controlled* the grill temperature with a special feedback-type thermostat. *We did* broiling in the ordinary manner, with the food placed about 8 cm below the electric element. In some experiments, *we measured* the temperature of the cooking surface and the temperature of the food. *We used* only the outer surface of cooked beef patties for analysis.

Adapted from "Mutagens in Cooked Food" (U.S. Department of Commerce, 1986)

MASS SPECTROMETRY

Scientists use mass spectrometry to help identify the compounds *they have purified. They ionize* the compounds first, so that *they can manipulate* them magnetically. *They accelerate* the ions in a magnetic field and *detect* them by a special detector. *A combination of the strength of the magnetic field and the inertia of the ion determines* the ion's path. *Scientists can therefore determine* the mass of the ions by the spatial distribution of the ion beam.

Adapted from "Optical Coatings by the Sol-Gel Process" (U.S. Department of Commerce, 1985)

E. Find the passive sentences in this passage. Why do you think the passive rather than the active was chosen?

MUTATION-CAUSING SUBSTANCES IN FOOD

The discovery, in the late 1970s, of mutation-causing substances in cooked beef is credited to Sugimura and to Commoner. Other cooked foods were later found by researchers at the Lawrence Livermore National Laboratory and elsewhere to contain significant amounts of these substances, with evidence that they were formed during the cooking process itself.

The idea that cultural practices are intimately connected with illness and disease is now well supported by epidemiological studies of cancer incidence in immigrants. Cancer incidence was known to be affected by diet, but the effect of cooking as a separate process had not previously been considered. The news that cooking could be dangerous stimulated considerable scientific interest, and several laboratories have been trying to identify the mutation-causing substances present and the conditions that affect their formation.

Adapted from "Mutagens in Cooked Food" (U.S. Department of Commerce, 1986)

F. The verbs have been removed from this passage. Decide whether to use the active or the passive of the verb in brackets. To choose the verb forms, remember that this is a report of a research project. Any specific action was in the past, but there are some general truth statements, too. Notice the use of the passive of *show* to refer to charts, illustrations, and graphs.

SOME COOKING METHODS PRODUCE MORE
MUTATION-CAUSING SUBSTANCES*

We _____ [cook] food by several common methods.
The results of cooking beefsteak in various ways _____
[show] in Figure 2. Pan-frying and broiling _____ [pro-
duce] much greater amounts of mutation-causing substances than other
cooking methods.

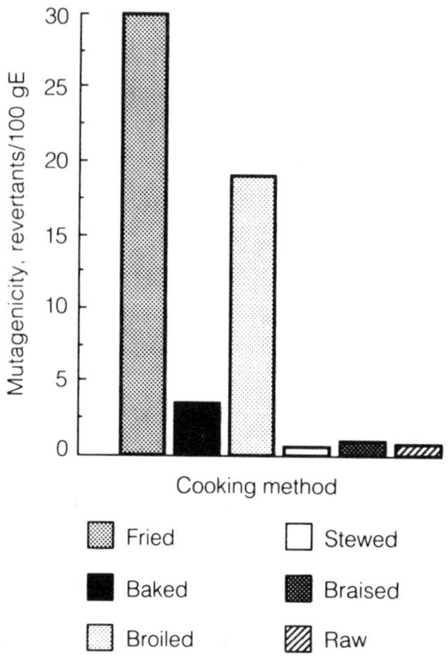

Figure 2 Mutagenicity of beefsteak cooked by different methods: frying at 300°C for 6 minutes a side, baking at 176°C for 90 minutes, broiling at 300°C for 9 minutes a side, stewing at 100°C for 165 minutes, and braising at 100°C for 165 minutes. (gE means gram equivalent of uncooked ground beef.)

Since it _____ [be] possible to avoid eating broiled
or pan-fried foods by using alternative cooking procedures (baking, stewing, microwaving, etc.), we _____ [study] a variety of
foods that _____ [cook] in various ways. We _____
_____ [use] the nine protein-rich, cooked foods that
_____ [eat] in this country—ground beef, beefsteak,

*Mutagens are substances that tend to increase the frequency or extent of mutation. In this case, mutagens result from certain food preparation techniques.

eggs, pork chops, fried chicken, pot-roasted beef, ham, roast beef, and bacon. We also _____ [study] other sources of protein in the American diet, including seafood, lamb, cheese, milk, beans, tofu, and organ meats (e.g., liver, kidney, tongue, and brain).

Quite complex results _____ [obtain], but a number of general statements _____ [can, make]. In many different studies, red meats cooked at moderately high temperatures _____ _____ [contain] mutation-causing substances while other foods not derived from animal muscle cooked by similar methods at similar temperatures _____ [contain] no mutation-causing substances or much smaller amounts. In general, when we _____ _____ [cook] any food longer or at higher temperatures, we _____ [find] more mutation-causing substances, just as we _____ [have] for beef. Some of these effects _____ [show] in Figure 3.

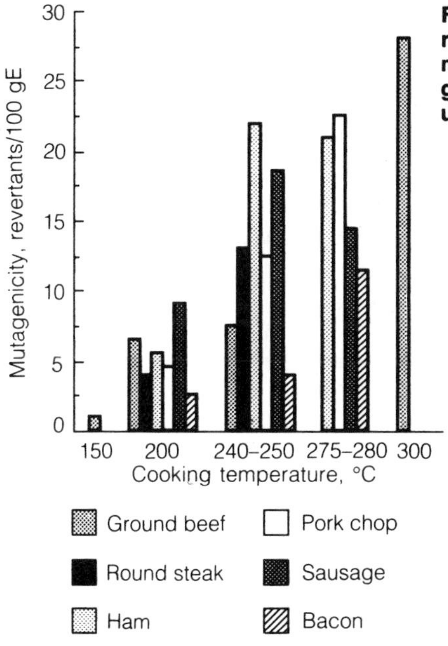

Figure 3 **Mutagenicity of various fried red meats. The meats were fried for 6 minutes a side on a stainless steel griddle. (gE means gram equivalent of uncooked ground beef.)**

Adapted from "Mutagens in Cooked Food" (U.S. Department of Commerce, 1986)

G. Look again at this sentence from the passage in exercise F, and then fill in the blanks to make the sentence complete. This sentence uses three reduced relative clauses that involve passives. The first one is *cooked at moderately high temperatures.* . . . What sentences have been combined to make this complex sentence?

In many different studies, red meats cooked at moderately high temper-

atures _____ [contain] mutation-causing substances

while other foods not derived from animal muscle cooked by similar

methods at similar temperatures _____ [contain] no

mutation-causing substances or much smaller amounts.

---

1. *Red meats contain mutation-causing substances.*

2. *These red meats are cooked at moderately high temperatures.*

3. *Other foods contain no mutation-causing substances or much smaller amounts.*

4. _____

5. _____

Here is another sentence that contains embedded passive sentences. List the different sentences that have been combined.

The original report suggested that meat prepared and served according to normal American dietary customs might contain mutation-causing substances, and biomedical scientists connected with the Lawrence Livermore National Laboratory were concerned.

1. _____

2. _____

3. _____

4. _____

5. _____

6. _____

If you have trouble doing exercise G, see Section 4, "Restrictive Relative Clauses," on p. 301.

H. Find five examples of the passive in today's newspaper. Why do you think passive voice was used? Share the sentences with another student and analyze them together. Show your analyses to your instructor.

I. Find an article of interest to you in a journal in your major field. Are any passives used? For what purposes? Do any of them include modals? Which meanings of the modals—social or inferential—are used? Show the article and the passive examples to your instructor to share with the rest of the class.

J. Use a copy of a textbook in a scientific or technical field. Select a chapter that is interesting to you to analyze for passives. Select five interesting examples to share with your class. Include at least one modal + passive combination in your examples. Which of the two basic modal meanings is involved—social (advice) or logical (inference)?

CHAPTER 4

Subjunctive Sentences

1 Introduction to the Subjunctive

Subjunctive refers to something that is unreal or hypothetical. Unlike some other languages, English does not always use a special verb to indicate the unreal/hypothetical meaning of the subjunctive. For example, these sentences have the subjunctive meaning (signaled by *if* and *wish*):

If they were here, we could begin the project immediately. (They are not here. We cannot begin the project immediately.)

I wish they were here. (They are not here.)

In very formal English, *were* is used with singular subjects to indicate the subjunctive meaning. (You will hear *was* in informal spoken English.)

If John were here, I could go home. (John is not here.)

I wish she were here. (She is not here.)

Another formal usage in English has the past tense of the verb used for an untrue meaning.

If I spoke French, I would be very pleased with myself. (I do not speak French.)

You must be careful that the sentence is actually subjunctive in meaning before using these forms. Compare the following sentences:

I was not in class myself, so I do not know if she was there. (Since the sentence is about possibilities rather than a hypothetical meaning, the subjunctive would be wrong.)

I was in the lab yesterday myself. If John was in the lab at that time, I did not see him. (This is conditional but not hypothetical. It is about reality rather than the wishes or imagined actions.)

If she were here, we could go to the library immediately. (This is a real subjunctive. She is not here. We cannot go immediately.)

We wish the computer lab were open more hours on the weekend. (Wishes are always subjunctive because by their very nature they are not real.)

2 Verbs that Require the Subjunctive

English has a small set of verbs that in formal written English are followed by subjunctives in their objects. Generally, these have meanings that involve the giving of commands or requirements. Notice that the main verb in the basic sentence is followed by *that* plus a complete sentence; the verb in the embedded sentence is the simple infinitive without *to*.

The university insists that each student have insurance.

The teacher suggested that John come to class on time.

We urge that you be more patient.

I recommend that the students be in the testing room 10 minutes early.

The verbs in this group include *advise, ask, command, forbid, insist, move* (the special parliamentary procedure meaning), *order, propose, recommend, request, stipulate, suggest, urge.*

3 Adjectives and the Subjunctive

English can form subjunctive sentences that center on an adjective such as *essential, imperative, important, necessary,* and *vital.* The pattern used is

It is (adjective) *that* (subject + base verb) . . .

It is vital that you be on time.

It is imperative that John attend the meeting.

As with other subjunctives, the special verb form is frequently ignored in conversations. You will find more use of the subjunctive in formal writing and in formal speaking.

4 EXERCISES: The Subjunctive

A. The verbs listed in Section 2 on p. 117 are very similar in meaning but they are all quite different in implication. *Suggest* is completely different from *stipulate.* Arrange the words in order from the weakest to the strongest. First, decide which word has the least force and which word has the strongest requirement. Second, place those two at the opposite ends of the continuum. Finally, use an English-English dictionary to decide on the placement of the other words.

B. Can you add to the adjectives listed in Section 3 on p. 117? Talk with the other students in your class to come up with a longer list of these words. Select three that you especially like. Write two sentences that clearly and cleverly illustrate the potential for meaning of each of your three favorites. Work with another student if you prefer. Then, share your list of six sentences with the class.

C. In the U.S. most programs, departments, and universities seek information from students about ways to improve. For example, at the end of the term, most students are given opportunities to fill out *student course evaluation forms.* The following activity should only be done when the administration of the program, department, or university is willing to accept suggestions from students. This should *not* be done as an "exercise," but only when communication and change can take place.

1. The purpose of this activity is to provide the administration with suggestions about changes that can improve the quality of your life and your education. The procedures involve your working together in small committees to brainstorm ideas on particular topics. You will then prepare, edit, and type a letter addressed to the chief administrative officer of the unit being discussed.

2. Divide into small committees with equal numbers of students. Each committee is responsible for discussion of one of these topics: the academic program, student-teacher relationships, social-cultural programming, or some other important topic. During the discussion, you must decide two major things: First, what are the problems? Second, what solutions can you suggest for the problems? To be helpful and get changes, you must think of positive (and possible) changes to suggest. Just being critical is not usually a very effective tactic. If possible, invite the chief administrative officer to this discussion session, so that he/she can help you be realistic about your choices.

3. Write a formal business letter to the chief administrative officer on your topic. Carefully explain the problem. Then, clearly express your group's suggestions for possible changes. In making the suggestions, you should use the formal versions of verbs such as *suggest that* and *recommend that.* Revise and edit the letter carefully. Sloppy work will not get good results. It is possible that the chief administrative officer will want to show the letter to higher levels of administrators, so it is important for the letters to be well written and well typed.

4. Present the letters to the chief administrative officer. You can expect this person to give you a formal written response in reply to your analysis and suggestions.

CHAPTER 5

Conditional and Hypothetical Sentences

1 Introduction to the Conditional and Hypothetical

In academic writing, students and scholars frequently use conditional and hypothetical evidence to support an argument or to think through a problem. You will also hear the conditional and the hypothetical in lectures as instructors explain processes and interpret events.

If you do this to this side of the equation, then you will see this result.

If we were able to predict the future, then human life would be both simpler and more complex.

If Napoleon had better understood the vast size and intense winters of Russia, he would never have attempted the Russian campaign. If Hitler and his generals had been better historians, they would not have been tempted into the same trap that led to Napoleon's Russian disaster.

Conditional refers to the things that are necessary to make something happen. These can be statements of scientific truth or personal habit. A conditional sentence explains that if one thing happens, then another thing is the result. Conditionals are also used to make predictions about the future—if one thing happens, then another will result in future time. They can, of course, also be used to talk about conditions that were true in the past.

If you go to the library, you can find excellent dictionaries. (general truth)

If I leave at 7:00, I'm home by 7:45. (habit)

If you study hard, you will pass the test. (prediction)

If you determine the values of "x" and "y" in the linear equation, you still do not know that a causal relationship exists. (general truth)

If you pour oil on water, it floats. (general truth)

If you pass this test, you will receive a scholarship. (prediction)

If the research project is funded, the university will extend your scholarship. (prediction)

If the emperor needed additional funds, he devised a new tax to get them. (general truth about a past time situation)

Hypothetical refers to assumptions made in order to test or evaluate ideas. You say to your audience, "assume that this is true and think about the results. I know that it is not true or that we cannot prove it yet. But, just think about the implications if things were different." These, for example, are hypothetical statements: The first hypothetical sentence refers to past time; the second, to the future.

If the president had approved the Clean Water Bill, the country's rivers would have been saved from further chemical and biological contamination.

If the government were to give every citizen a guaranteed minimum income, petty crime would immediately be lowered because the need for such crime would have been eliminated.

In the first hypothetical example, the writer wants to talk about the results of a past time action by the president. He is talking about something that did not happen. He is saying, "we cannot change the past, but if we could, what would happen?" In the second hypothetical example, the writer wants us to think about results of a guaranteed minimum income. She suggests a result that she would expect. These examples are part of an intellectual approach that is based on "what if" or "let's suppose."

2a Conditional Meanings

Sentences with conditional meanings can be divided into three large groups: (1) general truth/habit statements, (2) inferential statements, and (3) prediction statements.

If water freezes, it expands. If water freezes, it will expand. (general truth)

If I eat in the cafeteria, I spend too much for lunch. (habit)

If these projections are correct, the company must change its marketing strategies at once. (inference)

If it is 10:00, the calculus final examination has started. (inference)

If you do this project well, you will certainly receive a good grade and probably the annual research award. (prediction)

2b Verbs in Sentences with Conditional Meanings

General Truth Statements   Usually, general truth statements are made with simple present tense verbs. The same verb form is usually in the clause and in the main verb. However, sometimes *will* is used in the main clause in its general truth meaning—not its future time meaning.

If a fire is denied oxygen, it goes out.

If a fire is denied oxygen, it will go out.

These sentences mean "in all such situations." In fact, *when* or *whenever* can be substituted for *if.*

When a fire is denied oxygen, it goes out.

Whenever a fire is denied oxygen, it will go out.

Habit Statements   Statements of habits can be in the present tense for the general truth meaning or in the past tense for things that were true in the past. The same verb form is used in the clause and in the main verb.

If I miss class, I borrow notes from another student.

If John went to the library, Mary usually went with him.

When and *whenever* can be substituted for these uses of *if*:

When I miss class, I borrow notes from another student.

Whenever John went to the library, Mary usually went with him.

Inference Statements Inference statements are different from general truth and habit statements. General truth statements are certainties—if one thing happens, we are sure that the other happens. Inference statements are educated guesses based on the information given in the *if* clause. Generally, these have a type of parallel structure with the same verb form in the *if* clause and in the main verb.

If you can drive a car, you can drive this truck. (If you have the ability to drive a car, then you have the ability to drive this truck.)

If you will meet me at 12:00, I will have time to eat lunch with you. (If you promise to meet me, I promise to have lunch with you. Yes, it is possible to use *will* in the *if* clause in this type of sentence. *Will* means "have the determination" or "make a promise.")

If he was in class, he heard the lecture. (The lecture was given, so if he attended he heard it.)

If we are not so sure, then a modal such as *might* or *should* will be used in the main clause:

If you study hard, you might pass the test.

If anyone understands the situation, it should be the President of the United States.

It is also possible to have present perfect in the main clause if the meaning is a past time connected to the present.

If you live in a city, you have become accustomed to noise, dirt, and crowds.

Prediction Statements The type of conditional that you have studied most often is usually called the *future conditional.* For example,

If he studies hard, he will pass the test.

These sentences are used to make predictions about future events. Several modals are possible in the main clause. The *if* clause uses simple present tense. The modals range from the strong certainty of *will* to the weaker certainty of *might*.

If you study, you will pass the test. (certainty, promise)
        you should pass the test.
        you may pass the test.
        you could pass the test.
        you might pass the test. (not so sure)

2c Subordinators Other than *If*

If is the most commonly used subordinator for conditional grammar. However, other words can be used, for example, *when* and *whenever* in general truth or habitual conditionals:

When *water freezes, it expands.*

Whenever *I go home for a visit, I take long walks with my father.*

Unless is also frequently used to give conditions:

Unless *we get a computer with more memory, we cannot do this research project.*

Several subordinators combine time with condition for their meanings:

Before *you can complete this project, you will need more complete data.*

Once *you have joined the army, you cannot leave just because you do not like military life.*

Other subordinators used in formal English include *given (that), in case, in the event that, on condition (that), provided (that), providing (that),* and *supposing (that).* These are usually found with the main clause first, followed by the conditional clause.

Scholarships will be given to five students provided that *the money is available.*

He has been hired as a researcher on the condition that *he finish his dissertation by the end of the year.* (Notice the use of the subjunctive *finish* in the clause. See Chapter 4 for more information.)

In the event that *the students need additional time on the examination, the test monitor can extend the time period by 30 minutes.*

2d EXERCISE: The Conditional

Compare these sets of sentences. They look alike, but are very different in their meanings. What time is involved in each? How are the conditions different?

1a. *If water is heated to the temperature of 212 degrees F, it becomes a gas.* (general truth, all the time)

1b. *If he works hard, he might finish the project in three months.* (prediction, future time, but not completely sure)

2a. *If she can read English, she can understand this form.*

2b. *If she arrives on time, we will see the beginning of the movie.*

3a. *If you will agree to this plan, we will start the project tomorrow.*

3b. *If you move to New York, your living expenses should be much greater.*

4a. *If copper is heated to a temperature of 1,083 degrees C, it melts.*

4b. *If you will go, I will go.*

3a Present and Future Time Hypothetical

These sentences present some difficulty or barrier that prevents the action of the main clause. There are two major possibilities for these sentences— either the situation is open to change or the situation is closed to change. In the following sentence, the truth is that the university does not have enough money and that more students do not get scholarships.

If the university had more money, more students would be given scholarships.

However, the sentence has another implication: If the university ever gets the money, the scholarships will be given. That is, the situation is open to change.

If the computer were working today, we would finish our research project.

The computer is not working; we cannot finish the project. However, the situation could change suddenly; the computer could start to work, and the project could finish. Probably not, but predictions are seldom 100 percent sure. In the following sentence, however, no change is possible.

If George Washington were alive, he would be amazed at the changes in the United States.

George Washington has been dead for approximately 200 years. This is a completely hypothetical statement. Here is another completely hypothetical sentence that is a traditional saying.

If wishes were horses, we all would be kings.

Consider the following examples. Is either situation open to change?

1. *If we knew how to transform nuclear waste into harmless substances, we would not have the storage problems that limit the usefulness of nuclear power.*

2. *If they were able to talk, we could learn wonderful things from the animals of the African grasslands.*

It is difficult to give a time orientation to these hypothetical sentences. They are really about the present but frequently have implications for the future. The meaning is about a current situation or problem that might change in the future—or might not.

3b Verbs in Present and Future Time Hypothetical Sentences

One of the uses of the past tense of the verb is to talk about things that are not true. If you think about it, this makes a lot of sense. The past is not real anymore (or at least that is the way the past is viewed by English speakers), so the past tense verb carries two meanings—past time/not real anymore. From that meaning, it is an easy step to present time/not real.

If he spoke Spanish, he would be more effective in this job.

The *if* clause has simple past tense. The main clause uses a modal, frequently *would* but also *might* for lesser degrees of certainty. *Could* is used to talk about conditional abilities or skills.

If he spoke Spanish, he could be more effective in this job.
might be more effective in this job.
would be more effective in this job.

3c Subjunctive Use of *Were* in Hypothetical Sentences

Formal English uses *were* in sentences such as:

If she were here, she would tell us what to do.
If it were possible, he would go to class, but he is really very sick.
If he were president, he would change the tax laws.
If I were a millionaire, I would quit work.

This is a seeming violation of the subject-verb agreement rule that says to use *was* in these sentences. *Were* is used to say "this is not true" or "this is only a hypothesis, not a reality." Because of this use of *were*, it is possible to have two different sentences with two different meanings based on *was* vs. *were*:

1. *If he was in class, he heard the lecture.* (The speaker does not know. It is possible that he was in class. This is about past time.)

2. *If he were in class, he could help solve the problem.* (He is definitely not in class. Therefore, he cannot help solve the problem. This is a present-time situation.)

See Chapter 4 for more information on the subjunctive.

4 Past Time Hypothetical

In these sentences, we are talking about the past and about things that did not happen. (1) How would the present be different if the past had been different? (2) How would the past itself have been different if the past had been different?

If John Kennedy had gone to Houston rather than to Dallas, he might be alive today. (past influence on the present)

If the whole New World had been a Spanish colony, Spanish would be the language of the United States today. (past influence on the present)

If the computer had not been broken, we would have finished the research project yesterday. (past influence on the past)

If the NASA management had listened to the engineers, Challenger *would not have lifted off the launch pad. The astronauts would be alive today.* (past influence on the past and on the present)

Notice the grammar of these hypothetical sentences. The *if* clause uses past perfect to refer to past time. The main clause uses either modal + verb for present time or modal + perfect for past time meanings. This use of the perfect makes sense if you remember that the simple past tense is used for "not true" in present time hypothetical statements. (We cannot use simple past tense to talk about past time because that verb form is already reserved for another meaning.)

In hypothetical sentences,

If clause: simple past tense = not real in present time; past perfect = not real in past time

Main clause: modal + verb = result in present/future time; modal + perfective = result in past time

5 Change in Word Order for Hypothetical Sentences

For variety in word order, *if* can be removed from hypothetical sentences as in these examples:

If *the computer had been repaired by the time promised, we could have finished the research project on schedule.*

Had *the computer been repaired by the time promised, we could have finished the research project on schedule.*

When *if* is removed, the first auxiliary in the introductory clause is moved to the beginning—just as in the formation of questions. Notice that this is not possible with conditional sentences.

If he arrives on time, we will be surprised.

▼ *Arrives he on time, we will be surprised.*

Other hypothetical examples are given here to show various auxiliaries moved to the beginning of the sentence:

If I were President of the United States, I would work hard for world peace.

Were I President of the United States, I would work hard for world peace.

If the university should lower its tuition, more students could have academic training.

Should the university lower its tuition, more students could have academic training.

If the university had more instructors, class size could be smaller.

Had the university more instructors, class size could be smaller.

This change happens most often when the verb in the hypothetical clause is *were,* when *would, should,* or *could* is the auxiliary in the clause, or when *had* is used either as the main verb or as the auxiliary for the past perfect. The change almost never occurs when the verb is a simple past tense form, as in this example:

If he told the truth, we have a very serious problem.

▼ *Told he the truth, we have a very serious problem.*

Since this change is primarily used to give variety to formal written English, you should not use it more than once or twice in any composition.

6 Summary of Major Grammatical Patterns

Conditionals

If + present tense, present tense . . .

If + any verb type, same verb type . . .

If + present tense, *will/be going to* . . .

should
must
can
may
would
could
might

Hypotheticals

If + past tense, *would* . . .
        might
        could

If + *were, would* . . .
    could
    might

If + past perfect, *would* ⎫
        could ⎬ *have* + past participle . . .
        might ⎭

Had + subject + past participle . . .

Were + subject . . .

7 EXERCISES: The Conditional and the Hypothetical

A. Look at the following examples. Which are hypothetical? Which are conditional? What time reference does each have?

1. *It is necessary to think seriously about the results if this proposal were adopted. It could lead to a serious disruption of the economy.* (future time hypothetical)

2. *If we make this change, then we will have this immediate result.* (future time conditional)

3. *If the president had not listened to the military, the war could have been avoided.* (past time hypothetical)

4. *If we continue to pollute the rivers, the U.S. will have a water-supply crisis early in the 21st century—if not before.*

5. *If one were to radically change the environment of a child, what would be the changes in the child's ability to learn?*

6. *If the university had offered enough scholarships, it could have had more and better students than we now find.*

B. In your university work, you will find that the conditional and hypothetical have serious and important uses. Scholars do not use them just to talk about what they would do if they had a million dollars. Here are some examples of serious writing using this grammar. Find the *if* clauses. What kind of grammar is used? What kind of meanings?

WATER POLLUTION IN THE UNITED STATES

Across the United States, our water supplies are being destroyed. Salt water is seeping into the underground sources. Municipal and industrial wastes have led to the closing of beaches and fishing areas. In rural areas, water is contaminated by insecticides and pesticides. The list of local and regional water headaches is almost endless.

If these conditions are to be curbed; if we are, in the words of President Kennedy, "to have sufficient water to serve the range of human and industrial needs"; if we are to bequeath to our children and our country an adequate supply of clean water useful for recreational as well as industrial, municipal, and agricultural purposes; then civic and community organizations will have much to do.

Adapted from *Focus on Clean Water: An Action Program for Community Organizations* (U.S. Department of Health, Education, and Welfare, 1964)

ANTIREFLECTIVE OPTICAL COATINGS

Optical theory dictates that, for optimum performance, a single layer of antireflective coating for fused-silica optics have a refractive index of about 1.22. The refractive index of silica is about 1.46. Therefore, if we want to make the antireflective coating of silica, we will need to achieve a porosity of about 55 percent.

Adapted from "Optical Coatings by the Sol-Gel Process" (U.S. Department of Commerce, 1985)

TRAFFIC DEATHS IN THE U.S.

Only a national commitment can really solve the total problem of deaths in highway accidents. If the trend of the 1960s were allowed to continue, we could expect 85,000 deaths a year by 1980.

Adapted from *The Human Collision—How Injuries Occur . . . How Seat Belts Prevent Them* (U.S. Department of Transportation, 1976)

SHOPPING BY MAIL

It has been said that if you shop by mail, the whole world is your department store. You can buy hams from Virginia, handicrafts from New Hampshire, woolens from Maine, apple-peelers from Alabama, or oranges from Florida.

Adapted from *How to Write a Wrong: Complain Effectively and Get Results* (American Association of Retired Persons with the U.S. Federal Trade Commission, undated)

HIGHWAY NOISE

The automobile, when operated in a safe and sensible manner, is a relatively quiet machine. It is usually well muffled and is generally designed for the comfort of the driver and passengers. Noise control has become a prominent factor in auto design lately, because of the selective purchasing habits of the American people. Such curbs of internal vehicle noise have also resulted in a substantial benefit to the roadside community. However, if one doubts the inherent noise generating capability of an automobile, simply remove the muffler, open the hood, and remove the air cleaner from the family car and listen to the cacophony of engine sounds that result.

Adapted from *Transportation Noise and Its Control* (U.S. Department of Transportation, 1972)

HIGHWAY NOISE ABATEMENT

A number of measures are available to highway planners to curtail the undesirable noise from traffic that impinges on surrounding residential communities. Chief among these are:

Man-constructed barriers to obstruct or dissipate sound emissions
Elevated or depressed highway through grading
Absorption effects of landscaping (trees, bushes, shrubs, and so on)

A rigid and fairly massive barrier can be an effective means to reduce noise from highways depending upon the relative heights of the barrier, the noise source, and the affected area, as well as the horizontal distance between the source and the barrier and between the barrier and the noise-affected area. It should be noted, for example, that if a diesel truck with a 10-foot-high exhaust stack passes a 10-foot barrier, no exhaust noise reduction can be realized from the barrier, since the exhaust noise merely passes over the top of the barrier unimpeded.

Adapted from *Transportation Noise and Its Control* (U.S. Department of Transportation, 1972)

TEACHING A MONKEY TO REPORT ON DISCRIMINATIONS BETWEEN SOUNDS*

Figure 1 shows the testing array which confronts the monkey as one wall of his experimental cage (which is located inside a sound-shielded audiometric testing booth). A single press at the translucent "Observing Response" panel causes an acoustic stimulus to be delivered through a loudspeaker located above the testing array. At the end of the stimulus, the two lower panels become lit—one red and the other green—indicating to the animal that a discriminative response may be made. If the monkey's single press is "correct," i.e., if the particular color chosen demonstrates the proper conditional response to the stimulus presented, the subject receives a single banana-pellet food reinforcement at the food well. If the single discriminative response is "incorrect" for the sound just

*In this passage, a researcher describes the method used to train monkeys to press different colored lights when they hear different sounds. That is, for one sound the monkey presses red and for a different sound the monkey presses green. Using this system, the monkey can "talk" to the researcher about sound differences.

Figure 1 **Testing Array and Contingencies for Nonspatial Auditory Delayed Response Task.**

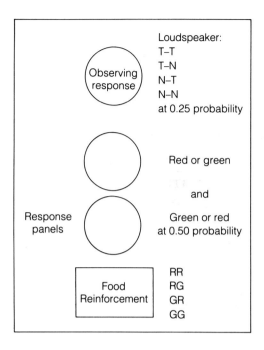

presented, no reinforcement is delivered and a timeout is enforced prior to the arming and relighting (with clear light) of the observing response panel. Thus the subject, in effect, paces himself throughout the testing session which typically involves 100–200 "trials" or discriminative choices.

Adapted from "Toward an Animal Model of Auditory Cognitive Function" (Dewson, 1979)

ONE METHOD FOR EVALUATION OF THE HEALTH OF CHILDREN

One way to evaluate the health of the nation's children is to determine whether changes have occurred in average heights and weights. Growth is characteristic of healthy, well-fed children. If illness or dietary inadequacy is chronic and mild, a child's linear growth will be slowed, and height will be low for age. If illness or dietary inadequacy is severe, the child will lose weight and will have a low weight-to-height ratio.

Adapted from *Charting the Nation's Health: Trends Since 1960* (U.S. Department of Health and Human Services, 1985)

INCREASED DEATHS IN THE UNITED STATES FROM CANCER: 1960 TO 1982

The major factor in the increased cancer death rates from 1960 to 1982 was respiratory cancer. In 1982 mortality from respiratory cancer among persons 55–64 was approaching two times what it was in 1960. If respiratory cancer were not considered, mortality from cancer for this age group would show a decline of 8 percent between 1960 and 1982.

Adapted from *Charting the Nation's Health: Trends Since 1960* (U.S. Department of Health and Human Services, 1985)

FEWER DEATHS FROM HEART DISEASE

In marked contrast to death rates for cancer, death rates for heart disease declined for the entire population of the U.S. between 1960 and 1970. Since the mid-1960s the decline in death rates for heart disease among persons 55–64 years of age has been steady and dramatic. If the 1960 death rates for heart disease had prevailed, heart disease would have claimed far more lives in 1982 than it actually did for this age group.

Adapted from *Charting the Nation's Health: Trends Since 1960* (U.S. Department of Health and Human Services, 1985)

C. How are conditionals and hypotheticals used in your major field? Select a journal in which research is reported. Look through the articles to find uses of *if* clauses. Are they conditional statements of scientific fact? Are they hypothetical examples given to illustrate a principle? Share these examples with another student majoring in the same field.

D. Work with another student to make a list of scientific generalizations using *if* clauses to create conditional sentences. Compare your list with those made by other students in the class.

E. The following passage shows how conditional and hypothetical examples are used in technical writing. Read this carefully to find and analyze the conditional and hypothetical examples. After you have analyzed this passage, do exercise F or G. Notice that the writer begins with an extended definition of the term *decibel.*

TECHNICAL PROPERTIES OF SOUND

The Decibel. An explanation is in order regarding some basic properties of any scale for stating the magnitude of a sound. The ear responds to sound pressure fluctuations with an increased sensory response for an increase in pressure. The range between the smallest sound pressure which is sensed by the human ear and the highest sound pressure physically tolerable covers a ratio of approximately 1,000,000 to 1. If we assign the number 1 to the sound pressure corresponding to the smallest sound that we can hear, the sound pressure from our voice in quiet conversational tones would correspond to the number 1,000. A loud voice would be approximately 30,000, and physical pain would be felt in the ear at a sound pressure of over 1,000,000.

While our brains have no trouble handling the range of sounds sensed by our ears, it is inconvenient for us to think in terms of numbers with all these zeros. It becomes more convenient, therefore, if we base our scale on the number of zeros rather than the actual number. The logarithm to the base 10 does just this. Thus, we may assign the zero on our scale to the number we can just hear, since the logarithm of 1 is zero. Our quiet conversational tones will then be assigned the number 3, since the logarithm of 1,000 is 3, and the highest pressure previously mentioned as causing physical pain would receive the number 6.

All of the numbers assigned—1, 3, and 6—are equal to the logarithm of the actual numbers, and the quantity measured in such a scale is called a level. Engineers and scientists prefer to work in terms of energy, which is proportional to sound pressure squared, instead of sound pressure. Thus, all the above numbers for sound pressure must be squared. Making this adjustment, 1 squared becomes 1; 1,000 squared becomes 1,000,000; and 1,000,000 squared becomes 1,000,000,000,000. Fortunately, the logarithm of a squared number is just two times the logarithm of the number; so, instead of the level ranging from 0 to 6, it ranges from 0 to 12. This scale is similar to the famous Richter scale for measuring earthquake magnitude, which is also logarithmic. In the fields of electronics and acoustics, the unit of the scale is called the "bel" in honor of Alexander Graham Bell. For convenience, the bel is divided up into 10 smaller units, so that the scale of the level now extends from 0 to 120 decibels, or tenths of bels. Figure A-1 provides an illustration of these concepts for

Figure A–1   The Logarithmic Nature of the Decibel.

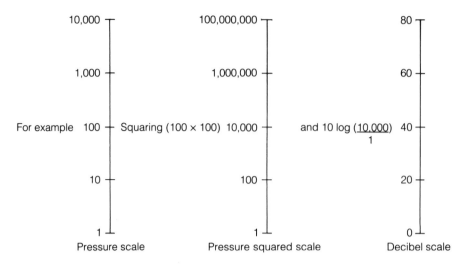

For example 100 Squaring (100 × 100) 10,000 and 10 log ($\frac{10,000}{1}$) 40

Pressure scale   Pressure squared scale   Decibel scale

converting from an inconvenient magnitude scale (linear pressure) to a more convenient scale of level (logarithmic) with decibels as the units.

Working with Decibels. The use of the decibel requires somewhat different mathematical operations than we are accustomed to using with linear scales. For example, if we have two similar noise sources operating simultaneously, the sound energy generated by the two sources will add together to give a value double that which would result from either course operating alone. The resulting sound pressure level in decibels from the combined sources will be only 3 decibels higher than the level produced by either source operating alone, as illustrated in Figure A-2. In other words, if we have two sounds of different magnitude, the level of the sum will always be less than 3 decibels above the level produced by the greater source alone. If the two sound sources produce individual levels that are different by 10 decibels or more, adding the two together will produce a level that is not significantly different from that produced by the greater source operating alone, as illustrated by Figure A-2.

Figure A-2 is useful to illustrate one of the frustrations of noise-control engineering. For example, imagine a machine which has a motor represented by the bar denoted as Sound No. 1 and a grinder or working apparatus represented by Sound No. 2. If the machine were considered too noisy, we would change the working apparatus Sound No. 2 by redesigning it, or by enclosing it in a "silencing box." If this effort were

Figure A–2 Addition of Sound Levels.

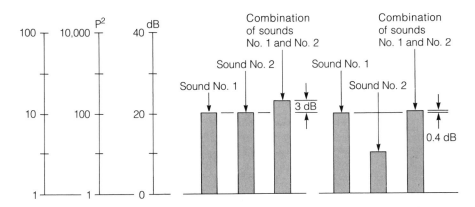

sufficiently successful for the noise heard from the apparatus to be 10 decibels less than before, we would in fact have reduced the total machine noise by an almost imperceptible 2.6 decibels. Further if we had completely silenced the grinder, a further "machine-noise reduction" of only 0.4 decibels could be achieved, unless additional measures were taken to reduce the noise generated by Sound No. 1 (the motor).

The same type of logic applies to community noise reduction. The noisiest sounds must be quieted in order to achieve real noise reductions in the surrounding area. Reduction of only one source of sound will not solve the problem.

Adapted from *Transportation Noise and Its Control* (U.S. Department of Transportation, 1972)

F. Write a description of a basic principle in your major field. For example, explain how the linear equation works. Illustrate the principle with a hypothetical example. (To see how this is done, study the passage "Technical Properties of Sound.")

G. Define a basic term from your field of study and illustrate it with a conditional or hypothetical example.

H. Describe a process that can have at least two different actions and responses. Use *if* conditionals to describe these. (For a model, see "Teaching a Monkey to Report on Discriminations Between Sounds" or "One Method for Evaluation of the Health of Children.")

I. Scholars in science and technology as well as in historical studies look to the past and think about what would have happened if things had been different. Look at the passage "Fewer Deaths from Heart Disease" to see a scientific example. Talk with another student and decide on some important past event. Think about what might be different today if the event had been different. Write a discussion of the event, the change you hypothesize, and the differences you imagine.

J. Instructors and testers frequently write essay topics in conditional or hypothetical form. Here are some essay topics that have been used to test the writing ability of college students. The students were expected to write a complete essay of at least five paragraphs on one of these topics; they had one hour to complete the essay. Study each of these topics carefully. What kind of question is being asked—conditional or hypothetical? Talk with another student about possible answers. Then, try writing one paragraph on some aspect of the topic. After you have revised your paragraph to be sure that it says what you want it to say, edit it carefully for the correct use of the conditional or the hypothetical.

1. Why would you like or dislike owning your own business? Explain.

2. If music reflects the mood of an age, what does current music say about America? Explain.

3. Discuss changes that would make the public less hesitant to report crime.

4. If you could pass one law, what would it be?

5. If you could hold any job for one year, what would you choose? Why?

6. If you could change any one thing about your childhood, what would it be?

7. If you could make one scientific discovery in your lifetime, what would it be? Why?

8. What would cause you to end a friendship? Explain.

9. What would you place in a time capsule to allow people opening the capsule 1,000 years from now to understand current life? Explain.

10. In your view, what would most impress (favorably or unfavorably) a foreign student spending his or her first weekend with an American family?

11. If your doctor told you that you had only a few months to live, to what extent and how would you alter your lifestyle? Why?

12. If you were asked to make a fair evaluation of your instructors, what criteria or standard would you use for the evaluation?

13. "If a man does not keep pace with his companions, perhaps it is because he hears a different drummer. Let him step to the music he hears." Attack or defend.

14. If, in your judgment, the leaders of this country are clearly wrong in adopting a particular policy, what should you do? Explain.

15. If you could have a conversation with a famous person (living or dead), whom would you choose and why?

16. If you were an employer, under what circumstances would you fire an employee?

17. If you had the power to change any event in history (outcome of an election, who won a war, and so on), which would you choose to change, and why?

18. If you were among the first colonizers of a new planet in the 21st century, what would you *not* want your fellow colonists to transport from planet Earth? Explain.

K. Review the information given in Section 5 on p. 128 about changes in the word order of hypothetical sentences. Working with another student, decide which of the sentences in exercise J can be changed to have the form without *if*. Compare your list to that of other students in the class.

L. After you have agreed on which sentences can have a different word order, rewrite those sentences. Compare your versions to those of other students.

M. Read a composition that you have written recently on a hypothetical topic. Find one or two sentences that you think could be changed to the word order discussed in Section 5 on p. 128—the hypothetical without *if*. Share your ideas with your instructor and the other students in your class before you make the changes. If you still like your plan after the discussion, then write new versions of the original sentences. Then, share those new sentences with the class to edit the grammar.

CHAPTER 6

Causative Verbs

1 Introduction to Causative Verbs

In many situations, we cause other people to do work for us or to act for us: We pay them, ask them, force them, talk them into doing what we want them to do. Secretaries type letters for their bosses. Mechanics repair our cars. Students write research papers for their courses (at the requirement of their instructors).

English has a small group of words that can be used in sentences to express this relationship in which one person causes and another person acts. The verbs used are *have, get, make, let,* and *help.* Other verbs have the same meanings, but these have grammatical peculiarities that make them a separate group.

When these verbs are used for a causative meaning, they take complete sentences as their objects. Thus, two sentences are combined into one causative sentence.

1. (The president had the vice president do something.)

2. (The vice president led the study group.)

        subject   verb   DO (sentence 2 is the DO)
3. The president had the vice president lead the study group.

In all of these combinations, the verb in the second sentence becomes either an infinitive or a simple form depending on the particular causative verb—no tense is used. Notice the use of *lead* in sentence 3. Also, if a pronoun is the subject of the second sentence, it becomes an object form—*me, him, her, you, us,* or *them.*

The president had her lead the study group.

2 *Have* and *Get*

There is little difference in meaning between these two causative verbs. *Get* is used mostly when we talk about convincing equals—roommates, friends, relatives, classmates—to do what we want. *Have* is used for more formal relationships. However, they are frequently felt to be interchangeable. Observe the following combinations: The object of *have* takes the simple form. *Get* needs *to* + verb.

(John causes something.)
(His secretary types his letters.)

John has his secretary type his letters.

John gets his secretary to type his letters.

Both *have* and *get* can take passive sentences in their complements. (See Chapter 3 for more on passive sentences.) In these sentences, the writer focuses on the action done or on the thing acted on rather than on the actor. When passive sentences are used in the objects, *have* and *get* have exactly the same grammar. The form of *be* is not used; only the past participle is left of the passive verb.

(John causes something.)
(His letters are typed.)

John has his letters typed.

John gets his letters typed.

(John caused something.)
(His car was repaired.)

John had his car repaired.

John got his car repaired.

3 Make

Make carries the meaning of "cause through force"; the force can be physical, moral, political, or legal.

(The university caused something.)
(The students bought health insurance.)

The university made the students buy health insurance.

Make does not have a passive sentence in its object.

4 Let

Let means "allow" or "give permission." The verb in the object is the simple form without *to*. There is no change of form for tense or subject-verb agreement. Passive sentences are rare in the object.

(The student asked to leave class early.)
(The instructor gave permission.)

The instructor let the student leave class early.

5 Help

Here the subject of the sentence is involved in the action. That is, in contrast to *have, get,* and *make,* the subject is more than a causer. The subject participates in the action. The verb in the object is usually the simple form without *to.* However, if the subject of the second sentence is complex, *to* may be used. Passive sentences are rare in the object.

(The student assistant helped. . . .)
(The secretary moved the computer.)

The student assistant helped the secretary move the computer.

(I helped. . . .)
(The student who lives near the bus station bought a new computer.)

I helped the student who lives near the bus station to buy a new computer. or,

I helped the student who lives near the bus station buy a new computer.

6 *See, Watch, Hear,* and *Feel*

Although they are not at all causative in meaning, it should be noticed that *see, watch, hear,* and *feel* can take complete sentences in their objects in much the same way as *have* and *make:* The verb in the second sentence becomes a simple form without *to.*

The instructor watched the student take the test.

Standing on the beach, John could feel the wind blow.

7 EXERCISES: The Causative Verbs

A. As members of an academic institution, instructors and students do things not because they want to but because they are required to. Sometimes we agree with these rules; sometimes we disagree; but the institution has the power to force our actions. Work with a group of students to write a list of five sentences to describe institutional requirements. Use the verb *make.* Then, compare lists to see how many different rules you can think of. For example, *The university makes students buy health insurance.*

B. Instructors and students are in a causative relationship. The instructor has, gets, makes, helps, lets students do things. In return, the students help, get instructors to do things. How do you feel about the sentence below? Explain a situation in which this might be written.

The students made the instructor change the date for the test.

C. Write a list of seven things that your instructor has caused you to do— use *have, get, make, help,* or *let.* At the same time that you are writing, your instructor will prepare a list of seven things that you have caused him/her to do. Compare your lists to see if you agree about the meaning. Edit the sentences for correct verb and pronoun forms.

D. The things that we own often need to be repaired. Usually when we write about those repairs, we use a passive sentence in the direct object of the causative verb because we are focused on the action rather than on the doer. That is, we are more interested in our car than in the mechanic.

I had my car repaired yesterday and am very unhappy about the cost.

I got my car fixed by a friend who is a great mechanic.

1. List anything you have had repaired in the past year. (bike? shoes? watch?)

2. Who did each repair?

3. Write a sentence to explain each situation.

4. Edit the sentences carefully for verb and pronoun forms. Then, share them with the class.

E. We all have an obligation to help relatives, friends, and other human beings (even strangers). Work with another student to answer these questions. Make notes to record your own answers.

1. Who have you helped recently? How? Why? What social relationships did you have with each person?

2. Did you help any strangers? How? When/where? Why?

3. Have any strangers helped you recently? How? When/where? Why?

F. Use the notes that you made in exercise E to write a composition about helping people. After you have revised and edited the passage, share it with the person you worked with to make your notes.

CHAPTER 7

Imperative Sentences

1 Introduction to the Imperative

English creates the *imperative* by using the simple dictionary form of the verb (the infinitive without *to*). Usually, no subject is given, but sometimes in emphatic spoken English *you* will be given as the subject:

Open the window.

Hand me the dictionary, please.

The mother said to her child: "You come here at once!"

The imperatives are used in some academic writing to give instructions for carrying out processes. This use is typically without a subject. The negative form can be either contracted or full depending on the formality of the writing.

Don't open the door. = Do not open the door.

Don't be late. = Do not be late.

2 EXERCISES: The Imperative

A. You can expect to find imperatives used in instruction manuals. Use a highlighter to mark all of the imperative verbs in this passage from a *First Aid Book* published by the U.S. Department of Labor in 1980 for use at coal mines and other types of mining operations. Do any of the instructions surprise you? What types of accidents seem to be common?

GENERAL PRINCIPLES

Besides being trained in proper first aid methods, all first-aiders should know what first aid equipment is available at the mine site and where it is kept. The equipment should be checked periodically. First-aiders should also know the operator's policy for calling medical assistance and transporting the injured.

No two situations requiring first aid are the same, and first-aiders must be able to select and apply appropriate first aid measures in different circumstances. However, the following procedures are generally applicable:

Take charge: Instruct someone to obtain medical help and others to assist as directed.

Make a primary survey of the victim.

Care for life-threatening conditions.

Care for all injuries in order of need.

If several people have been injured, decide upon priorities in caring for each victim.

Keep the injured person lying down.

Loosen restricting clothing when necessary.

Keep onlookers away from the victim.

When necessary, improvise first aid materials using the most appropriate material available.

Cover all wounds completely.

Use a tourniquet only as necessary.

Exclude air from burned surfaces as quickly as possible by using a suitable dressing.

Remove small, loose foreign objects from a wound by brushing away from the wound with a piece of sterile gauze.

Do not attempt to remove embedded objects.

Place a bandage compress and a bandage over an open fracture without undue pressure before applying splints.

Support and immobilize fractures and dislocations.

Leave the reduction of fractures or dislocations to a doctor except lower jaw dislocations when help is delayed.

Never move a victim, unless absolutely necessary, until fractures have been immobilized.

Test a stretcher before use, and carefully place an injured person on the stretcher.

Carry the victim on a stretcher without any unnecessary rough movements.

Adapted from *First Aid Book* (U.S. Department of Labor, 1980)

B. Using the imperative style, write out the instructions for a traditional game in your country. Give enough detail so that a person could learn to play the game following the instructions. After you have written them, teach the game to a student from another country. Revise the instructions as necessary.

C. Get a copy of the application form used by your university. Find all of the imperatives that are used to give instructions for completing the form.

D. If you still have them, bring to class the instructions that came with any mechanical, electrical, or electronic device that you have purchased recently. Look over the instructions with another student to find all of the uses of the imperative.

E. If you are taking a lab course, bring the lab manual to class. What style is used to give the instructions for various lab activities and experiments?

CHAPTER 8

Nouns, Noun Phrases, and Adjectives

1 Introduction to Nouns, Noun Phrases, and Adjectives

Nouns are words like *book, child, coffee, mathematics, John, New York,* and *IBM*. Three aspects of the use of these words will be considered in this section:

1. Grammatical classes of nouns such as common, proper, count, noncount, and so forth

2. Noun phrase structure, especially of technical and scientific vocabulary

3. Noun phrases modified by prepositional phrases

See Chapter 9 for information on the use of determiners and articles with nouns. See Chapter 1 for information on the use of nouns and noun phrases as subjects and objects. See Section 15 on p. 88 for a discussion of the influence of nouns on the form of the present tense verb.

2a Grammatical Classes of Nouns

Nouns can be subdivided into many different groups depending upon your point of view and purposes. For example, nouns can be classified as *common* or *proper, count* or *noncount, singular* or *plural, abstract* or *concrete.* Nouns can also be classified as *collectives.* Each of these categories will be discussed in the order listed here.

2b Common vs. Proper Nouns

Perhaps the most basic division is into common versus proper nouns. Common nouns are words like *book, child, action,* and *investigation.* Proper nouns are words like *John, New York,* and *IBM.*

2c Count vs. Noncount Nouns

Another basic group divides common nouns into the categories count and noncount (or *mass*). Count nouns have singulars and plurals. Noncount nouns have neither singular nor plural.

count: *book/books, apple/apples, child/children*

noncount: *mathematics, information, happiness*

You will recall that the form of the subject determines the form of the present tense verb: noncount nouns and singular count nouns are followed by the singular form of the verb while plural count nouns are followed by the plural form. (See Section 15, "Subject-Verb Agreement," on p. 88).

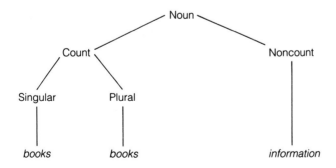

English Noncount Nouns that Are Count Nouns in Other Languages Some English noncount nouns have countable counterparts in other languages. For example, *chalk* is noncount in English, but the word that means "chalk" has a singular and a plural in some other languages. An American would not write ▼*The instructor needed some chalks.* (See Appendix I for a list of these words.)

Phrases Used with Noncount Nouns to Measure and Count To edit the incorrect example above, an American would write *The instructor needed some chalk.* Or more specifically, *The instructor needed a box of chalk.* Or, *The instructor needed 10 pieces of chalk.* English has many of these phrases that can be used with noncount nouns to measure or count the substance. Some of these are limited in use while others can be used for many different substances. (An alphabetized list of common measurement and counting phrases is given in Appendix J.)

Limited in use: *a head of lettuce, a head of cabbage,* and many others

Capable of broader use: *a box of . . ., a pound of . . ., a piece of . . .,* and many others

When used with a noncount noun, these phrases become the main subject of the sentence; the verb agrees with them rather than with the noncount noun.

Two boxes of chalk were left on the instructor's desk.

A box of chalk was on the tray at the bottom of the blackboard.

2d Singular vs. Plural Nouns

Most nouns are common count nouns. That is, most nouns have both singular and plural forms. The major problem for some advanced students is learning the correct spelling for the plural forms.

Many nouns that are usually noncount can be used as count nouns for special meanings. *Colombia grows many different coffees.* In this example, *coffees* means "varieties of coffee."

Proper nouns can be either singular or plural.

John Smith is a professor of chemistry.

The John Smiths live at 2000 Main St. (all the members of the John Smith family)

Spelling of Plural for Regular Nouns This section explains and illustrates the rules for spelling of noun plurals that are formed by adding *-s.* These nouns are usually called *regular nouns* (in contrast to the *irregular nouns* that use other methods to form their plurals).

Most nouns simply add -s to spell their plural forms: *book/books, bee/ bees, paper/papers, constitution/constitutions.*

The exceptions to the general rule include the following:

1. Nouns that end with a hissing, sibilant sound (-*s, -x, -z, -ch, -sh*), add -*es: glass/glasses, box/boxes.*

2. Most nouns that end with -*o*, add -*es: potato/potatoes.* However, *pianos, zoos,* and *radios.*

3. Nouns that end in a consonant + *y*, change the *y* to *i* and add *es: pully/pullies, baby/babies.*

4. Nouns that end in -*fe* or -*f*, change the *f* to *v* and add *es: wife/wives, knife/knives, shelf/shelves, leaf/leaves, wolf/wolves, life/lives, thief/ thieves.*

Spelling of Plural for Irregular Nouns   The following rules explain how to spell *irregular nouns*; these nouns do not use -*s* to form their plurals.

Some nouns form their plural with an internal vowel change rather than adding a form of -*s*. You already know most of these. As a review, write the plural in the space provided. If you are not sure, look up the spelling in your dictionary.

child/ _____   *mouse/* _____

foot/ _____   *ox/* _____

goose/ _____   *tooth/* _____

louse/ _____   *woman/* _____

man/ _____

Some nouns use the same form for both singular and plural: *deer, fish, sheep, species, means, series.* The plural *fishes* is used to refer to species of *fish: There are many different kinds of fishes in the ocean.* But, *He caught two fish.*

Spelling of Plural for Nouns Adopted from Other Languages
English has taken many nouns from other languages (especially Latin, Greek, and French) and continues to use the original plural form rather than the English pattern. Many of these words are important in formal academic writing. In learning these, notice that seven different patterns occur:

1. The singular ends in *-sis* and the plural in *-ses*: *analysis/analyses, basis/bases.* Write in the plural.

crisis/ _____   *oasis/* _____

thesis/ _____   *parenthesis/* _____

hypothesis/ _____   *paralysis/* _____

axis/ _____   *synopsis/* _____

diagnosis/ _____   *synthesis/* _____

ellipsis/ _____

2. The singular ends in *-um* and the plural in *-a*: *datum/data, bacterium/bacteria, medium/media.* These words can cause some problems.

Data is used both for the singular and the plural by many Americans: *This data is important. These data are important.* You will only rarely see *datum.* Use whichever form is commonly used in your major field and by the individual instructors of your courses.

Bacteria tend to come in sets of more than one, so the singular is not a common word except in technical contexts. *Media* has taken on a special meaning in referring to modern systems of communication—TV, newspapers, radio are referred to collectively as *the media. Representatives of the media interviewed the president. Media representatives met with the president. Medium* and *media* have specialized uses in biology and other scientific fields. Learn to use the terms as they are used in your reading and by your professors.

3. The singular ends in *-on;* the plural ends in *-a*: *criterion/criteria.*

phenomenon/ _____

4. The singular ends in *-a;* the plural ends in *-ae*: *vita/vitae.* Look up these and write in the plural.

formula/ _____ (However, in everyday English rather than in technical English, the plural is *formulas.*)

vertebra/ _____ (In everyday English, however, *vertebras* is used.)

antenna/ _____ (The Latin plural is used in biology, but the regular English plural *antennas* is used generally and in electronics.)

5. The singular ends in *-ex* or *-ix;* the plural ends in *-ices: appendix/ appendices.*

index/ _____ (But, *indexes* is used when referring to parts of books.)

matrix/ _____

6. The singular ends in *-us* and the foreign plural in *-i: stimulus/stimuli, fungus/fungi* or *funguses.*

focus/foci or *focuses (Foci* is used mostly in optical studies; *focuses* is more commonly used elsewhere.)

7. The singular ends in *-us* and the foreign plural in *-a: corpus/corpora* or *corpuses, genus/genera.*

An alphabetized list of these and other irregular nouns is given in Appendix H of Ready Reference.

Nouns that Have Only Plurals   Some nouns have only a plural form—and require a plural form of the verb. (Compare these to the "false plurals" in Section 15b on p. 90.) These can be divided into three groups:

1. Nouns for things that come in **pairs**. Some of these refer to tools: *glasses, scissors, binoculars, forceps, tongs, tweezers.* Others are clothing: *jeans, pants, pajamas, shorts, trousers.*

2. Nouns that **end in -s** but have no singular: *accommodations, amends, archives, arms* ("weapons"), *bowels, intestines, brains* ("intellect"—*use your brains*), *clothes, communications* ("means of communication"—*communications network*), *congratulations, contents, stairs, thanks.*

3. Nouns that are **plural but do not end in -s:** *people, police, cattle.* (Note: one person, one policeman, one policewoman, one cow)

2e Abstract vs. Concrete Nouns

Nouns can also be divided based on their meaning. *Abstract nouns* are words that refer to abstract concepts (things that would be impossible to touch, for example) like *liberty, brotherhood, kindness. Concrete nouns* are words that refer to objects that are easier to think of as having physical reality—such as *child, book, apple.* Obviously, this is a continuum over which we can have much disagreement. Is *kindness* more or less abstract than *freedom?* Is *apple* more abstract than *Winesap apple?*

The category is mentioned here because it can be of use in deciding if a word is count or noncount. Generally, count nouns are concrete in meaning while noncount nouns are abstract.

count/concrete: *child, apple*

noncount/abstract: *freedom, motherhood*

(This generalization does not work so well for *gold, salt, coffee*, and other concrete noncount nouns. But, it can be a useful guide in dealing with new words.)

2f Collective Nouns

Some nouns refer to groups of individuals, for example *committee, jury, team*. When a collective noun is the subject of a sentence, selection of the verb can be a problem. If you are thinking of the group as a whole, acting together as a unit, then the singular verb is used: *The committee meets again next Wednesday*. If you are thinking of the individuals in the group acting individually rather than in a united way, you use the plural verb: *The jury disagree about the verdict*. In the U.S., these collective nouns are generally used with the singular verb. (See Section 15, "Subject-Verb Agreement," on p. 88.)

You already know many of these nouns. Working with the other students in your class, make as complete a list as possible to use for later reference. Write the list in the space below.

committee, jury

_____

_____

_____

2g EXERCISES: Nouns

A. Analyze the nouns that have been underlined in the following passages. Answer these questions about each noun:

1. Is the noun common or proper?

2. If it is common, is it singular, plural, or noncount?

TECHNOLOGIC DISASTERS

In modern times, technologic <u>disasters</u> have become a new <u>threat</u>. This <u>class</u> of disaster contains all great <u>accidents</u> that are caused by human inventions. Such incidents include <u>fires</u>, explosions, releases of toxic substances, transport accidents, dam failures, and a <u>myriad</u> of other mishaps. The toxic chemical incidents that occurred in <u>Bhopal</u>, India, and in Seveso, <u>Italy</u>, demonstrate what the consequences might be.

The United States has never experienced any great disaster comparable in <u>magnitude</u> to the 1984 Bhopal toxic gas release. While disasters have occurred, each event was in a relatively unpopulated <u>area,</u> and this limited the number of casualties caused by the incident. Similar incidents will recur in the future, however, and as American cities increase in area and in <u>population</u>, a significant mass casualty incident becomes much more likely.

Adapted from *Disaster Medical Assistance Team Organization Guide* (U.S. Department of Defense, 1986)

NUTRITION AND ISOLATION

Why does poor <u>nutrition</u> sometimes result from <u>isolation</u>? Poor nutrition can be caused in part by isolation and <u>loneliness</u> which make it seem hardly worthwhile to prepare <u>food</u> to eat alone.

Good nutrition, however, provided in a group setting, can offer a partial <u>solution</u> to loneliness. Through much of <u>life,</u> eating is a social occasion, a time for family <u>gatherings</u> and meetings with friends. Birthday parties, holidays, picnics, and other occasions are associated with pleasant times and food. When the social element is removed entirely, many <u>people</u> abandon regular mealtimes and turn to sporadic snacks to satisfy their <u>hunger.</u>

Adapted from *Let's End Isolation* (U.S. Department of Health, Education, and Welfare, 1971)

COMMERCIALIZATION OF BIOTECHNOLOGY

Biotechnology has entered the phase of commercialization. Although the competitive position of the United States is currently strong, it is increasingly challenged by the aggressive growth of biotechnological industries in foreign countries, particularly in Japan. These challenges are not surprising since Japan and other countries have established the development and commercialization of biotechnology as a national goal.

Adapted from *Biotechnology*. *High Technology Industries: Profiles and Outlooks* (U.S. Department of Commerce, 1984)

B. Work with another student to analyze the noncount nouns listed in Appendix I. First, divide the words into two groups based on the concreteness or abstractness of their meanings. Then, compare your list to those of other students in the class. Be prepared to defend your choices.

C. Your instructor will bring a copy of a newspaper advertisement for a supermarket that gives pictures of items on sale. Using the list in Appendix J, decide on the correct counting phrase to use in buying each item pictured—a pound of cheese, a package of hamburger, and so forth. Add to the list in Appendix J any new phrases that you learn from other students or from your instructor.

3a Noun Phrase Structure

While nouns can be used alone or with a single article, they are frequently combined with other words to make longer and more complex phrases that have the same functions as the simple noun—subject, object of a verb, or object of a preposition.

The book cost too much. (subject)

The new book cost too much. (subject)

The new calculus book cost too much. (subject)

The new calculus book that is required for Business Calculus 305 cost too much. (subject)

I paid too much for *this new calculus book that is required for Business Calculus 305.* (object of preposition)

I lost *that expensive new calculus book that is required for Business Calculus 305.* (direct object)

These examples also illustrate three of the types of words that can be combined with nouns to make noun phrases: (1) articles and other determiners, (2) adjectives, and (3) nouns.

For more information on the structure and use of relative clauses, see Section 4, "Restrictive Relative Clauses," on p. 301 and Section 5, "Nonrestrictive Relative Clauses," on p. 307. Also, see Chapter 9, "Determiners and Articles," for more information on the structure of noun phrases.

3b Order of Modifiers in Front of a Noun

The order in which prenoun modifiers are placed is relatively fixed. English speakers do not put them together in random order but usually arrange them according to a set pattern. The following rule gives the pattern generally followed:

determiner + sequence + number + quality or character + size + shape + age + temperature + shape + color + origin + location + noun + NOUN

Determiners are words like *a/an, the, this/that/these/those* (see Chapter 9). *Sequence* refers to words that give numerical ordering—all of the ordinal numbers (*first, second*), *last, next,* and many others. *Number* words include all the cardinal numbers—*one, two, three,* and so on. Quality, character, size, shape, age, temperature, color, origin, and location are categories of adjectives. NOUN is the main noun in the noun phrase.

Remember
Possessive personal pronouns and possessive nouns can be used as determiners (see Chapter 9).   *my computer*   *John's computer*   *the instructor of the calculus course's computer*

Here are some noun phrases to illustrate the rule given above:

the first three beautiful small hot round brown Southern biscuits

the = determiner

first = sequence

three = number

beautiful = quality or character

small = size

hot = temperature

round = shape

brown = color

Southern = origin

biscuits = NOUN

the second four happy little old rotund university instructors

the = determiner

second = sequence

four = number

happy = quality or character

little = size

old = age

rotund = shape

university = noun

instructors = NOUN

the first ten Spanish olives

the = _____

first = _____

ten = _____

Spanish = _____

olives = _____

those first ten historical Spanish buildings

those = _____

first = _____

ten = _____

historical = _____

Spanish = _____

buildings = _____

Madrid's first historical monument

Madrid's = _____

first = _____

historical = _____

monument = _____

Notice that this noun phrase rule can be subdivided into six parts:

1. determiner +

2. [sequence + number] +

3. [quality or character + size + shape + age + temperature + shape + color] +

4. [origin + location] +

5. noun +

6. NOUN

That is, this generalization about English might be easier to learn if you divide the rule into these parts:

(determiner) + (sequence + number) + (age) + (origin) + (noun) + (NOUN)
    the   *first three*   *new*   *Japanese*   *car*   *radios*

3c Adjectives in Front of a Noun

Adjectives can be classified as

quality or character: *beautiful, happy, intelligent*
size: *tall, big, huge, short, small; tiny*
shape: *round, square*
age: *old, young*
temperature: *hot, cold*
color: *red, purple*
origin and location: *American (the diplomat from the United States), central (a central location)*

Adjectives of shape have more flexibility in their location than the other types. For that reason, the category is given twice in the rule. Evidently, the adjective that is emphasized comes first.

the old round box   *the round old box*

Adjectives can, of course, be compounded, for example, *the red, white, and blue flag, his hot and cold reactions,* and *the friendly and helpful secretary.* Notice that the compounds are made up of two or more adjectives from the same category.

When *but* is used to compound the adjectives, the order puts the adjectives in a different relationship because of *but's* meaning of "however." The first adjective is some problem or negative quality, for example, *the old but healthy man* or *the expensive but worthwhile trip.*

Technically, there is no limit on the number of adjectives that can be placed in front of a noun to modify its meaning. In reality, you will seldom read or write more than two or three.

3d EXERCISES: Noun Phrase Structure

A. Work with another student to agree on combinations of these words to make noun phrases:

dress (stylish, new, a)

stamps (some, old, valuable)

cars (foreign, those, small)

operation (economical, their)

car (long, strange, black, a)

cousin (mother's, my, distant)

book (new, this, picture)

pictures (other, interesting, several)

buildings (old, some, historical)

house (that, gray, other)

crowd (young, a, enthusiastic)

game (the, exciting, first, basketball)

jokes (funny, many, comedian's, a)

information (useless, old, that)

cars (new, two)

B. Analyze these noun phrases with another student. What kinds of adjectives are used? Is the adjective ordering rule followed?

a young American writer

other recent calculus books

an important five-year labor research project

a profound young California researcher

the long quiet winter months

the central mountain range

the first three American presidents

the first and last company president

the important but difficult-to-follow research report

the big old rectangular library reading room table

C. Look again at the passage "Technologic Disasters" on p. 155. Analyze the noun phrases. What combinations of words are used?

D. Look again at the passages "Nutrition and Isolation" (p. 155) and "Commercialization of Biotechnology" (p. 156). Find the two uses of possessive personal pronouns or possessive noun phrases as determiners.

E. Look at the front page of today's newspaper. Make a list of 15 noun phrases that have three or more words. How many have possessives as determiners? What kinds of words are combined? Do many of them have two or more adjectives? Do many of them have the noun + noun combination?

4a Nouns Modifying Nouns

You have already seen that nouns can be used to modify other nouns. Consider these noun phrases:

the computer terminal

the library book

the laboratory schedule

English very often uses one noun to modify the meaning of another noun. This system can result in quite long and complex noun phrases because the first noun can have modifiers of its own:

the computer software catalog

These three nouns have this relationship: *computer* modifies *software* to make the combination *computer software;* then that combination modifies *catalog* to mean "the catalog of computer software."

These combinations can be ambiguous. In this phrase, what is "modern"? The computer? The software? The catalog?

the modern computer software catalog

Usually, context will make the meaning clear. Sometimes, the phrase will have to be rewritten so that the meaning is clear.

the modern catalog of computer software

the catalog of software for modern computers

the catalog of modern software for computers

Technical and scientific English frequently uses these complex noun phrases. Many of the specialized terms of your field of study will have this structure.

Sometimes, the two nouns are so closely related and so often used together that they have actually become one compound noun even though they are still written as two words. The key to the difference is in pronunciation. If the first of the nouns is stressed, the word is a compound: *interest rates,* for example.

4b Analyzing Noun + Noun Combinations for Meaning and Grammar

Most of these combinations can be analyzed as a noun followed by a prepositional phrase.

a computer catalog means a catalog for computers

the Brooklyn Bridge means the bridge to Brooklyn

a paper plate means a plate made of paper

However, some of these noun phrases are difficult to rephrase:

consumer goods (perhaps, goods for the consumer, but that is not quite accurate because it really means something like goods made to be consumed)

Sometimes prefixes correspond to the prepositional phrase:

preregistration procedures means procedures prior to registration

antiwar speeches means speeches against (the) war

Grammarians have identified the following major categories of these noun + noun combinations. This list is not complete but only suggests the kinds of relationships you will find.

1. The modifying noun refers to the source or material out of which something is made: *a clay tablet, a paper napkin, a lead pencil* (which is now made of graphite because lead is poisonous), *a rubber band, plastic glasses.*

2. The modifying noun gives the purpose to which the main noun is put: *water glass, wine glass, vegetable dish, water fountain.*

3. The modifying noun names something that makes up part of the whole: *clay soil, salt water.*

4. The modifying noun gives location or place: *a street sign, an apartment office, the university library.*

5. The modifying noun gives the direction that a street or road goes: *the Atlanta Highway, the Santa Ana Freeway.*

6. The modifying noun refers to time: *a morning flight, an evening class, an afternoon appointment.*

7. The modifying noun names the larger group for a whole/part relationship: *a board member, a class member, an airline pilot, a university instructor, a computer terminal, a computer keyboard.*

8. The modifying noun tells the purpose of the main noun: *a tiger hunt, a physics test, a chemistry class.*

There is some overlapping of these categories. Purpose and group membership, for example, are sometimes hard to distinguish.

4c EXERCISES: Noun Phrases

A. Analyze the meanings of these noun phrases. What is the meaning relationship between the two nouns?

afternoon class

grammar class

student center or *student union*

car factory

action plan

typewriter paper

coke machine

apple juice

bus station

fast food restaurant

department office

Brooklyn Bridge

cheese sandwich

coffee pot

English dictionary

English-Turkish dictionary

B. Work with another student who is majoring in your field of study. Together go through an introductory textbook in your field to find 10 important noun phrases. Analyze the meaning relationship between the nouns. For example, a management major might find *the management functions, the planning process,* and many others. Share the terms that you find with any other students in your class who are majoring in your field.

5a Plural Nouns as Noun Modifiers

Some advanced students have problems with a grammatical change that occurs when plurals are used as the modifying noun. Typically, a noun loses the plural when it is used as a modifier. This loss is probably the result of the more general English rule that adjectives do not agree with their nouns. (That is, ▼*the bigs cars.*)

The report is 200 pages long becomes *the 200-page report.*

The gear has 500 teeth becomes *the 500-tooth gear.*

The mountain is 2,000 feet high becomes *the 2,000-foot mountain.*

There are some exceptions to this rule when the loss of plural would be ambiguous. The use of this pattern seems to be increasing.

a systems analyst (They analyze more than one system.)

the parks department (They manage more than one park.)

a Blues band (*Blues* is a kind of music. *A blue band* would have a different meaning.)

5b EXERCISES: Plural Nouns as Noun Modifiers

A. Change these phrases following the model:

1. The book has 200 pages = the 200-page book

2. The company has 2,000 employees = _____

3. The garage holds three cars = _____

4. The statue is 1,500 years old = _____

5. The formal plan has 35 subdivisions = _____

6. The family has five children = _____

7. The car has four doors = _____

B. Find the noun + noun phrases in these sentences. Has the plural been dropped from the first noun? If not, why do you think the plural was kept?

The sales division prepared a 250-page report on the 10-year period from 1975 to 1985. The report shows a 2.5 million dollar increase in costs accompanied by a 3.0 million dollar increase in sales.

6a Noun Phrases Modified by Prepositional Phrases

Noun phrases are frequently followed by prepositional phrases that modify their meaning. All prepositions are capable of being used in this way. However, *of* is the most commonly used preposition for modifying a noun phrase.

a book about U.S. history

a research project with serious implications

the president of the student government

the front of the room

Noun phrases can develop into long chains of nouns connected to other nouns with prepositions.

the need for information

the need for information about computer costs

the need at our institution for information about computer costs

The following sentences from a report on the shift of U.S. population from cities to smaller towns is typical in its use of prepositional phrases. Use a highlighter to mark all of the prepositional phrases. How many did you find?

Understanding these changes requires an analysis of reasons for moving and the motivations that underlie decisions to live in one place rather than another. Some insights into reasons for the new patterns of the 1970s have been gleaned from examination of the types of nonmetropolitan counties that had net inmigration.*

---

*Inmigration means a move of people into a place; *county* means a subdivision of a state.

List here the noun + prepositional phrase combinations that are used in these two sentences:

1. *an analysis of reasons*
2. *reasons for moving*
3. _____

4. _____

5. _____

6. _____

6b *Of* vs. the Possessive Noun

Look at these noun phrases:

Mary's book
John's foot
the instructor's lecture
the politician's son
Einstein's theories
two dollars' worth of candy
last year's Federal budget
the top of the page
the arrival of the bus

These are all usually called *possessives*. However, they are not all referring to ownership. Mary owns the book, but does John own his foot? Does the instructor own the lecture? Does the politician own his son? Does Einstein own his theories? Does the page own its top? Does the bus own its arrival? Obviously other kinds of meanings are involved.

1. relationship
   my mother's oldest sister
2. part/whole
   the bottom of the application form
   Mary's elbow
3. origin/agent
   Poe's short stories
   my professor's research report
4. amount/quantity/time
   today's test
   next month's rent
   two dollars' worth of candy

5. measurement/classification
   a pound of coffee
   a kind of research
   a type of fish
6. ownership
   Mike's house
7. association/use
   Mary's apartment
   my advisor's office
8. description
   the train's departure

6c EXERCISE: *Of* vs. the Possessive Noun

Analyze the list of noun phrases given at the beginning of Section 6b on p. 166. What meanings do you think are involved?

6d Selection of the Correct Form of the Possessive

The *possessive* can be signaled either by *'s* or by *of*. While the rules that control your choice are complex, generally you can follow these guidelines:

1. *'s* must be used with a proper noun that refers to ownership or relationship: *Mike's house, John's foot, Mary's car.*

   Notice that English refers to parts of the body using the possessive when talking about an individual's body, but the articles are used to talk about bodies in general: *my nose itches* or *John's long crooked nose* versus *the nose is a sensitive organ.*

2. *'s* is preferred when the noun refers to human beings or to the higher animals: *the instructor's research report, the cat's paw, the elephant's valuable tusk.*

   However, *of* is possible for formal use or for long, complex noun phrases: *the paw of the Bengal Tiger, the car of the student who lives next to me.*

3. *'s* is preferred when the noun refers to something that is seen as related to human beings, especially geographical nouns: *France's wine country, China's rural roads.*

   However, prepositions can be substituted: *the wine country of France, the rural roads in China.*

4. Two *'s* can be used for complex relationships: *John's sister, John's sister's husband, John's sister's husband's mother. Of* can be used beyond the basic relationship: *the husband of John's sister, the mother of the husband of John's sister.*

5. *Of* is preferred for inanimate nouns (except as in 6 and 7 below): *the top of the page, the results of the report, the end of the term.*

6. *'s* is possible for time and location uses: *this month's rent, Japan's northern islands.*

   Other prepositions could be used: *the rent for this month, the northern islands of Japan.*

7. *'s* is used with collective nouns having human or animal reference: *the committee's report, the flock's feeding time.*

   Prepositions can also be used: *the report from the committee, the feeding time for the flock.*

8. In addition, complex phrases can have *of* rather than the possessive noun: *the car of my brother's wife's first cousin, the theories of the researchers who are working on this project.*

9. Also, *of* is felt to be more formal than *'s* and is sometimes used for that reason: *the theories of Einstein* is more formal than *Einstein's theories.*

   However, this choice cannot ever be made when referring to ownership, possession, relationship with proper names: you can never write ▼*the foot of John,* ▼*the car of Mary,* ▼*the sister of Mike.*

6e EXERCISES: The Possessive

A. Combine the words listed below by using the appropriate possessive form.

CALMING FEARS

_____ (1) to the nuclear accident puzzled many people

because of _____ (2). In addition, _____

(3) did not calm _____ (4). She announced that

_____ (5) had fled the accident scene and that the

army had been placed in control of the disaster area. _____

(6) would probably never be known. This accident could certainly be

compared to _____ (7) at Chernobyl.

---

1. the reaction, government
2. the lack, decisive action
3. the television appearance, the prime minister
4. the fear, people living near the power plant
5. the managers, facility
6. the cause, the explosion
7. last year, disaster

B. To see the importance of <u>of</u> phrases, look at this passage. The <u>of</u> phrases have been marked in the first paragraph. Find the <u>of</u> phrases in the other paragraphs. How many are used? Also, mark any uses of *'s*. Why is the *'s* used rather than an <u>of</u> phrase?

BIOTECHNOLOGY IN JAPAN

In a survey <u>of over 600</u> <u>of the leading companies</u> in Japan, biotechnology was rated as having the greatest growth potential <u>of all new emerging industries</u>. Both the Japanese government and industry have accorded a high priority to the rapid development <u>of an internationally competitive level</u> of technology.

The Japanese government has made the commercialization of biotechnology a national priority in order to ensure Japan's economic competitiveness and to decrease dependence on imports of foreign technology. Biotechnology is seen as a way to decrease imports of energy and raw materials for feedstocks, as well as a way to develop new export markets. The Ministry of Industry and Trade's (MITI) vision for the future includes the establishment of Japan as a world leader in science and technology innovation. In October 1982, MITI led a biotechnology mission (representing government, industry, and academia) to visit research institutes, government agencies, and private firms in the United States, West Germany, France, Switzerland, and the U.K. The purpose of the mission was to investigate the possibilities for international cooperation in biotechnology research and development and to learn the state of research and development in biotechnology, government promotion plans, and private industry strategies.

Unlike the early development of biotechnology in the United States, most of which was done by small firms, the biotechnology drive in Japan is spearheaded by established firms, primarily from the food processing, pharmaceutical, and chemical industries. The leading firms include Aji-nomot and Kyowa Hakko Kogyo (food processing); Takeda and Shionogi (pharmaceuticals); Toray (synthetic fibers); Sumitomo Chemicals; and Suntory (brewing). The trading houses have started partnerships with many of these firms. There are no venture capital funded start-up bio-technology firms in Japan, although the recent surge of interest in ven-ture capital funding by the financial sector, including domestic and foreign venture capital firms, and the formation of venture capital funded firms in the electronics sector may be an indication that some will be formed in the biotechnology sector as well. The government's recent easing of capital and earnings requirements will make it easier for new and unprofitable firms to sell stocks on the Japanese stock exchange and thereby obtain equity financing.

_____

Adapted from "A Study of the U.S. Competitive Position in Biotechnology" (Arakaki, 1984)

C. The length of some of the noun phrases in the passage in exercise B is typical of the writing found in formal, academic English, especially in scientific and technical areas. Analyze these noun phrases: the first two are done as models.

1. the/ greatest/ growth/ potential
   article + quality adjective + noun + noun

2. an/ internationally competitive/ level
   article + (adverb + quality adjective) + noun

3. the Ministry of Industry and Trade

   _____

4. the Ministry of Industry and Trade's vision

   _____

5. the food processing, pharmaceutical, and chemical industries

   _____

6. no venture capital funded start-up biotechnology firms

   _____

7. capital and earnings requirements

   _____

8. new and unprofitable firms

   _____

7 EXERCISES: Noun Phrase

A. Noun phrases from this passage on countertrade are listed below. Analyze the phrases. What kinds of words have been combined to make these phrases? Then, locate each noun phrase in the text. How is it used? Subject? Object of verb? Object of preposition?

COUNTERTRADE

A basic and necessary characteristic of an expanding world economy is the market-oriented, unfettered flow of capital, goods, and services across national boundaries.

However, when sluggish economic conditions, which affect national trade balances, market access privileges, convertible currency transfer patterns, and which result in unemployment and low utilization of industrial production capacities, prevail in world markets, some countries find it expedient to impose various reciprocal conditions on their foreign trade. These conditions may link purchases of foreign goods and services to exports of domestic goods and services ("countertrade"), and/or, increasingly, to other asset transfers which result in benefits for the importing country. The latter conditions may involve technology transfers, investments, and other domestic requirements and are known as "offsets" in government procurement parlance.

Adapted from *International Countertrade: A Guide for Managers and Executives* (Verzariu, 1984)

---

basic and necessary characteristic

an expanding world economy

the market-oriented, unfettered flow

national boundaries

sluggish economic conditions

national trade balances

market access privileges

convertible currency transfer patterns

low utilization

industrial production capacities

world markets

some countries

various reciprocal conditions

their foreign trade

these conditions	the latter conditions
foreign goods	technology transfer
domestic goods	other domestic requirements
other asset transfers	government procurement parlance
the importing country	

B. First, use a highlighter to mark the noun phrases in this passage. Then, analyze the structure of the noun phrases. Notice how prepositions are used to tie noun phrases together to make larger noun phrases.

URBAN TRENDS IN THE U.S.

One of the major urban trends in the United States during recent decades has been the growing disparity between residents of the central city and suburban portions of metropolitan areas. Cities and suburbs in the aggregate have tended to become increasingly dissimilar in a number of respects, perhaps most notably in terms of racial composition and socioeconomic status. The percentage of blacks in many central cities has increased greatly since World War II, and the income level of central city residents has tended to fall further behind that of suburbanites. The growing socioeconomic disparity within metropolitan areas stands in sharp contrast to the many decreasing socioeconomic differences between metropolitan and nonmetropolitan populations during the 1970s.

Adapted from *The City-Suburb Income Gap: Is It Being Narrowed by a Back-to-the-City Movement?* (Long and Dahmann, 1980)

C. The following noun phrases were taken from a textbook used in introduction to management courses. The phrases were found in the first three pages of a chapter on the importance of planning as a management function. Analyze these using the modifier ordering rule. What kinds of noun phrases seem most popular?

future time periods	top management
two major segments	the objectives
the management function	business and functional strategies
three basic questions	the previous chapter
the first question	the upper levels
the present situation	the very top levels

the second question	the primary management function
the desired objectives	the other management functions
the final question	high employee turnover
the financial impact	a British planning consultant
current decisions	an ever-longer planning horizon
many authors	an informal or casual basis
the objective-setting situation	a formal planning system
the planning process	short-range plans
the more narrow sense	long-range plans
some predetermined goal	day-by-day problems

D. Use a highlighter to mark the noun phrases in the passages. Then, analyze their structure.

MOTHERS BECOME DOCTORS

Women in the U.S. have been at the vortex of sweeping changes in demographic, social, and economic patterns. During the 15 immediate post-World War II years, American women bore and nurtured the massive baby boom generation. Indeed, in the early 1960s, most American women seemed to be reading Dr. Benjamin Spock's *Common Sense Book of Baby and Child Care*. After its publication in 1946, over one million paperback copies were sold every year, or approximately one for every 2.6 women aged 15 to 44 by 1960. By 1980, however, there had been a complete reversal. Childbearing had fallen below natural replacement levels, and many women were concentrating on jobs and education. Indeed, many American women were becoming doctors themselves. Between 1950 and 1979, the number of female physicians in the United States increased from 584 to 3,405, and for the first time, more women than men were enrolled in college in 1980.

Adapted from *American Women: Three Decades of Change* (Bianchi and Spain, 1983)

FROM CITY TO COUNTRY: THE U.S. POPULATION PATTERN

One of the most unexpected demographic developments in the United States in the 1970s was the shift of nonmetropolitan areas to net inmigration. Partly because of this change, the nonmetropolitan sector, which includes many small towns and rural areas, experienced noticeably faster rates of total population growth in the aggregate than did metropolitan areas. To many people, these changes seemed to imply a reversal of the longstanding association of rural-to-urban migration with rapid growth of large urban areas, and there was even a suggestion in the data and discussions that new forces might be governing population redistribution in the United States and new motives might be shaping the residential location decisions of individuals.

Adapted from *The City-Suburb Income Gap: Is It Being Narrowed by a Back-to-the-City Movement?* (Long and Dahmann, 1980)

E. To see how noun phrases are used in your major field of study, find and analyze the noun phrases on two pages of a textbook for a course you will take.

F. Words in the noun phrases in this passage have been scrambled—they are presented in alphabetical order in the list below. Some of the noun phrases include prepositional phrases. Put them into the correct order.

NEED FOR A NATIONAL DISASTER MEDICAL SYSTEM IN THE U.S.

The United States has never experienced _____ (1) comparable in magnitude to _____ (2), _____ (3), _____ (4), or _____ (5). Nevertheless, the nation is at risk of such catastrophes.

Each of these disasters has _____ (6): _____ (7), the eruption of Mt. St. Helens in 1980, or the explosions that devastated Port Chicago, California, in 1944 or Texas City, Texas, in 1947. In each of these examples, the event occurred in _____ (8), and this limited the number of casualties caused by the incident. Similar incidents will recur in the future, however, and as American cities increase in area and in population, _____ (9) becomes much more likely.

Adapted from *Disaster Medical Assistance Team Organization Guide* (U.S. Department of Defense, 1986)

---

1. any/disaster/great

2. Bhopal/1984/gas/release/toxic/the

3. China/earthquake/1976/in/Tangshan/the

4. eruption/Mt. Pelee/Martinique/of/on/1904/the

5. explosion/Halifax, Nova Scotia/in/1917/ship/the

6. a/American/analogue/recent

7. Alaskan/earthquake/of/1964/the

8. a/area/relatively/unpopulated

9. a/casualty/incident/mass/significant

CHAPTER 9

Determiners and Articles

1 Introduction to Determiners and Articles

The *determiners* are members of a group of words that precede nouns and modify the meaning of the nouns in various ways. There can be only one determiner for each noun. (See Chapter 8 for more information on nouns and the words that go with them to make noun phrases.)

Determiners				
a/an	any	this/that	my	noun + *'s*
the	each	these/	his	noun + *s'*
some	every	those	her	
	much		its	
	many		your	
			our	
			their	

the book	*each book*	*these books*	*their books*	*Dr. Lund's book*
				the students' books

As you can see, the articles *a/an, the, some* are included in the determiner system. Since most advanced students have more problems with the articles than with the other determiners, this chapter will focus primarily on the articles.

Correct use of *the* and *a/an* is one of the most difficult areas of English—both for instructors to explain and for students to learn. Various causes for the problems can be given: Some languages do not have articles. Languages that do have articles use them differently from English. The English system is complex. Unlike some areas of grammar, articles cannot be avoided. They are everywhere—in just about every sentence. Certainly, few paragraphs will be written without the writer making choices about articles.

These difficulties cannot be allowed to stop your attempt to improve your written English. In conversation, the lack of articles or the wrong use of articles might not be noticed. However, as soon as you begin to write, your lack of control over the system is easy to observe.

First, the broad outlines of the system will be presented. Then, details of particular forms will be discussed and illustrated.

2a The Basic Article System

These are the facts:

Articles are words that go with nouns.

Articles are used to indicate definiteness or indefiniteness.

Articles are used to indicate generic or nongeneric meaning.

The choice of article or no article is controlled by

    the type of noun,

    meaning, and

    the knowledge shared between writer and reader.

The basic article system gives you four choices: *the, a/an, some,* or no article (called the *zero form* by grammarians). When those choices are combined with the categories of nouns, you get this system:*

	Singular	Plural	Noncount	Proper
zero form		books	money	John Smith
a/some	a book	some books	some money	
the form	the book	the books	the money	the Smiths

This chart can be interpreted in the following way:

1. If a noun is singular, it must have an article.

2. A plural noun has *the* if its meaning is definite; *some* is used for indefinite meanings; either *the* or zero article (no article) can be used for generic meaning.

   Since most nouns are count nouns, these singular and plural uses are what you will encounter most often.

3. Noncount nouns have three choices—

   the for definite meanings

   some for indefinite meanings

   zero for generic meanings

4. Proper nouns have only two choices—

   the for plural meanings

   zero for the singular meaning

The proper noun category is made complex because of the geographic names that must be learned. (See Section 3 on p. 184 for special and idiomatic uses of the articles, including geographic names.)

---

*If you do not understand the difference between *count* and *noncount nouns,* turn immediately to Section 2c on p. 149 before continuing with your study of articles.

2b Definite vs. Indefinite

To fully understand the article system, you must think about the meaning of *definite, indefinite,* and *generic.* What does it mean to say that a noun is definite? It means that the writer thinks that the reader understands the particular thing, person, or idea that is being referred to. It means that the writer does not think the particular thing, person, or idea is new to the reader.

When is a noun definite? When you think the reader knows the same information that you do, the noun is definite.

When can I be sure that the reader knows the same things I do? Grammarians have suggested a number of different situations in which a writer can assume that the reader would understand a noun as definite. While this list is not complete, it can help you understand the concept "definite" more clearly.

Situations that Are Definite

1. The noun refers to something that is unique for everyone in the world: *the sun, the moon, the universe, the stars.*

2. The noun is made specific by its setting. For example, in the classroom you can say: *the blackboard, the instructor, the students.* Any reader who is in that context will understand the same meaning that you do.

3. Members of a particular group share common meanings. For example, if you say *the president,* Americans will assume that you mean the President of the U.S.

4. A speaker can point (with a finger, a nod of the head) at something and use *the* because he/she assumes that the listener then understands the particular object being talked about. This is almost impossible for a writer.

5. The nouns refer to the parts of some whole that is being talked about. If you are describing a house, then you can write *the windows, the doors.* If you are describing a computer, you can write *the diskdrive, the monitor.*

6. A writer can mention something one time, using *a* or *an,* because the reader does not share the same information. But after that first use, the writer changes to *the* because the information is now shared with the reader. Grammar texts usually illustrate this use with the beginning sentences of a story: *Long ago, an old woman lived in a village. The old woman had two grandchildren who came to the village to visit her every Sunday.* This use is not, however, restricted to folk tales. *To carry out this procedure, a new computer program had*

to be written. While the *program was extremely expensive, it has been found to have many other applications.*

7. A writer can make a noun definite by adding phrases to define it: *the president of our organization, the house next door to mine, the car I hit in the parking lot.*

8. The parts of sets are considered definite: *the first page, the last question.* This group includes the superlative adjective form because it marks a definite member of a set: *the slowest walker, the biggest mountain.*

2c Generic vs. Indefinite

1. Definite: *I know the teacher of this class.*

2. Generic: *Teachers usually receive long years of training.*

3. Indefinite: *I know a teacher who can help you.*

4. Indefinite: *This school needs some teachers.*

Sometimes a noun refers to a particular individual, as in the first example of *the teacher of this class.* In other instances, the noun can be used to refer to a kind of person rather than an individual, as in the second example—*Teachers usually receive long years of training. Generic* is the term grammarians use when they are talking about this second use of nouns. The generic can refer to categories of people or things; the generic can also refer to all of the members of a set together.

Generic is different from indefinite. The indefinite, in the third example, refers to a particular teacher, but the speaker does not think the listener shares the information. In the fourth example, the writer is giving an indefinite count but is not thinking about all teachers.

2d Five Types of Generic Uses of Nouns

Unfortunately, the generic is not as simple as suggested above. Singular, plural, noncount, and proper nouns can be used for generic meaning.

1. A teacher *must have years of training.*

2. The teacher *has much responsibility to society.*

3. Teachers *are seldom paid as much as businessmen.*

4. *Thus, we can generalize that* the Americans *see life in terms of doing rather than being.*

5. Sugar *is Cuba's most important agricultural product.*

Generic-1   This first type has the pattern of *a/an* + singular noun. It is used in less formal situations, especially in conversations, to give generalities about a type of thing or group of people. *What are the responsibilities of a student? A student should . . .*

Generic-2   The second pattern is *the* + singular noun. This is the formal way that writers indicate generic meaning. The pattern can be used for just about all nouns. However, it is not used for simple inanimate objects, such as *book*. Research has shown that this generic type is the one preferred in technical or informative writing on plants, animals, inventions.

The computer has altered the ways in which business is conducted.
The tiger is greatly feared by rural Indians.

Generic-3   The third pattern is *plural noun*—with zero article. This generic type is a less formal version of the second pattern. It can be used anywhere that pattern 2 is used. In addition, it can be used to generalize about simple inanimate objects: *Books are basic for a student's life.*

Computers have altered the ways in which business is conducted.
Tigers are greatly feared by rural Indians.

Generic-4   The fourth generic type is the rarest—*the* + plural noun. This pattern is used to talk about human groups, usually political, national, religious, social, or occupational. The pattern is used to express generalities about the group as a whole. Social scientists use this pattern to talk about characteristics of groups.

The middle class Catholics give significantly different explanations from those offered by the middle class Baptists. (The group "the middle class Catholics" is defined in economic and religious terms; it is a social group.)

Generic-5   *Sugar* in the example refers to this product as a kind of thing. The indefinite would be *I need some sugar for my coffee.* The definite would be *Please, pass the sugar.* Another way to state the rule says: noncount nouns form their generic without any article at all.

2e Learning to Recognize Different Types of Generic Uses of Nouns

The following passages were selected to show you the various types of generic uses of nouns. Which type of generic is used in each of the nouns printed in bold type?

Buying Used Cars

Each year, **Americans** spend about $54 billion to buy more than 17 million used cars. The Federal Trade Commission's Used Car Rule requires **used car dealers** to place large stickers, called "Buyers Guides," in the left front windows of used vehicles they offer for sale.

Edgar Allan Poe

Edgar Allan Poe, born in Boston in 1809, is still famous as **a poet** and **a short story writer**. During his brief life, he also worked as an editor and was **a soldier** (at a point when he could not find any other way to earn a living).

Water

Water is a chemical compound of **hydrogen** and **oxygen**. Occurring almost everywhere in nature, it takes the form of ice, snow, water, and **steam**. The purest natural form of water is **snow**.

The Human Hand

The human hand is made up of **skin**, fatty tissue, **nerves**, muscles, bones, tendons, and joints. The basic divisions of the hand are commonly called "the fingers." In scientific writing, **the thumb** is "finger I."

Survey of Opinion

In sum, our survey reveals that **the Japanese** view of their role in their country's economic plans is quite different from the attitudes of **the Americans** or the Chinese.

Tigers

Tigers are the largest member of the cat family. Confined to Asia, tigers can be divided into several geographic subgroups. While tigers usually eat wild animals, old or wounded tigers may attack **human beings**. **The tiger** is, however, no match for **the elephant**.

2f Telling Indefinite Singular from Generic-1

The same singular noun phrase can be used for two different meanings. Notice how *a poet* is different in these two sentences:

Last night I went to a poetry reading by a poet *from Poland.*

My father is very upset because I want to be a poet *rather than an engineer.*

Indefinite nouns are used when the writer thinks the following:

1. The reader does not have the same information he/she does. A particular thing is being written about, but the reader is not yet informed about that particular thing. That is, the reference is specific for the writer but not yet specific for the reader. For example, this is the first sentence of a passage about finding interesting books in strange places:

   Last year in Paris I found a beautiful and fascinating book *about Russian bridges. The book cost only $15.*

2. The writer does not yet have specific information but thinks the reader does. That is, the reference is indefinite for the writer but specific for the reader/listener.

   You write a note to leave for your advisor: *I need* a book *or* an article *on engineering applications of calculus.*

   You say to a professor, *"I understand that you have written* an article *about the problems of foreign students in American universities."*

3. The writer is communicating about something that is not specific for him/her and also not specific for the reader, but the writer is not writing generalizations about categories. The writer is talking about "one of these objects or people but not a specific one."

   I need a new notebook.

   John does not have a computer, *but he really needs one.*

Generic-1 is used to write about categories, especially in talking about the work, skills, training of a person. It is frequently used to give definitions.

My brother is a lawyer.

A machine *is* a mechanical device *for doing work.*

Within each of these sets of sentences, compare the different meanings possible for *a/an.*

Set A

1. A student *entered the vice president's office and asked for an appointment with the vice president.*

2. *My roommate is* a student.

3. A student *is a person who studies.*

4. *I know* a student *from Venezuela.*

Set B

1. A machine *is a mechanical device for doing work.*

2. An inventor *is a person who makes new machines.*

3. *Edison worked on* a machine *to record the human voice.*

4. *Edison was* an inventor.

3a Special Uses of the Articles

In addition to the general system, the articles are also used in special situations with geographical names, the names of universities, the names of diseases, the names of the parts of the body, and other idiomatic uses. Each of these is discussed and illustrated in turn.

3b The Articles and Geographical Names

Most place names are proper nouns with zero article: *South America, Russia, Atlanta, Lake Erie.*

Some proper names are plurals or collectives that take *the: the United States, the Soviet Union, the People's Republic of China, the United Kingdom.* This second category also includes sets of places—*the Great Lakes* and *the Alps,* for example.

The third group is made up of singular nouns that take *the.* These nouns are the names for bodies of water (oceans, seas, gulfs, rivers, channels, canals), regions of the world, deserts, and peninsulas. Researchers suggest that these geographic features are alike in being relatively hard to define—where does an ocean, or a desert, or a peninsula begin or end? Space has been left for you in the list below to add other names that you consider important to know.

Oceans: *the Atlantic Ocean,* _____

Seas: *the Mediterranean Sea,* _____

Gulfs: *the Gulf of Mexico,* _____

Rivers: *the Mississippi River,* _____

Channels/Canals: *the English Channel, the Erie Canal,* _____

Regions: *the American West,* _____

Deserts: *the Sahara,* _____

Peninsulas: *the Iberian Peninsula,* _____

3c Academic Names

U.S. colleges and universities have these patterns in their names. Most states have a university with the name the University of _____, for example, *the University of Michigan* or *the University of Florida.* Many states also have a second university with the name *State University—Michigan State University, Florida State University, Georgia State University.*

Because the word *the* carries meaning of uniqueness, some of the state universities add that word to their official titles: *the Florida State University, the Ohio State University.* That wording is usually limited to the official publications of the institution. Americans still refer to *Ohio State University* or *Florida State University.* At least one university uses a different naming pattern: *the Ohio University.*

Some states have a university system in which all the institutions have the same basic name; the only difference is the location. California and New York use this naming method: *California State University— Chico, the University of California—Davis, the State University of New*

York—Buffalo. The more common name for the New York schools uses the initials of the longer name: *SUNY—Buffalo* or *SUNY—Albany.*

Some universities are named for the city where they are located: *Atlanta University, Boston University.* Other city universities use the *University of . . .* pattern: *the University of Toledo, the University of San Francisco, the University of Miami.* These city universities do not necessarily belong to that city. *The University of Miami,* for instance, is a private institution.

Many colleges and universities have been named to honor prominent individuals: *Washington and Lee University, George Washington University, Stanford University.*

What pattern does your institution use? What are the names of the other colleges and universities in the area? In the state? What other colleges or universities have you heard of?

3d The Articles with Names of Diseases

All five different noun types are used in naming diseases—*the* + singular noun, *a/an* + singular noun, *the* + plural noun, zero + plural noun, zero + noncount noun.

1. *the* + singular: *the flu, the plague*

2. *a/an* + singular: *a cold, a headache* (all the *ache* names); zero + plural: *colds, headaches*

3. *the* + plural: *the mumps, the measles, the chickenpox* (all the *pox* names)

4. zero + plural: *mumps, measles* (an optional form of pattern 3)

5. zero + noncount: *influenza, pneumonia, cancer, AIDS* (The Latinate names such as *tuberculosis,* while technically count nouns, fit pattern 5 better than pattern 4.)

In general, you can remember this overall pattern: The everyday "achy" diseases use *a/an* for singular and no article for plural. The diseases of childhood are given plural names with either *the* or zero. The scientific or Latinate names for diseases have no article. Pattern 1, however, includes both common and rare diseases that are named using *the.*

3e The Articles with Names of Body Parts

Most of the names given parts of human and animal bodies are common count nouns. When English speakers are talking about their own bodies— or the bodies of other individuals—possessive personal pronouns are used:

He broke his arm.

Please raise your hand if you know the answer.

There is something in my eye.

For animals, forms of *it* are usually preferred—unless the animal is a deeply loved pet.

The racehorse broke its leg.

My cat, Rosebud, broke her front leg.

For generic use, these count nouns that name the body parts use *the* plus either the singular or the plural—depending on how many of the parts exist in any one body:

the heart	*the eyes*
the stomach	*the ears*
the nose	*the lungs*
the liver	*the teeth*

These generic forms are used in technical and nontechnical writing about health and physical matters. Scientists and health journalists share the same vocabulary when writing on these topics.

3f Other Idiomatic Uses of the Articles

When talking or writing about telephones, radios, trains, and buses, English speakers use *the* where you might have expected *a/an*.

We heard the announcement on the radio.

He rides the train to work.

She took the bus to the mall.

I talked with my mother on the phone.

I am taking a cab to the bank.

> *the church.*
>
> *the university.*
>
> *the park.*
>
> *the movies.*
>
> *the store.*

All of these seem to mean something like "the particular one that I always use or go to." While the speaker does not expect the listener to know the particular one, it is reasonable to expect your audience to know that you have particular habits and places that you go. That is, if someone says "I'm going to the store," he/she means "I'm going to the store that I usually go to."

But remember we do not use articles with *home, school,* or *church* in sentences such as

We are going home.

We are going to school.

We are going to church.

4 Nouns in Sets

It is possible to use *the* or *a/an* at the beginning of a set of parallel nouns without repeating the article for every noun. The English speaker understands that you mean the same thing as if you had repeated the articles each time. For other information on parallel structure, see the Index.

The schedule tells us the building, date, and time for our classes.

5a Editing for Articles

Remember to use the following steps when you are editing for articles and determiners.

1. Check each noun in the passage. Is it singular, plural, noncount, proper?

2. If the noun is a proper noun, decide if it is one of the names that requires *the*. See Section 3 on p. 184 for information.

3. If the noun is a singular count noun, it *must* have an article or determiner.

   Decide on the proper meaning—definite, indefinite, or generic.

   Select *a/an, the,* or a determiner.

4. If the noun is plural or noncount, it *may* need an article or determiner.

   Decide on the meaning—definite, indefinite, or generic.

   Select the proper form—zero, *the, some,* or a determiner.

Definite = *the*

Indefinite = *a/an, some*

Generic = *the, a/an, some,* or zero form depending on type being used

For other meanings, use the determiners—*this/that, many, your,* and so forth.

5b A Chart to Use When Editing for Articles

Following the steps outlined above, use this chart to decide which article to use with each noun in your writing.

count singular	indefinite	*a/an*
	definite	*the*
	Generic-1	*a/an*
	Generic-2	*the*
count plural	indefinite	*some*
	definite	*the*
	Generic-3	(no article)
	Generic-4*	*the*
noncount	indefinite	*some*
	definite	*the*
	Generic-5	(no article)
proper		(no article)
		the

---

*Rarely used outside social sciences.

To practice using the chart and following the steps outlined on p. 188, do this exercise. Decide on the article needed for each noun in bold type. For example,

1. **boy** is a singular count noun so you look in the first section of the chart. Your choices are *a* for indefinite, *the* for definite, *a* for Generic-1, or *the* for Generic-2.

2. In this situation, *boy* is indefinite. This is a particular boy, but the writer must use indefinite for the first mention of the boy; the reader does not share the writer's information.

3. Therefore, your choice is *a*.

THOMAS EDISON

1. When he was 21, _____ small-town **boy** from

   _____ **Ohio** was issued _____

   patent for _____ electrical vote **recorder** that was

   intended for use by _____ **United States Congress.**

2. Within _____ next few **years**, he had improved

   _____ **telegraph.**

3. Then he set himself up in _____ **workshop** in

   _____ **Menlo Park, New Jersey,** to produce

   _____ useful and marketable new **ideas.**

4. In 1877, one year after _____ **invention** of

   _____ **telephone,** Thomas A. Edison was working

   in his workshop to develop _____ **machine** for rec-

   ording telephone messages.

5. _____ **machine** was _____ **pin**

   attached to _____ **diaphragm.**

6. _____ **pin** made _____ **marks**

   on waxed **paper.**

7. By substituting _____ grooved **cylinder** covered

with _____ tin **foil**, he discovered that

_____ **sound waves** could be recorded and played

back.

8. _____ **certitude** and _____

stubbornness helped Edison become _____

innovative **genius**. But, they did not always serve him well as

_____ **businessman**.

9. Edison holds _____ **record** for _____

number of patents issued to anyone in _____

United States.

Adapted from *Eureka!* (U.S. Small Business Administration, 1982)

6a Determiners

At the beginning of this chapter, a chart is given which lists examples of
the words called *determiners* (see p. 176). Words such as *this/that, much/
many, little/few,* and *his/her* are used to count, measure, and collect nouns
into sets. They are called *determiners* because they determine the meaning of nouns. Of these, the determiners that cause advanced students the
most difficulty are the group called *quantifiers*. (See the Index for information on other determiners.)

6b Words and Phrases Used for Counting

Quantifiers are the words that are used to specify the amount or quantity
of the noun. This group includes words like *much, many, little, few, a
lot of,* and many others.

The quantifiers with a positive meaning can be arranged in two groups.
The first group refers to larger amounts, and the second group is used for
more limited amounts.

Group 1	Group 2
a great deal of	some
much	a couple of
many	several
a great many	a few
a lot of	a little
lots of	
plenty of	
most	
all	

The negative quantifiers can also be divided into two groups. The first group is the most negative. The second group refers to smaller amounts but from a negative point of view.

Group 3	Group 4
none	few
no	little
not any	hardly any
not all	scarcely any
	not many
	not much
	not a lot of

Quantifiers can also be divided into groups according to the kinds of nouns they can be used with. Some can only go with noncount nouns; some can only be used with plural count nouns; and others can be used with either. (See Section 2 on p. 149 for information on noun types.)

Only with noncount nouns: *a little, little, much, a great deal of*

Only with plural count nouns: *a couple of, several, a few, few, many*

With noncount and plural: *some, a lot of, lots of, plenty of, most, all, not all, no, none, hardly any, scarcely any*

A question often asked by advanced students involves the differences among *much, many,* and *a lot of.* The situation is complex because not all educated writers of English agree about how to use the words. Generally, you can use the following information as a guide.

Much is used with noncount nouns in very formal writing in positive as well as negative sentences. However, many writers actually prefer to use the quantifier *a great deal of.*

We have much experience with economic development.

We have a great deal of experience with economic development.

We do not have much experience with banking.

Many is used with count nouns in formal writing in positive as well as negative sentences.

You will face many problems in this area.

You will not have many problems with calculus.

In informal usage, *a lot of* is the preferred use with positive statements while *much* and *many* are preferred in negative sentences.

I have a lot of time but not much money.

Experts disagree about the use of *a lot of* in formal writing. You should ask your instructor about his/her attitudes and follow those in your own writing. Many composition instructors think that *a lot of* is too informal for use in academic writing.

The use of *many* and *much* in spoken English involves other issues that we will not consider here—for example, they are not much used in short answers to questions.

6c EXERCISE: Quantifiers

Working with the other students in your class and your instructor, arrange the quantifiers on a scale with *none* on one end and *all* on the other.

7 EXERCISES: Articles and Determiners

A. To select the correct article, you must be able to recognize the various types of nouns—count (singular/plural), noncount, proper.

1. In the following passage, the nouns have been underlined in the first paragraph. Name each noun's category.

2. In the second paragraph, underline each noun; then decide on the category of each.

If you have trouble with this exercise, study the materials on nouns in Chapter 8 before continuing to study articles. Keep your analysis simple; do not try to decide on the definite/indefinite/generic meanings. Just decide if the noun is singular, plural, noncount, or proper.

THE ICE CREAM CONE

The <u>ice cream cone</u>! Simple in design, delicious to eat, it is perhaps the most ecologically-sound <u>packaging</u> devised by modern <u>man</u>. The <u>cone</u> is such a good <u>idea</u>, in fact, that several <u>people</u> have claimed to be the first to invent it. But many <u>historians</u> agree that the <u>ice cream</u> cone was born at the <u>St. Louis World's Fair</u> in 1905. It was there that <u>Ernest A. Hamwi,</u> a Syrian-born <u>salesman</u>, opened a <u>stand</u> to sell "<u>zalabia,</u>" a crisp, <u>wafer</u>like <u>pastry</u> baked on a flat waffle <u>iron</u> and served with <u>sugar</u>.

Close to Hamwi's stand stood a merchant, selling scoops of ice cream. One day, the ice cream seller ran out of dishes. The resourceful Hamwi took one of his thin zalabia, rolled it into a cone, and scooped in some ice cream. Thus, the birth of the ice cream cone! Everyone loved the idea. Before the fair was over, factories were turning out cones for ice cream. Hamwi himself began the Cornucopia Waffle Company in St. Louis. The cone survives today in its basic simplicity, consumed at the rate of three billion a year in the United States alone.

Adapted from *Eureka!* (U.S. Small Business Administration, 1982)

B. Take a paragraph that you have written. Underline all the nouns. Then analyze them as singular, plural, noncount, proper. How many of each type did you use? Compare your analysis to that of another student in the class.

C. In the passage about Elijah McCoy given on p. 14, use a highlighter to mark all the singular nouns. What determiner or article is used with each?

D. What does the word *definite* mean? If you are not sure, look it up. Also, read Section 2b on p. 179. English marks nouns as definite by using *the*. Determiners such as *this*, *that*, *my*, and *our* are also definite in their meaning. Why does the writer of each of these sentences use *the*? What makes the noun definite?

1. San Antonio is *the* 14th largest city in *the* United States.

2. Last night *the* clouds blocked *the* light from *the* moon.

3. *The* dean of our college supports international education.

4. I looked for a new apartment last weekend because I'm having trouble with my current apartment. *The* windows don't close. *The* heat doesn't work well. *The* refrigerator makes too much noise.

5. *The* last chapter of this book was very helpful for my report.

6. *The* teacher who taught me when I was 12 years old was a remarkable human being.

E. What does *indefinite* mean? English marks a noun as indefinite by using *a* (or *an* before a vowel) and *some*. The following sentences mix definite with indefinite meanings. Use *the* for the definite and *a/an* or *some* for the indefinite meanings.

1. San Antonio is _____ city in southern Texas.

2. San Antonio is _____ city where I was born.

3. The teacher said that he needs _____ chalk.

4. I went to the library to get _____ book on geography.

5. To complete the report, you will need _____ information on current educational policy.

6. I can't find _____ book you lent me for my report.

F. What does *generic* mean? You might have noticed the word being used at the supermarket for products that are not a particular brand. In grammar, we mean that we are talking about the noun as a representative of a whole class or group. Scientific and technical writing frequently uses the generic with *the* plus a singular count noun (Generic-2) to give generalizations and definitions: *The horse originated in Asia.* A plural noun without *the* (Generic-3) can be used for a less formal version of the same meaning: *Horses originated in Asia.* Working with another student, write two different generalizations for each of the words listed below, one in the formal scientific style and one in the less formal plural style. Use an English-English dictionary or an encyclopedia to gather accurate and interesting information before writing the generalizations.

computer   grapefruit

knee   moose

abacus

G. Generic-1 can be used for giving definitions: *A horse is "a large solid-hoofed herbivorous mammal domesticated as a draft and saddle animal"* (p. 341 of *The Merriam-Webster Dictionary*). This type of definition can be used only with count nouns because only singular count nouns can have *a* or *an*. How does the dictionary give definitions of noncount nouns? With your class, brainstorm a list of nouns that are usually noncount.

Then, select two of those to analyze by looking up their definitions in an English-English dictionary. Compare your analysis of the grammar used in the definition with that of the rest of your class.

H. Formal definitions generally have three parts: (1) the word or phrase that needs to be defined, (2) the words that tell the large general category that the term belongs to, and (3) the details that distinguish the things from all other members of the general category. The terms that are used for these parts are (1) item, (2) genus, and (3) differentia. Look at this definition from the *Merriam-Webster Dictionary*:

bayonet: a daggerlike weapon made to fit on the muzzle end of a rifle

The item is *bayonet*. The genus is *weapon*. Everything else is given to distinguish this type of weapon from other weapons. A definition describes how a thing or person looks, or smells, or functions. For example, in the definition of *bayonet* the dictionary tells how it looks—*daggerlike*—and how it functions—*to fit on the muzzle end of a rifle*.

Notice that *bayonet* is a count noun—it can be either singular or plural. The dictionary defines count nouns in the singular form and explains how the plural is spelled if it is irregular.

Brainstorm with the rest of the class a list of interesting and unusual count nouns. Select two to look up in an English-English dictionary. Analyze the definitions in terms of term, genus, differentia. What senses are appealed to in the definitions—sight, sound, smell, taste, touch?

I. In your English writing, you will at some point write about your own culture or country. Americans are frequently very interested to learn more about your background so you can expect to get their attention and to interest your readers by including information that is unfamiliar to Americans. However, you will immediately have the problem of defining words and phrases from your language. For example, an Iranian student wrote the following paragraph as part of a comparison of his country and the U.S. Without definitions for the names of the foods, the American reader has no idea what is meant.

> *Food in my country is generally more flavorful and spicy than that I have eaten in the U.S. For example, a favorite dish is* bagali polo. *This is a rice, lamb, and lima bean dish flavored with pepper, cinnamon, and dill. Another example is* tah chin, *a rice and lamb dish flavored with saffron in addition to pepper and cinnamon.*

Notice that each is defined as "a dish."

Writing about food is especially difficult because even the names of the ingredients can be unfamiliar to Americans—or you might not yet know the English for these things. Rather than writing about food, select another cultural area such as a famous holiday. Plan a paragraph in which you discuss some aspect of the topic and include two or three words or phrases from your language to define. Share the words and your definitions with the rest of the class.

J. Generalizations are not, of course, always definitions but are frequently general statements about a class of people or things: *A teacher must have a great deal of patience—so should a student.* You will hear this form used in discussions in the classroom. Provide a generalization (using Generic-1) that you think is true about each of the following. Be prepared to defend your statement.

university	teacher
politician	student
child	newspaper
parent	medical doctor

K. Generalizations with count nouns can take another form—*the* + plural. *The most common stereotype about the Germans is that they love classical music and war.* This style is found most often in research written in the social sciences. If you are majoring in sociology, psychology, education, or some other area in the social sciences, find a journal of importance in your field. Look at the conclusions of several research reports to see what types of generalizations are preferred. Share some of these generalizations with other social scientists in your class.

L. Generic statements can also be made using noncount nouns without any article or determiner: *Sugar is bad for your teeth. Sugar is an agricultural product.* Indefinite statements with noncount nouns use *some—I need some sugar.* Definite statements use *the—Please, pass the sugar.* Decide whether each statement given below is generic, indefinite, or definite. Then, use no article, *some*, or *the* in the blank space. Different interpretations of meaning will lead to different selections.

1. I needed _____ furniture for my apartment.

2. At the store, I realized that _____ furniture is more expensive than I had thought.

3. Why, I thought, is having _____ furniture so important?

4. So, I borrowed _____ old furniture from a friend.

5. _____ furniture in my apartment is very old but very cheap.

M. Generalizations can be made in many forms. Write a generic statement about each of these nouns. Do not change the form of the noun from singular or plural.

a microscope	education
a professor	money
airports	the television
computers	the manager

N. Look at the generic statements you wrote in exercise M. What are the differences in grammar? When would you expect each style to be used?

O. Using your knowledge of noun classes and of the differences among *definite/indefinite/generic,* classify the nouns in exercise A on p. 193. For example,

1. *ice cream*—it is noncount and is used as an adjective

2. *cone*—it is singular, count, and generic (like Generic-2)

3. *packaging*—noncount and definite (superlative use of *the*)

P. Go back to your own paragraph that you analyzed in exercise B on p. 194. Check each noun to see if it should or should not have an article.

Q. Select another short passage of your own writing; find all of the nouns and mark them with a highlighter. Edit the passage for articles using the steps listed in Section 5 on p. 188. Talk with your instructor about any changes that you think should be made.

R. Look again at the passage about Elijah McCoy (p. 14). Although many of the nouns in the passage are preceded by *the, a,* or *an,* many other nouns have other determining words. In exercise C, you marked all the singular nouns. Now, mark all the rest of the nouns in the passage. Then, check to see what determiners and articles are used. List the determiners (other than the articles) that you find in the passage.

S. How many of the nouns in the passage on Elijah McCoy do not have any article or determiner? What meanings do they have? What kinds of nouns can occur without an article or without a determiner?

T. Unfortunately, at some point you will probably need to visit a doctor. Before you actually talk with him or her about your problems, you will be asked to fill out a complete medical history that lists all of the diseases and illnesses that you have ever had. Translating the names of childhood diseases while you are sick is not an easy task. Take time now to practice with the names of common diseases by filling out this medical history form.

Notice that Section I has only childhood diseases and Latinate named diseases—none of the everyday *achy* names. Can *the* be used with any of the names in Section I?

```
Medical History Form

Name:_____         Date:_____

I. Check past illnesses:

☐ chickenpox          ☐ pneumonia          ☐ mononucleosis
☐ measles             ☐ bronchitis         ☐ meningitis
☐ German measles      ☐ pleurisy           ☐ heart attack
☐ mumps               ☐ tuberculosis       ☐ kidney trouble
☐ scarlet fever       ☐ malaria            ☐ stroke
☐ rheumatic fever     ☐ ulcer              ☐ phlebitis
☐ hay fever           ☐ hepatitis          ☐ high blood pressure
☐ asthma              ☐ cancer

II. Check if anyone in your family has ever had the following:

  Disease            Relationship      Disease            Relationship
☐ diabetes          _____      ☐ hay fever/asthma  _____
☐ heart disease     _____      ☐ ulcers            _____
☐ stroke            _____      ☐ cancer            _____
☐ high blood pressure _____    ☐ anemia            _____
☐ migraine headaches _____     ☐ epilepsy          _____
```

U. Your instructor will bring a selection of popular magazines to class. Find all of the advertisements for medicines. What are the diseases or symptoms that the medicines are supposed to help? What articles are used with those names? Write the list here to use for reference. What kinds of illnesses seem common in the U.S.?

_____

_____

_____

V. Look for generalizations and definitions in a textbook in your major field. What styles do you find? Share your list with other students from the same field of study. Also, show the rest of the class what you have found about academic writing in your profession.

W. Many students have difficulties using Generic-5. This is the type of generic that uses noncount nouns. For example,

Water is necessary for human life.

Both *water* and *life* are noncount nouns. A common error is to use *the* for this meaning, as in

▼ *The water is necessary for the human life.*

Write a passage in which you discuss the things that are necessary for human life. After revising it, edit it for articles.

X. Read again an essay that you wrote earlier in the term. Do you have trouble using Generic-5? If so, add it to your editing list.

Y. In a chapter of a textbook in a scientific or technical field, look for examples of noncount generics (Generic-5). Share those examples with the rest of the class.

CHAPTER 10

Pronouns

1 Introduction to Pronouns

Pronouns are, of course, words like *I, you, her; who, whom; this, that,* and *there.* This chapter first reviews the personal pronouns such as *I, me, my, mine* and then discusses various problems with pronouns.

Advanced students should already know the forms of the personal pronouns such as *I, you, he, she,* and so forth. Fill in these charts to check for any problems you might have.

Subject Form	Object Form	Possessive Forms
I	me	my, mine
you	_____	_____
it	_____	_____
_____	_____	her
_____	him	_____
we	_____	_____
they	_____	_____

The reflexive forms are used in sentences such as

He opened the door himself.

Fill in the reflexive forms that correspond to each of these personal pronouns:

Subject	Reflexive
I	_____
you	_____
he	_____
she	_____
it	_____
we	_____
they	_____

2 Problems with Pronoun Reference

One of the most serious pronoun problems for advanced users of English is *pronoun reference*. This means getting the right pronoun to refer back to the right noun. In general, the pronoun reference problems include the following:

1. Matching correct sex to correct noun—*she/her* for females, *he/him* for males, and *it* for things not considered as either male or female

   She *brought* her *research report to* her *professor.*

   My brother *put* his *research report in* his *briefcase.*

   The research report *is excellent;* it *provides new information about the pollution of water by industry.*

2. Matching correct singular or plural forms

   The scientists *made* their *reports at a meeting in March.*

   The researcher *made* her *report at the same meeting.*

3. Selecting correct forms for irregular or confusing forms, especially when the choice is between a singular and a plural form

Either this report or those books *are wrong in* their *conclusions.*

Either those books or this report *is wrong in* its *conclusion.*

He broke his *arm. She raised* her *arm to ask a question.* (English uses personal pronouns for reference to body parts in nontechnical usage. See Section 6 on p. 165 for more information on the possessive forms.)

Handling types 1 and 2 correctly is relatively easy except when the pronoun is a long way away from its noun. Type 3 is more difficult because of complexities both of subject-verb agreement and of pronoun choice. (See Section 15 on p. 88 for more information on subject-verb agreement.)

3a *Who* vs. *Whom*

Whom is the object form of the pronoun *who.* Both words can be used in information questions and in relative clauses.

Who will teach calculus next term?

To whom did you give the information?

The instructor who will teach calculus next quarter is one of my favorite teachers.

The instructor to whom you give the information will teach calculus next quarter.

In speaking, it is the usual style to use *who* for both subject and object.

subject
Who teaches calculus?

DO   subject
Who did you talk to about your problem?

The usual spoken version of a question would leave the preposition at the end; a more formal spoken version moves the preposition to the beginning and uses *whom:*

Who did the student discuss this problem with? (spoken)

With whom did the student discuss this problem? (written)

3b Using *Whom*

In formal written English, most writers will use *whom* when the word has an objective function (object of a preposition or object of a verb). They will also usually move prepositions to the front of the question along with the pronoun.

With whom did the student discuss this problem?

We wanted to know with whom the student discussed this problem.

3c A Danger with *Whom*

Be careful in using *whom* in sentences such as this:

I want to know. . . .

The student asked. . . .

Many times the next word is the subject of a subordinate or embedded clause rather than the object of the verb.

                 subject of embedded question
I wanted to know who will teach the class.

                 subject of embedded question
The president asked who should be on the committee.

         DO   subject
The president asked whom he should appoint to the committee.

    Writers sometimes make the error of using *whom* to create sentences such as:

▼ *The president asked whom should be on the committee.* (Who must be used because the word is the subject rather than the object of the embedded question.)

4a Nonreferential *There* vs. *It* in the Subject Position

Many students have trouble with sentences like these:

There are five computers in the department.

It is very cold in the computer lab.

In these sentences, *there* and *it* function in the subject position, but they do not have meaning. They are used to be sure the sentence has a word in the subject position—remember, English sentences must have subjects.

While *it* and *there* do not have meaning in these sentences, they do have grammatical work. Most importantly, they provide the sentence with a subject. In addition, in forming tag questions, they function as the subject.

There are five computers in the department, aren't there?

It is very cold in the computer lab, isn't it?

Also, in yes-no questions, they function as the subject:

Are there five computers in the department?

Is it very cold in the computer lab?

On the other hand, *there* does not control subject-verb agreement; the noun phrase in the direct object position controls the form of the verb:

There is one computer in the office.

There are five computers in the lab.

Many advanced students have two problems with this topic. First, they sometimes confuse *there* and *it*. Second, they sometimes make subject-verb agreement errors with *there*.

▼ *It is five computers in the department.*

▼ *There is very cold in the computer lab.*

▼ *There is five computers in the department.*

4b Nonreferential *It* for Weather, Time, Distance, and Other Environmental Meanings

First, compare the use of *it* in these two little conversations:

Mary: Where's the library?

John: **It's** across the street from the classroom building.

Mary: You look really unhappy. What's wrong?

John: I'm freezing. **It's** too cold in here.

In the first example, *it* is a personal pronoun that refers back to the noun phrase *the library*. However, in the second example, *it* does not refer back to anything; *it* is the nonreferential subject in a sentence about weather.

It is used in a variety of ways to communicate about the environment.

1. *It* for precipitation (for forms of falling water) with various verb forms.

   It is raining.

   It snowed yesterday.

   It was hailing.

   It has rained for two hours straight.

2. *It* for other weather conditions—using *be* + adjective or a verb such as *feel* or *seem.*

   It is foggy.

   It has been snowy.

   It may be cloudy.

   It feels hot in here.

   It seems rainy/chilly/cold/warm/hot now.

3. *It* for the temperature—using *be* + temperature. Notice that verbs such as *seem* and *feel* can be used. (Remember that in everyday use, Americans probably will refer to the temperature in Fahrenheit. But, in scientific and technical contexts, the centigrade scale will be used.)

   Fahrenheit examples—from everyday, nontechnical use:

   It is 32 outside right now.

   It has been almost 100 all afternoon.

   It feels about 70, but I'm not really sure of the temperature.

   Centigrade examples—from technical contexts:

   Water boils at 100 C.

   Water has the unusual characteristic of having greater density at 3.98 C than at any higher or lower temperature.

4. *It* to communicate about time. Notice that *be* is the most commonly used verb, but others are possible.

   What time is it? It is 10 o'clock.

   It was 8 a.m. when the bomb exploded.

   It seems like it ought to be later than it is.

5. *It* for distance. Notice that *be* is the most commonly used verb, but others such as *seems like* are possible.

   It is five miles from my house to the grocery store.

   It is a long way from his home to the university.

   It feels like a longer walk than it really is.

6. Other, related uses of *it* to talk about the environment.

   It is crowded in the library on Sunday afternoons.

   It is noisy in the cafeteria.

   It is quiet in the library, especially on Friday afternoons.

   It seems too quiet in here.

4c Nonreferential *It* in Complex Sentences

In academic writing, you will find other, more complicated uses of *it*.

1. *It* followed by an adjective plus an embedded sentence. *It is important that* + *sentence*. (Other words that can be substituted for *important* include *vital, imperative, essential*, and so on. Notice that the subjunctive is used in the embedded sentence. See Chapter 4 for more information on the subjunctive.)

   It is important that the process be followed exactly.

   It is imperative that the government live up to its obligations.

2. *It* followed by a verb plus an embedded sentence.

   It is surprising that our results are so inconclusive.

   It confused me that I could not find any information on my topic in the library.

3. *It* followed by a noun phrase plus an embedded sentence.

   It is a fact that the university does not have adequate computer labs.

   It is a problem that our results do not agree with previous observations.

   It is not much of a problem that we can use the computer lab only at night.

   It is a mistake to think that this process is not important.

4. *It* followed by an adjective plus an infinitive. *It is important to* + *verb* + *sentence*.

   It is important to note that the correct process was followed.

   It is useful to divide market forces into supply and demand.

5. *It* followed by a passive verb plus an embedded sentence.

It was announced that the library would be closed for the holidays.

It was reported that the university would receive new scholarship funds.

It is suspected that the politician will run for president.

4d Nonreferential Uses of *There*

Remember, *there* in this use has none of the place meaning of *there* used as an adverb:

place
He saw her standing there in the corner of the room.

subject
There were three students in the lab when the instructor arrived.

The usual verb is the simple present or simple past of *be*, although others are possible.

There exist numerous explanations for this phenomena.

The major purpose of *there* sentences is to introduce new material. They tell the reader that you are presenting new material for consideration, and they imply that you will discuss each of the topics raised. For example, you will frequently see them used for thesis statements such as:

There are three major subdivisions of . . . that need to be considered here. (Discussion of all three should follow.)

There were five important military leaders involved in making these decisions. The role of each will be discussed in the following five chapters of this book. (The reader knows that the next five chapters will discuss the military leaders in order.)

Composition teachers often advise (and even require) that nonreferential *there* be avoided. The reason is that the word is empty of meaning and is wasting space. They would recommend changing the sentences above to the following:

Three major subdivisions of . . . need to be considered here.

Five important military leaders were involved in making these decisions.

5 EXERCISES: Pronouns

A. Look back over several things that you have written recently. List here any problems that you had with pronouns.

—What pronouns did you misspell?

—Did you ever choose the wrong sex form (*he* rather than *she*, for example)? If so, why do you think you made the mistake?

—Did you choose the wrong singular or plural? Why did you make the mistake?

—Did you choose the wrong form—subject rather than object? Why did you make that particular wrong choice?

B. If you think it would help you, write the correct forms of the sentences from exercise A. For some students, rewriting sentences is a way of learning to use the correct grammar. For other students, this is not an effective method because they do not learn well from work that is not in the context of the whole paper.

C. All of the personal pronouns have been left out of the following passage. Fill in the blanks.

"What dressing will you have on your salad?" the waiter said.

"R-r-r-r-r-ro-ro-roque-roque, I'll have the roque—I think I'd like to try the ro-ro-ro—Thousand Island."

Stutterers laugh at that joke, too. For _____, however, stuttering has far more serious consequences than not getting

_____ favorite salad dressing. The frustration and struggle to get the words out can embarrass and exhaust both speaker and listener. Some stutterers avoid the struggle by dodging situations where

_____ have to speak. Children may say "Don't know," to the teacher—even when _____ do know—rather than face laughter and teasing from their classmates. Other stutterers keep _____ minds a phrase or two ahead of

_____ mouths. That way _____ can pick out problem words and find substitutes. In either case the stutterer suffers the loss of smooth and easy speech, the spontaneous exchange of feelings and ideas so important at school or work, among family and friends.

"_____ is like a sharp mmmmmomentary twist of pain that I eexxsss—perience again and again throughout eeeevery dddday ah ah of _____ life. _____ ss-sss-sometimes ssssssee _____ as a as a nnnnnnnnail in _____ shoe that iiiis thththere and p-p-pro-bab-bly always www-ww-wi-ll be there . . ." says a 36-year-old woman.

Yet there is reason to hope that that woman, and others, particularly young stutterers, will be able to escape the twist of pain. With therapy—and sometimes without _____—many stutterers achieve more normal speech. Studies describing the differences in the way normal and stuttered speech are produced are pointing to new directions in therapy.

Adapted from *Stuttering: Hope Through Research* (U.S. Department of Health and Human Services, 1981)

D. Select a passage from today's newspaper. Use white-out to mark out all of the pronouns. (Be sure to write out a list of them first to aid your memory.) Exchange passages with another student in your class. After you have filled in the blanks with your choice of pronouns, talk with the other student to see if you got the right answers. Show him/her the correct answers for your passage, too.

E. Decide if the use of *whom* is correct or incorrect in each of these sentences.

1. The report showed whom was responsible for the accident.

2. The audit recommended those whom the president should hold responsible for the accident.

3. The president will meet only with those whom have been recommended by the vice president.

4. The president will meet only with those whom are innocent.

5. The president will meet only with those whom the vice president recommended.

6. The letter began with the phrase "To Whom It May Concern."

7. The dean asked, "Whom is the university going to give the reward to?"

8. The university is going to give the reward to whomever meets its standards.

9. The university is going to give the reward to whomever the president recommends.

F. Work with another student to complete the sentences given below. Write one version using *who* and another using *whom* for each sentence. Share your four sentences with the rest of the class to edit together.

1. I want the President of the U.S. to know _____.

2. I want the President of the U.S. to know _____.

3. I understand _____.

4. I understand _____.

G. In the following sentence, the writer has used *whom*. Did he make the correct choice? Explain your answer.

Students at the university have developed a list of professors whom, they think, are difficult to understand because of their foreign accents.

H. This passage from a university textbook on economics is part of a larger discussion of supply and demand. The passage illustrates well the uses of nonreferential *there* and *it* in academic writing. First, read the complete passage to understand its meaning and purpose. Then, find the *there* sentences. What purpose do they serve? What organization does the second one promise? Is that organization followed? After looking at the *there* sentences, find the examples of nonreferential *it*. How are those sentences used?

SHIFT VARIABLES

Economists use the term *shift variables* to refer to variables that cause a curve to be relocated—to "shift"—on a graph. Clearly, there can be a great many shift variables for any function or curve, since there is no limit to the number of variables that are covered by the *ceteris paribus**

---

* Ceteris paribus is a technical term for an assumption used when economists want to compare two variables at a particular time without having to worry about any other variables. The Latin words mean "other things being equal."

assumption. There are three especially important shift variables for an individual's demand curve.*

An increase in a consumer's *taste* for a good or service will cause the demand curve to shift to the right,† and a decrease in taste will bring about a shift to the left, other things being equal. If Alex, who has been wearing dress pants to work, suddenly decides that jeans are more comfortable and just as appropriate, his demand curve for jeans will shift to the right. On the other hand, if Alex has been wearing jeans to work and his boss "suggests" that dress pants are more correct, his demand curve for jeans will probably shift to the left.

An increase in a consumer's *income* will usually cause his or her demand curve to shift to the right, and a decrease in income usually brings about a shift to the left. Alex can afford to buy more jeans when his income is higher and fewer when it is lower. Only in rare cases will higher income cause people to demand less and lower income cause them to demand more. It is possible, however, that at very much higher income levels some people will demand fewer hamburgers since they will have switched to steak.

Shifts in demand for a good also result from *price changes of other goods,* especially closely related goods. Such "other" goods may be grouped into two categories: substitutes and complements.

Substitutes are goods that may be used instead of one another. Examples of good substitutes are beer and ale, Coca-Cola and Pepsi-Cola, and vinyl kitchen flooring and kitchen carpeting. An increase in the price of a substitute will cause the demand curve for the other good to shift to the right, and a decrease in the price of a subsitute brings about a shift to the left. If Alex finds that jeans and cords are fairly good substitutes, and if cords go up in price, he will buy more jeans and fewer cords. In this case, Alex's *quantity demanded* for cords goes down and his *demand* for jeans goes up. Similarly, a decrease in the price of cords will cause Alex to

---

*In economics, *demand* is a technical term used to talk about the ability and willingness of consumers to make purchases. That is, it does not have quite the same meaning as the everyday use of the word.

†A "shift to the right" means a greater demand; for example, if the price of jeans goes down, consumers will buy more pairs. A "shift to the left" means a decrease in demand; for example, if the price of jeans increases, consumers will buy fewer pairs. These terms are used because economists use graphs of supply and demand to develop curves that illustrate supply and demand at various prices.

demand fewer jeans and more cords. This time Alex's *quantity demanded* for cords goes up and his *demand* for jeans goes down.

Complements are goods that are used with each other. Examples are automobiles and gasoline, ski boots and ski poles, and kites and string. Alex will demand fewer jeans if the type of belt that he wears with jeans, but not with other pants, goes up in price. That is, if the package, made up of a pair of jeans and one of these belts, has gone up in price, he will demand fewer jeans. Also, if the price of these belts decreases, Alex may demand more jeans.

When goods have several uses, they may be complementary in some cases and substitutable in others. It is then a complicated problem in economic statistics (econometrics) to discover which relation dominates at any particular time or place. And, of course, the answer may vary from time to time or from place to place. At a time or place where soft drinks like Coca-Cola or Pepsi-Cola are never used as mixers for alcoholic drinks, soft drinks will be substitutes for alcoholic ones. At a time or place where soft drinks are used almost entirely as mixers and almost never consumed by themselves, the dominant relation will be complementary.

This discussion of complementary and substitute goods has been limited to the demand side of the market. As you will see, there are similar relationships on the supply side, and it will be useful to distinguish between the effects of complementarity and substitutability in supply.

Adapted from *Economics* (Bronfenbrenner, Sichel, and Gardner, 1987)

I. In a textbook from your major field of study, find five examples of nonreferential *it*. Bring those examples to share with the class so that you can better understand when academic writers use this type of sentence. Do any of the examples refer to weather, temperature, time, distance, or other environmental factors? What other uses do you find?

J. In a textbook from your major field of study, find five examples of nonreferential *there*. Bring those examples to share with the class so that you can better understand when academic writers use this type of sentence. Do any of the sentences function as thesis statements, topic sentences, or paragraph hooks?

CHAPTER 11

Gerunds, Infinitives, and Participles

1a Introduction to Gerunds, Infinitives, and Participles

A *verb* is, of course, a word that can function as the verb of a sentence. For instance, *go* is a verb that can be used in sentences such as

We go to the library every weekend.

We will go to the library every weekend.

We have gone to the library every weekend.

The problem is finding a way to use verbs for other grammatical functions. How can *go* be used when you want that word and its meaning in the subject or object position?

English solves this problem by changing the form of the verb. *To* is added to make the *infinitive*, or *-ing* is added to make the *gerund*.

Going to the library takes a lot of time.

I like to go to the library to study.

A similar problem arises when a verb and its meaning are needed for use as adjectives or adverbs. In this case, English uses the participle forms. In the first example, a present participle is used as an adverbial. In the second example, a past participle is used as an adjective.

Opening *the door, the instructor entered the room.*

I returned the damaged *package to the Post Office.*

Because infinitives, gerunds, and participles involve verb forms, they are sometimes referred to as *verbals.*

Advanced students have a minor problem and a major problem because of this system. The minor problem has to do with the formation and spelling of the gerund and the two kinds of participles. The major problem is knowing which to use when.

The spelling rules for the formation of the gerund and participles are exactly the same as for the formation of the other *-ing* or past participle forms. (See Section 14a on p. 85 for information on the spelling of verb forms.)

1b Functions of Infinitives

Infinitives can be used as (1) subject, (2) direct object, (3) complement, (4) appositive, (5) adjective modifier, and (6) adverbial.

1. *To prepare carefully for class is a student's responsibility.*

2. *He needs to go to the library after class.*

3. *The answer is to talk with your instructor about an extension of the deadline.*

4. *His answer, to talk with the instructor about an extension, is really not very reasonable.*

5. *She is eager to make a good grade.*

6. *He came to the United States to get a Ph.D. in physics.*

1c Functions of Gerunds

A gerund is an *-ing* form of the verb that is used in the same function as a noun. Gerunds can be used as (1) subject, (2) direct object, (3) object of a preposition, (4) complement, and (5) appositive.

1. *Studying in the library takes discipline.*

2. *He avoids studying in the library.*

3. *The instructor warned us against turning the papers in late.*
   I am looking forward to studying in the library.

4. *The first stage in the project should be reading the relevant research reports.*

5. *The first stage, reading the research reports, will take about one week.*

Gerunds have two possible meanings. They can refer to activities or actions with a meaning much like the progressive form of the verb. Or they can refer to things, facts, or types of activities. For example, *swimming* can be the name of a sport much as *baseball, soccer,* and *tennis* are names of sports. *Swimming* can also be used to talk about the action or doing the activity itself.

1. *Studying in the library is part of the life of most students.*

2. *John's studying in the library last night meant that he could not attend the party.*

In these examples, (1) is about a type of activity (the way *swimming* can name a sport) while (2) is about John doing something.

1d Infinitive vs. Gerund as the Object of Verbs

You are probably aware that (1) some verbs take gerunds as their objects, (2) some verbs take infinitives, (3) some verbs can take either but with a change of meaning, and (4) some verbs can take either with the same meaning.

1. *He wants to take Business Calculus next term.*

2. *She enjoys studying in the library.*

3. *He stopped to buy a newspaper* is different from *He stopped buying the newspaper.*

4. *I like to go to the library. = I like going to the library.*

In Appendixes C, D, E, and F of Ready Reference, you will find an alphabetized list of the most commonly used verbs divided into these four categories. Learning the verbs in those lists is a challenging task. In the discussion below, we suggest a method that should be more helpful than just memorizing lists of words.

Grammarians have found a meaning difference that explains the choice of gerund or infinitive as direct object for many verbs. For these verbs, the infinitive expresses something that is potential, not yet true, future, hypothetical. The gerund expresses something that is real, true, fulfilled, experienced. For example, when you *hope*, the thing you hope for is not true yet, so the infinitive is used.

He hopes to make an "A" in Business Calculus.

But, when you *enjoy*, the thing you enjoy is something that you know or have already experienced, so

She enjoys studying in the library because it is quiet.

This explanation also helps us understand the difference in meaning between these two sentences:

He remembered reading the book. (The reading came first, was already experienced.)

He remembered to read the book. (The reading came after the remembering; it was not fulfilled at the moment he remembered to do it.)

The problem is that grammarians have not yet found a rule to explain all of the choices of infinitive or gerund. For example, these verbs can take either the gerund or the infinitive as direct object with no change in meaning: *begin, start, continue, like, prefer, hate, can't stand, intend, try.* Usually, the gerund implies some of the same meaning as the progressive form of the verb—that the action is in progress, ongoing.

He likes studying in the library.

He likes to study in the library.

In addition, there are some choices that are best explained as idiomatic—all the uses of gerunds for sporting activities for example: I go swimming every weekend. (See Section 7 on p. 225 for more information.)

However, the rule works for enough verbs to make it worth learning. For most students, it is easier to learn this rule than to memorize hundreds of verbs in the lists in Ready Reference.

1e EXERCISES: Infinitives and Gerunds

A. In Section 1d on p. 216, a rule was given to explain the meaning difference between infinitives and gerunds. Use that rule to analyze the difference in meaning between these two sentences:

1. *He stopped smoking after he read the article on lung cancer.*

2. *He stopped to smoke a cigarette before he went to class.*

B. Use the rule given in Section 1d to write sentences using these verbs that can take either the infinitive or the gerund with a difference in meaning. Then, share the sentences with the class to practice recognition of the difference in meaning. Here are the verbs to use: *stop, remember, forget, regret, prefer, try.*

C. These sentences use verbs that can have only the infinitive or only the gerund. Does the meaning rule help to explain why?

1. *We finished studying by 10:00 p.m.*

2. *Actually, we stopped reading at 9:45 so we could check out some books.*

3. *My brain had quit working at 9:30 anyway.*

4. *I had hoped to leave the library by 9:00 p.m.*

5. *But, I also wanted to finish the project before I went home.*

D. Your instructor will provide an article from a popular magazine. Use a highlighter to mark the infinitives and gerunds. Can the meaning rule explain all of them? Most of them? Any of them?

E. What functions do the infinitives and gerunds have in the article analyzed in exercise D?

2a Gerunds with Prepositions; *To* as a Preposition

A very common use of the gerund is as object of a preposition. Infinitives cannot ever have this function.

Lack of funding discourages many cities from developing more recreational facilities.

A fact of English can confuse some advanced students: *to* can be a preposition as well as a part of the infinitive. There are some two- and three-word verbs that have the preposition *to* and must be followed by a gerund.

I am looking forward to studying calculus.

He is used to studying in the library.

Students generally object to having increases in tuition.

They are accustomed to taking multiple-choice examinations.

2b EXERCISES: Gerunds with Prepositions

A. To practice using the gerund after the preposition *to*, interview a friend or another student. Find out about things he/she is used to doing, looks forward to doing, objects to doing, and is accustomed to doing. Write a 10–15 sentence description using the information. Use these verb + preposition + gerund forms as part of the description. Carefully edit the revised description. Share the completed version of the description with the whole class.

B. Look at the front page of a recent newspaper—today's if possible. Find any sentences with preposition + gerund. Share your list with the rest of the class. If you find any that are not listed in Section 2a on p. 218, keep a record of them here.

_____

_____

_____

3a Gerunds and Infinitives as Subjects of Sentences

subject
To deal with stress is a requirement of modern urban life.

subject
Dealing with stress is a requirement of modern urban life.

Both infinitives and gerunds can be used as subjects. However, the infinitive is much rarer in this function than the gerund. Each type is discussed in detail in the following sections.

3b Infinitives as Subjects of Sentences

English grammar allows infinitives to function as the subject of sentences.

To write well is a significant part of being educated.

Notice that two infinitives balance each other in the following type of sentence.

To study is not always to learn.
To seek is to find.

To love is not always to be loved.

To study should be to learn.

However, this use is not as common as another type of sentence that uses *it* as the subject and moves the infinitive after the verb.

To study in the library is necessary for many students.

It is necessary for many students to study in the library.

3c EXERCISE: Infinitives as Subjects

Work with another student to complete these sentences. Compare your ideas to those of other students in the class. Then, revise the sentences to make their meaning clearer. Finally, edit the sentences for correct use of the infinitive.

1. To work _____

2. To know _____

3. To feel _____

4. To think _____

5. To love _____

6. To have children _____

3d Gerunds as Subjects of Sentences

Gerunds are more likely to be found as subjects of sentences than infinitives are.

Maintaining a clean water supply is vital to the health of our citizens.

3e EXERCISE: Gerunds as Subjects

Find the gerunds in this passage. What grammatical functions do they have?

STOPPING SMOKING

It is not easy to stop smoking, but the moment you quit, your body begins to make repairs. If you make the choice to quit, you will not only feel better, but you will also improve your health. Excess risk for heart disease will be minimized in just two years.

Quitting will bring on physical and psychological withdrawal symptoms. Neither set of symptoms is pleasant. The physical symptoms will probably dissipate first, but all the negative points will fade away with time.

There are three proven approaches to stopping. They are listed from the most successful to least successful:

1. Cold Turkey
2. Tapering
3. Postponing

Going cold turkey means stopping abruptly. In this way, you do not prolong the withdrawal time. Tapering means predetermining a lesser number of cigarettes each day and smoking no more than that number. Postponing means each day you postpone the initial cigarette by a certain number of hours.

Whichever method you choose, remember—no one has ever died as a result of stopping smoking, only as a result of continuing to smoke.

Adapted from the *Drug Enforcement Administration: Physical Fitness Handbook* (U.S. Drug Enforcement Administration, undated)

---

4 Infinitives with *Too* and *Enough*

The infinitive is used in sentences such as

1. *The student has enough information to write a 20-page report.*

2. *He has been in class long enough to evaluate the instructor.*

3. *This test is too difficult to complete in one hour.*

Enough can be used with nouns or with adjectives. The pattern in sentence 1 is

enough + noun + infinitive.

The infinitive is really a modifier that tells the purpose or result of having *enough* of something.

In sentence 2, the pattern with *enough* is

adjective + *enough* + infinitive.

Sentence 3 shows the pattern with *too* as

too + adjective + infinitive.

5 Infinitives as Adverbs

Infinitives are frequently used to answer the question *Why?* or *For what purpose?* in sentences such as

The instructor gave the assignment to test the students' diligence.

The test machine can be accelerated and stopped suddenly to simulate the forces that occur in real collisions.

Some advanced students can have trouble with this particular use of the infinitive. The common mistake is to use the gerund here when the infinitive is required. For example, what is the answer to this question: *Why did you come to the U.S.?* A common mistake is to answer ▼*I came for studying English.* The answer should be *I came to study English.*

6a Nouns and Pronouns as Subjects of Infinitives and Gerunds

Infinitives and gerunds can, like verbs, have objects. *Mathematics* is the direct object of *to study* in this sentence: *I like to study mathematics.* The complete infinitive is *to study mathematics.* An example with a gerund is *Studying mathematics is a matter of discipline.*

Infinitives and gerunds can also have subjects. But, the grammar of these subjects is different from the grammar of the main subject of a sentence. The next two sections discuss and illustrate the subjects with infinitives and with gerunds.

6b Subjects of Infinitives

In these sentences, the infinitives have subjects:

1. *He wanted Mary to go to the library.*

2. *He wanted his friend to go to the library.*

Compare their meanings to

3. *He wanted to go to the library.*

In the first sentence, the person wanted Mary to go to the library, and in the second sentence, he wanted his friend to go. In the third sentence, he wanted to go himself.

Notice the form of the subject of the infinitive. If it is a noun, the form is the same as for the main subject of a sentence. But, if the infinitive's subject is a pronoun, the form is the objective. If the infinitive is itself the main subject of a sentence, *for* + pronoun is added to give the subject of the infinitive.

He told me to answer the question.

She asked them to go to the library.

For us to go to the library today is impossible.

Verb Type 1a   Some verbs can have only the infinitive without a noun or pronoun as subject. These include *hope, decide, agree, offer, refuse, remember, seem, appear.*

He hopes to finish the paper on Saturday afternoon.

Verb Type 1b   However, for some of these *for* + pronoun can be used.

He hopes for us to take business calculus together next term.

Hope, decide, agree, offer, refuse, remember can add *for* + pronoun.

Verb Type 2   Some verbs require a noun or pronoun along with the infinitive in the direct object. These verbs include *tell, remind, advise, encourage, permit, allow, require, force, order.*

He told the student to turn the paper in on time.

He told her to turn the paper in on time.

Verb Type 3   The third group of verbs can have either a plain infinitive or an infinitive with a subject: *ask, want, expect, need.*

The instructor asked to teach business calculus.

The instructor asked the student to answer the question.

6c EXERCISE: Subjects of Infinitives

Study these examples carefully. How many people are involved in each sentence?

1. *He hoped to make an "A."*

2. *She told the students to bring their textbooks to the test.*

3. *She told Mary to make an appointment to talk about the project.*

In sentence 1 the "A" will perhaps be made by the subject of the sentence, but in sentence 2 the students bring their textbooks, or in sentence 3 Mary makes an appointment.

Who finishes the project quickly in sentences 4, 5, and 6?

4. *He wanted to finish the project quickly.*

5. *He wanted us to finish the project quickly.*

6. *He wanted John to finish the project quickly.*

6d Possessive Nouns and Pronouns with the Gerund

In formal English, a subject can be added to many gerunds by using a possessive noun or possessive personal pronoun:

Mary's finishing the test early put a lot of pressure on the other students. (gerund is subject of sentence)

I admire his going to the library on Saturday nights even though I cannot imagine my doing it. (both gerunds are direct objects)

We are looking forward to the president's speaking to the student body at graduation. (gerund is object of preposition)

In informal spoken English, the objective form is frequently substituted: "My father will be in town next week. I am really excited about him coming to visit."

6e EXERCISE: Subjects for the Gerund

For practice at supplying a subject for the gerund, fill in these blanks with the correct form. To make the gerund, take the verb of the second sentence. Then, use the rest of the sentence to form the rest of the gerund phrase. The first one is done as an example.

1. We are looking forward to . . .
   The inventor will lecture on his discovery methods.

   We are looking forward to the inventor's lecturing on his discovery methods.

2. We are accustomed to . . .
   The instructor brings interesting guest speakers to class.

   _____

   _____

3. No one objects to . . .
   We give class time for these lectures.

   _____

   _____

4. We appreciate . . .
   He shares his professional contacts with us.

   _____

   _____

7 Gerunds for Recreational and Sporting Activities

The gerund is used with *go* for these phrases, which might be more common in speaking and informal writing than in formal written English. *Go* can, of course, be in any appropriate form:

He goes shopping every Saturday.

They went mountain climbing.

She has gone swimming.

We will go jogging.

John is going fishing.

Other phrases include: *go hunting, go bowling, go skiing, go dancing, go hiking,* and more.

8a Participles

The term *participle* is used to name two different verb forms: the *present participle* and the *past participle*. The present participle is the *-ing* form used to make the present and past progressive verbs:

He is studying *physics.*

She was reading *in the library.*

The past participle is the form used to make the present and past perfect verb and also to create the passive verb:

She has been *in the library since noon.*

He had studied *in the library before he went to class.*

The nuclear laboratory was closed *by the safety committee.*

In addition to these uses in verb phrases, the present and past participles can be used as adjectives and adverbials.

She stood in front of the closed *elevator.*

He bought an interesting *book.*

Running *into the room, he knocked over a chair.*

8b Participles as Adjectives with Verbs that Refer to Emotions

Certain verbs that refer to emotions (*interest, amuse,* and others listed below) have special uses involving their present and past participles. For example, look at these sentences:

I am very interested *in computer science.*

Computer science is very interesting *to me.*

Many advanced students still have trouble with these forms and write sentences such as the following:

▼ *I am very interesting in computer science.*

▼ *Computer science is very interested to me.*

To edit sentences using these participles, remember this rule. If the adjective refers to the person (or animal) that experienced the emotion, then the past participle form is used:

I = interested (The **experiencer** = past participle)

I am very interested *in computer science*

If the adjective refers to the cause of the emotion, then the *-ing* form is used:

computer science = interesting (The **cause** = present participle)

Computer science is very interesting to me.

The verbs involved in this pattern include *amuse, annoy, bewilder, bother, captivate, interest, intrigue, irritate, puzzle, surprise,* and others.

8c EXERCISE: Participles as Adjectives with Verbs

Working with other students from your class, write example sentences to illustrate the use of each of the verbs listed above. You will probably need to write a two- or three-sentence description of the context to make the meaning of the example sentence clear. Try to make the examples as vivid and exact as possible. Write the best of the examples in the spaces below to use when you are editing for these verbs as a reminder of their different meanings.

1. *amuse*

   Context:　I tell very good and very funny stories.
   Examples:　I am amusing to my friends. I am amusing at parties. I am an amusing teacher.

   Context:　I went to the concert by the famous comic. I listened to her funny stories and enjoyed them.
   Examples:　I was amused at the concert. The amused spectator laughed at the comic's jokes.

2. *annoy*

   Context: _____

   _____

   Examples: _____

   _____

   _____

3. *bewilder*

   Context: _____

   _____

   Examples: _____

   _____

   _____

4. *bother*

   Context: _____

   _____

   Examples: _____

   _____

   _____

5. *captivate*

   Context: _____

   _____

   Examples: _____

   _____

   _____

6. *interest*

   Context: _____

   _____

   Examples: _____

   _____

   _____

7. *intrigue*

   Context: _____

   _____

   Examples: _____

   _____

   _____

8. *irritate*

   Context: _____

   _____

   Examples: _____

   _____

   _____

9. *puzzle*

   Context: _____

   _____

   Examples: _____

   _____

   _____

10. *surprise*

    Context: _____

    _____

    Examples: _____

    _____

    _____

9a Participle Phrases

Participle phrases can be used to combine two related sentences into one sentence. Both present participles and past participles can be used for this purpose.

Opening the door, *the instructor entered the room.*

Tired and hungry, *the student left the library to go to class.*

Advanced students have two problems with this area of grammar: First, they need to recognize opportunities to use the participle phrase to add to the sophistication of their writing; second, they need to avoid the mistake called the *dangling participle.*

9b The Basic Present Participle Phrase

The basic type of present participle phrase can be used in the following contexts:

1. Two or more sentences have the same subject.

2. These sentences also have the same verb forms.

For example, analyze the following pairs of sentences:

1a. He opened the door.

1b. He entered the room.

2a. She will complete her courses in May.

2b. She will graduate from the university in June.

These two pairs can easily be combined using a participle phrase. Drop the subject of the first sentence; change the verb into the *-ing* form; add the phrase to the second sentence.

Opening the door, he entered the room.

Finishing her courses in May, she will graduate from the university in June.

Usually the participle phrase comes at the beginning of the sentence; however, it can sometimes be added at the end. Notice that the comma is still required, in contrast to adverbial clauses (see Section 3 on p. 298).

He entered the room, dragging a heavy box behind him.

Try combining these sentences yourself:

1a. The politician moved slowly into the auditorium.

1b. The politician shook hands with people in the crowd.

_____

_____

2a. The politician's wife smiled graciously at the crowd.

2b. The politician's wife waited on the stage.

_____

_____

9c The Perfect Form
of the Participle Phrase

To show that the action in the phrase occurred before the action of the main verb, a perfect form of the phrase is created using *have* + past participle. In this example, he finished eating before he went to the library.

Having eaten dinner, he went to the library to study.

Try making one combined sentence out of these sets. Be careful to have the sentences in a logical time order.

1a. She returned to her home country.

1b. She graduated from a university in the United States.

_____

_____

2a. She returned to her home country.

2b. She got an excellent position with the government.

_____

_____

9d Past Participle Phrases

Past participle phrases can be used to combine two or more sentences in the following contexts:

1. The sentences have the same subject.

2. One of the sentences has past participles in the verb phrases (either perfect verb forms or passive verb forms).

The subject and any verb auxiliaries are left out; the past participle is used to head the participle phrase.

1a. John was tired from playing soccer all afternoon.

1b. John went to bed immediately after dinner.

Tired from playing soccer all afternoon, John went to bed immediately after dinner.

2a. The pieces of the wrecked airplane were scattered over a three-mile area.

2b. The pieces of the wrecked airplane were needed by the investigators to determine the cause of the crash.

Scattered all over a three-mile area, the pieces of the wrecked airplane were needed by the investigators to determine the cause of the crash.

Try combining the following pairs of sentences:

1a. The package was torn and ripped.

1b. The package arrived two months late.

_____

_____

2a. She was exhausted from the tension as well as the effort.

2b. She finished the examination.

_____

_____

9e Dangling Participles

The danger in combining sentences by the method shown in Sections 9b, 9c, and 9d on p. 230 is that you can create illogical statements if you are not careful. Remember, the subject of both sentences *must* be the same! Why are the following sentences illogical and somewhat foolish? *Dangling* means that the phrase does not have the same subject as the main sentence—so it is just hanging there without any logical purpose in the sentence.

▼ *Reading the newspaper, the dog began to howl.*
▼ *Bruised and battered, the wife of the boxer held her husband's head.*

Who is reading the newspaper? Who is bruised and battered?

9f EXERCISES: Participles

A. Select a page from today's newspaper that is interesting to you—news, business, sports, comics. Find all the *-ing* verbs on the page. Are any of them used in participle phrases? With the other students in your class, make a list of at least five sentences that have participle phrases. Then, analyze the sentences to see if they are correctly constructed. What does the participle phrase mean? Did you find any dangling participles?

B. Look back at two compositions that you have written this term. Did you use any participle phrases? Could you have combined any short sentences by this method? Did you have any dangling participle phrases? If you are not using this method in your writing, try to add one participle phrase to the work that you are currently doing. Check your sentence with your instructor.

10 The Many Uses of the *-ing* Form of the Verb

Whatever the technical name given by grammarians, the *-ing* form of the verb has these uses:

1. In the progressive forms of the verb:
   The library was closing *when I arrived.*
   John is working *in the library this term.*

2. As a noun (*gerund*), in subjects and objects:

Studying in the library gives many students a quiet environment with excellent resources for research.

He hates studying *in the library.*

He looks forward to finishing his research project.

3. As an adjective (*present participle*):

The exciting *movie was extremely popular.*

4. As an adverbial (*present participle*):

Opening the door, he entered the library.

11 EXERCISES: Gerunds, Infinitives, and Participles

A. Infinitives are often found in statements like these that express general truths.

To make mistakes is necessary in order to learn.

To learn from mistakes is a sign of intelligence.

To fail to learn from mistakes seems foolish.

Work with two or three other students to write a list of five *truisms* that use infinitives. Share your list with the rest of the class.

B. Working with another student discuss possibilities for a composition modeled on the one entitled "Stopping Smoking" in the exercise on p. 221. In your composition, give three methods for one of the following: (1) learning new vocabulary, (2) getting an instructor to postpone a test, (3) meeting a new person, (4) borrowing $5 from an older brother/sister, or some other topic. After you have your ideas for the three approaches, write the composition by yourself. Revise and edit it before sharing it with the class.

C. Here is a list of the basic steps to check out a book from a university library. To each step, add an infinitive that explains why the step is being taken. Number 1 has been done as an example.

1. You first check on the computerized catalog system.

2. You write down all the information about the call number.

3. You go to the stacks.

4. You take the book to the circulation desk.

1. *You first check on the computerized catalog system to see if the library owns the book you need.*

2. _____

_____

3. _____

_____

4. _____

_____

D. Select a process that you know well. For example, how to load software into a personal computer, how to cook rice, how to do some laboratory process, how to buy a used car, how to get a passport. Write 10 sentences about parts of that process. Then, add to each sentence an infinitive that explains why that step is done or the result of that step.

E. Some advanced students continue to have trouble with the verbs used to talk about talking: *ask, say, tell.* Look at these examples. What kind of objects can each verb have?

He asked to leave the class early.

He asked John to meet him in the library.

He asked the instructor for permission to leave class early.

She said that she was going to the library.

She said, "I am going to the library."

She said to meet her at the library.

He told me that he was going to the lab.

He told John to go to the lab.

The instructor told him to go to the lab.

Based on that evidence, first decide what is wrong with these sentences and then correct each:

▼ *The president said the secretary of state to represent him at the meeting.*

What's wrong? _____

How should it be written? _____

▼ *The president told to demand a change in the treaty.*

What's wrong? _____

How should it be written? _____

▼ *The president asked their changing of the agreement.*

What's wrong? _____

How should it be written? _____

F. Find the *-ing* forms in the first two paragraphs of the passage "How Do Seat Belts Work?" Which are main verbs using the progressive? Which are used as nouns? Which are used as adjectives?

G. Find the infinitives in the first two paragraphs of this passage. How many different ways are they used?

H. Starting with the third paragraph, fill in the correct forms.

HOW DO SEAT BELTS WORK?

In a 30-mile-per-hour crash test, the car takes about two feet to come to a stop. This is a fairly abrupt stop. The occupants usually stop over a much shorter distance, perhaps one to two inches. This difference in stopping distance means that the occupants will stop much more abruptly than the car. To allow the person to come to a more gradual stop, all of the *car's* stopping distance has to be used. Holding the person in his/her seat with belts allows him/her to stop within about the same distance as the car. As a result, the forces on the body are greatly reduced.

The difference between the belted person's stopping distance and the unbelted person's stopping distance is often the difference between life and death. This is like the difference between a fall in which you land on a sidewalk or in garden soil. The soft ground gives the person a few inches in which to come to a stop. Seat belts give the person in the car an additional couple of feet in which to stop.

The lap belt keeps a person inside the car, protecting him/her from the many dangers of _____ (be) thrown out of the car. Even if used alone, the lap belt usually keeps the head from _____ (strike) the windshield or windshield frame. It allows the body _____ (bend) forward so that the head hits only the steering wheel or dashboard. These parts of the car are designed _____ (absorb) energy, and although their cushioning effect is somewhat limited, they cause much less damage than harder structures. The lap belt allows the hips _____ (absorb) much of the force of the collision and thus reduces the force that the head or chest must absorb in _____ (hit) the steering wheel or dashboard.

The shoulder belt prevents the head from _____ (hit) the steering wheel or dashboard. The shoulder belt provides a great deal of extra protection, particularly in _____ (prevent) injuries to the head and face. These are very dangerous and disfiguring injuries. The shoulder belt prevents these injuries by _____ (restrain) the upper part of the body and _____ (keep) the head from _____ (hit) the interior of the car.

Many people find the shoulder belt uncomfortable and inconvenient when they first start _____ (use) their belts, particularly in older cars with separate shoulder belts. In order _____ (prevent) the injuries to the head and face, it is worth the trouble _____ (wear) the shoulder belt whenever possible. A shoulder belt should never be worn without a lap belt. Together, the lap and shoulder belts work _____ (keep) a person in his/her seat and _____ (distribute) the force of the collision over the hips and shoulders—the parts of the body that can best withstand the force.

Adapted from *The Human Collision—How Injuries Occur . . . How Seat Belts Prevent Them* (U.S. Department of Transportation, 1976)

I. Analyze two passages that you wrote earlier this term. Find all the infinitives, gerunds, and participles. Do you need to make any corrections? What kinds of problems do you have? Show those to your instructor. Add any information about this editing step to your list of things that you need to edit for.

CHAPTER 12

Adverbs and Adverbials

1 Introduction to Adverbs and Adverbials

From your study of English sentences, you are aware that the fourth major part of the basic sentence is called the *adverb* or the *modifier*.

subject + verb + direct object + adverb of place
He studies English in the library.

Why are adverbs important? They are the third most common part of an English sentence. Adverbs make up about 15 percent of written English. They are the most common sentence element after subjects and verbs. Because they have so many different meanings (time, place, manner, reason, and others), more than one adverb can occur in a single sentence.

Adverbs can be divided into many different types. One of the most important distinctions is between (1) adverbs that occur at the end or the beginning of the sentence and (2) adverbs of frequency that occur in the middle of the sentence as part of the verb phrase.

1a. *He studies in the library from 2:00 to 4:00.*

1b. *From 2:00 to 4:00, he studies in the library.*

2. *He has never studied chemistry.*

This chapter will discuss and illustrate both of these types of adverbs. Infinitives and other forms can be used for *adverbial* meaning. For information on other adverbials, check the Index. Also, see Section 3a on p. 298 for information on adverbial clauses.

2 Forms of Adverbs

Adverbs can take many different forms—from single words to whole clauses. Technically, the word *adverb* is reserved for the single word forms, such as *quickly* or *never*, while *adverbial* refers to other forms that are used for adverb meanings, such as the subordinate clause in *We are required to take calculus **because it is a basic intellectual tool for science and technology***.

single word
He writes quickly.

noun phrase
The lab was open last night.

prepositional phrase
We must make our report in the morning.

infinitive
He went home to get his car.

phrase
Confused about her test grade, she asked for an appointment.

clause
The library closed before we finished our report.

3 Location of Adverbs and Adverbials

Adverbs can occur at the beginning, middle, and end of sentences. The most common location is at the end. The next most common location is at the beginning. Of course, preverb adverbs of frequency (*never, often*—see Section 8a on p. 246) are usually in the middle of the sentence in the verb phrase. Very often prepositional phrases of space or time are given at the beginning of a sentence, especially if other prepositional phrases occur at the end of the sentence.

He went to the library yesterday.

Yesterday he went to the library.

In the morning, we will go to the library to study for the final examination.

In the library, we can study in peace and quiet.

4a Order of Subcategories of Adverbs

A major issue is the order of adverbs when more than one is used in a sentence. Which comes first? You have probably studied rules about the order of adverbs of manner, place, and time. In this section, a more advanced version of those rules is given.

Adverbs of Direction and Position Adverbs of place really include several different types of meaning. Two of these are adverbs of *direction* and adverbs of *position*. Direction adverbs are used with verbs of action for sentences such as

He walked to the library.

Position adverbs are used with verbs that indicate being located in a place (rather than moving in a direction).

He sat in his office.

Adverbs of Purpose and Reason Adverbs that answer the question *Why?* can also be subdivided into two or more exact categories—adverbs of *purpose* and adverbs of *reason.* Purpose adverbs can best be paraphrased with the words *in order to.*

He sat in his office in order to read the report.

She went to New York to visit her sister.

Adverbs of reason go another step beyond purpose to explain the reason for doing the action.

purpose   reason
He sat in his office in order to read the report because he had to explain it at a 1:00 meeting.

purpose   reason
She went to New York to visit her sister because her mother was at her sister's house.

Adverbs of Time and Frequency Adverbs of time can be subdivided into adverbs of time and of frequency. They tell *when* and *how often.*

how often + when
He studies in the library everyday from 1 to 3.

Adverbs of Manner Adverbs of manner are used to describe *how* something was done.

She does her work quickly but carefully.

To summarize the types of adverbs:

1. place = direction or position

2. reason = reason or purpose

3. time = time or frequency

4. manner

By the way, this adverb of frequency is different from the preverb adverbs of frequency discussed in Section 8a on p. 246.

4b Ordering of These Adverbs

It would be easier for you if this rule were more exact. The truth, however, is that adverbs *tend* to take certain orders but that the orders can vary.

Adverbs of Direction, Manner, and Position: Where, How, Where

1. Direction tends to go before manner.
   He walked to school slowly.

2. Direction tends to go before position. They usually are kept together if another adverb is added.
   He went to the reading room at the library.
   He went to the reading room at the library at 10:00 a.m.

3. Manner varies with position—either one can come first.
   He sat in the library quietly.
   He sat quietly in the library.

Adverbs of Time and Frequency: When, How Often

4. Time/frequency usually come after direction, manner, position.
   He goes to the library at 10:00 a.m. every morning.
   He goes to the library unhappily at 10:00 a.m. every morning.
   He goes to the library on campus at 10:00 a.m. every morning.

5. Time varies with frequency—either one can come first.
   He goes to the library every morning at 10:00 a.m.
   He goes to the library at 10:00 a.m. every morning.

Adverbs of Purpose and Reason

6. Purpose usually comes before reason.

   He goes to the library to study because he wants to make an "A" in his economics course.

7. Purpose and reason usually come after all the other types of adverbs.

   He walks into the library slowly every morning because he is tired.

Other Influences on Ordering

8. Shorter adverbs usually come before longer ones—no matter what type of meaning is involved.

   He walked slowly into the large library of his new university.

9. If the writer wants to emphasize a particular adverb, that one tends to come first.

   He goes—because he wants to make an "A"—to the library every morning. (However, a less awkward sentence would be: *Because he wants to make an "A," he goes to the library every morning.* Putting the adverb first emphasizes it.)

10. If two or more adverbs of the same kind occur in a sentence, the more specific comes first and the more general comes last.

    2 time adverbs
    The bomb exploded at 2:00 p.m. on October 22, 1985.

    2 position adverbs
    She studies in her room at home.

5 Adverbial Clauses

Often adverbial meaning is given with subordinate clauses. For example, in the following sentence, the subordinated clause gives the reason for the woman's hard work:

She studies many hours because she is determined to graduate in only three years.

For more information about adverbial clauses, see Section 3 on p. 298.

6 EXERCISES: Adverbs and Adverbials

A. To review what you know and the rules listed above, decide which rule is illustrated by each of these sentences.

1. He started school at 8:00 a.m. on September 5, 1972.

2. He walked to a school in his neighborhood.

3. He walked to school slowly.

4. He walked to school slowly because he hated his teacher.

5. He sat quietly at his desk.

6. He walked to school every morning.

7. He got up at 6:30 every morning.

8. He got up at 6:30 every morning to get ready to go to school.

9. He got up early to go to school because his parents made him.

10. Quietly, unhappily, and sleepily, he walked every morning to a place that he hated.

B. Choose a topic—weather, education, love, money, anything of interest to you. Write one sentence on that topic to illustrate each of the rules given above. Compare your sentences to those of other students writing on the same topic. Select five or six of the most interesting sentences to put on the board to share with the whole class.

C. Very commonly writers will use more than one adverb in a single sentence. Find the adverbs in the following sentences. What types are used? What ordering rules are being followed?

1. In Canada in 1974, 2,529 drivers died in accidents.

2. Children often resist using seat belts when they are first introduced to them.

3. In recent years, motor vehicle collisions have been studied in an effort to reduce the severity of injuries.

4. When a car strikes a solid object, it stops very abruptly.

5. On impact, the car begins to crush and to slow down. The person inside the car has nothing to slow him down so he continues to move forward inside the car at 30 mph.

6. One study looked at all the fatal accidents in Metropolitan Toronto in 1970. During that year, 35 drivers and 22 passengers were killed.

7. One major study of 28,000 accident records was conducted in the mid-1960s in Sweden.

D. You would expect a newspaper article to have adverbs and adverbials to tell when, where, and perhaps why something happened. Generally this information is given in the first few sentences. Here are the first sentences from all the front-page stories in the *Atlanta Constitution* for Wednesday, March 18, 1987. Underline the adverbs of time, place, and reason used in these sentences. (Remember that infinitives can function as adverbs.)

1. Several million dollars in profits from arms sales to Iran were paid to an Iranian group that financed the kidnappers of Americans in Lebanon, according to U.S. officials and associates of an Iranian middleman. [Why is a passive used in this sentence?]

2. The Soviet Union proposed Tuesday that international inspectors monitor space launches to prevent an arms race in space.

3. Government investigators warned Congress on Tuesday that some of the government's nuclear weapons plants may be "irreversibly contaminated" and that billions of dollars will be needed to control the problem at the facilities.

4. Under pressure from Congress, the Internal Revenue Service on Tuesday agreed to begin a pilot program to determine if corporations are avoiding as much as $8 billion a year in taxes on interest and dividend income.

5. Under government pressure to reduce delays, airline representatives agreed Tuesday to shift 128 flights off peak times at Atlanta's Hartsfield International Airport.

6. Piedmont Airlines Flight 74 will lift off from Greensboro, N.C., Wednesday afternoon, headed for Washington, D.C., as the first regularly scheduled commercial flight to carry an airborne computer system that warns pilots of potential inflight collisions and gives directions on how to avoid them.

7. An argument between teenagers at a high school track meet Friday afternoon may have been the start of it.

E. In a textbook from a course other than English, study any two pages. What adverbs and adverbials are used? Is one type more frequently used than another? Why do you think that might be true?

F. Look back at several passages that you have written recently. What errors did you make that involved adverbs? The possibilities include wrong word choice for meaning, wrong form, and wrong place in the sentence. If adverb use is a serious problem in your writing, add it to your personal editing list.

7 Split Infinitives

Very often you will wish to include an adverb with the infinitive form of a verb.

It is necessary to solve this problem. Add *quickly.*

We will have to think about the problem. Add *carefully.*

A split infinitive would put the adverb between *to* and the verb:

It is necessary to quickly solve this problem.

We will have to carefully think about the problem.

In spoken English and in informal written English, you will generally not be criticized for this usage—most educated Americans do it all the time. In formal written English, it is frequently better to rewrite the sentence to move the adverb to another position if doing so does not change the meaning of the sentence.

It is necessary to solve this problem quickly.

We will have to think carefully about this problem.

We will have to think about this problem carefully.

Another choice is to decide if the adverb is essential to your meaning. If it is not necessary, then edit it out of the sentence or find another way to say the same thing.

This problem should be solved quickly.

We should think about this problem carefully.

8a Preverb Adverbs of Frequency

Preverb adverbs are words such as *never, seldom,* and *always.* That these adverbs are so important might say something about American society. We seem to like to establish *how often* or *how many times* actions occur.

8b Meaning System of the Preverb Adverbs of Frequency

These adverbs are a system based on meanings that range between the extremes of *always* and *never*:

always
usually, generally, regularly
often, frequently
sometimes
occasionally
not always
not usually, not generally, not regularly
rarely, seldom, hardly ever, scarcely ever, not often
never, not ever

Discussions can focus on a contrast between two or more of these adverbs:

John always studies in the library, but he never studies at home.

The government has seldom ignored the will of the people completely, but it has often been slow in understanding what the people wanted.

Discussions can also be about the accuracy of the adverb:

John: *I'm always on time to class.*

Instructor: *Well, that isn't quite accurate. You were sometimes late and frequently absent.*

While previous research claimed that working wives always make less money than their husbands, our research has found a new trend: working wives who are highly educated frequently earn more than their husbands if the husbands have less education.

8c Preverb Adverbs of Frequency and the Progressive Verb Form

Preverb adverbs of frequency are about repetition. Therefore, they are usually used with verbs that mean "habit"—that is, they are frequently found with simple present tense forms of the verb.

English majors seldom study calculus.

Preverb adverbs of frequency are, thus, seldom used with progressives because of the present time meaning often associated with the progressive.

▼ *He is never going to the library right now.*

However, progressives can be used for emotional meanings—for emphatic statements such as

John is always *complaining about something.*
Mary is constantly *arriving late for class.*

These are found more in speech than in writing. When spoken, strong emphasis is placed on the preverb adverb of frequency.

8d Location of the Preverb Adverbs of Frequency

Preverb adverbs are usually found in the middle of the sentence—in the verb phrase. Some of them can be used in other locations. This section will first discuss the rules for use in the verb phrase and then will show other locations.

The adverb of frequency is usually found (1) after the first auxiliary, (2) before the simple present/past tense, and (3) after *be* as the main verb:

1. *She has rarely visited the library.*
   He can always find time to play soccer.

2. *He frequently studies in the library.*
   She seldom worked in the lab.

3. *He is always late to work.*

For imperatives, the preverb adverb of frequency comes before the verb:

Always turn off the lights.
Never try to register late.

8e EXERCISES: Preverb Adverbs of Frequency

A. To review your understanding of the basic preverb adverbs, write in the blank space an adverb that has the *opposite* meaning of the one in the sentence. Use a different adverb for each sentence.

1. He always studies in the library.

   No, that's not right. He _____ studies in the library.

2. He usually eats lunch in the cafeteria.

No, that's not right. He _____ eats lunch in the cafeteria.

3. He has never worked with a computer.

No, that's not right. He has _____ worked with a computer.

4. He sometimes meets his friends to study in an empty classroom.

No, that's not right. He _____ meets his friends to study in an empty classroom.

5. He hardly ever studies at home.

No, that's not right. He _____ studies at home.

B. To continue your review of these adverbs, write seven sentences about a city or town that you know well. You can write about the physical features of the city, the weather, the people, the government, anything you have accurate information about. Use the adverb in parenthesis in the sentence. The sentences will range from *always* to *never*. Share the description with the rest of the class.

1. (always) _____

   _____

2. (usually) _____

   _____

3. (frequently) _____

   _____

4. (sometimes) _____

   _____

5. (occasionally) _____

   _____

6. (rarely) _____

_____

7. (never) _____

_____

C. Select a passage that you have written. Would it be made more explicit by adding any preverb adverbs? Try adding appropriate words. Then, share the passage with your instructor to talk about the results of the changes that you made.

D. Select a front-page story that interests you from today's newspaper. Find the preverb adverbs in the story. Which words are used most frequently? How many are used?

E. Select two pages from a college textbook. Find the preverb adverbs. Which are used most frequently? How many are used? Compare these results with those in exercise D. Are there any differences?

8f Double Negatives

The preverb adverbs with negative meaning (*never, rarely, seldom, hardly ever, scarcely ever, not often*) cannot be used with *not* for a negative meaning in formal written English (although you will certainly hear some Americans talk this way).

▼ *She isn't never on time for class.*
She is never on time for class.

8g Negative Preverb Adverbs at the Beginning of Sentences

For variety and emphasis, writers can move the negative preverb adverbs to the beginning of the sentence. This move forces another change: the subject and auxiliary change places just as in the formation of questions.

adverb + aux. + subject   +   verb   +   DO
Never has our university made such a terrible mistake.

8h EXERCISES: Preverb Adverbs

A. Add the preverb adverb to the front of the sentence. Then, adjust the grammar.

1. The government has wasted money on such a ridiculous project. (never)

2. Many students will be in the library on Friday nights. (rarely)

3. Businessmen place ethics above economics. (seldom)

B. Complete these sentences on a topic of your choice. Use simple present tense verbs to make general truth statements.

1. Never _____

_____

2. Seldom _____

_____

3. Rarely _____

_____

C. Complete these sentences on a topic of your choice. Use any of the modals for future time meaning (*will, can, may, should, must*). Work with another student to revise and then edit both of your sets of sentences. Then, share your sentences with the rest of the class.

1. Rarely _____

_____

2. Hardly ever _____

_____

3. Seldom _____

_____

CHAPTER 13

Prepositions and Prepositional Phrases

1 Introduction to Prepositions and Prepositional Phrases

Prepositions are words like *in, on, to,* and *at* that are used to express relationships between a noun phrase and some other part of a sentence. For example, in *He threw the paper into the trashcan,* what is the relationship between *trashcan* and the rest of the sentence? One possible answer is that the trashcan is the direction of the action. What is the relationship between *on foot* and the rest of the sentence in *She walked to the store on foot?* Method or means of transportation?

2 The Nine Most Common Prepositions

The nine most common prepositions are

at	*from*	*on*
by	*in*	*to*
for	*of*	*with*

Each of these has many different uses and meanings. For example, *at* has been found to have at least six different meanings. A good resource for finding out about the meanings of the various prepositions is an English-English dictionary, especially one of the dictionaries prepared for students of ESL.

This chapter will present information to help you be more accurate in your use of prepositions by helping you understand the system. You should be looking for insights that will make it easier for you to learn to use these words.

3 Uses of Prepositional Phrases

English uses prepositional phrases as:

1. Modifiers of nouns or noun phrases
   The book on the table is mine.

2. Adverbs
   He studies in the library.

3. Complements of verbs and adjectives
   We argued about his ideas.
   I am angry with him.

4a Meanings of Prepositions

Grammarians point out two major ways in which prepositions are used for meaning. First, prepositions are used to talk about ideas and relationships of time and space: *at noon, in class, on the moon*. Second, prepositions are used to talk about relationships among people, between people and objects, or among objects: *The book was written by Dickens*, or *We covered the table with a cloth.*

4b Space and Time

You already know many of these meanings of prepositions. To remember what you know and to discover what you need to learn, fill in this chart with examples of each preposition for each meaning. You can write either phrases or complete sentences as long as the meaning of the example is clear. Many times you will be able to think of two or more different but

related meanings. For example, *at* can mean different types of space—
"intersection," "target," or "general area."

The supermarket is at the corner of Main St. and First Ave.

Look at this example.

He is at the library.

Do this preposition chart from your memory at first. You might find
it useful to work with another student to get additional examples.

	Space	Time	Other (idioms, too)
at	*at the corner*	*at 3:00*	*work at learning English*
by			
for			
from			
in			
of			
on			
to			
with			

4c Relationships Between People and/or Objects

Here are some of the kinds of relationship meanings that common prepositions have. This list is not complete but gives basic examples to help
you understand the system better. In the exercises, you will look at prepositions to see what meaning relationships seem to be used.

by "agent" in passive sentences

Paper was invented by the Chinese.

by "means" or "method"

　He comes to school by bus.

for "to do something helpful for someone" with the indirect object

　He bought the book for his brother.

for "to replace someone" or "to do someone's work"

　He taught the class for his professor.

from "source" or "person/place one gets something from"

　He got the book from his instructor.

　He brought the rug from Turkey.

to "receiver" of direct object

　I gave the money to my sister.

with "instrument"

　I wrote the letter with a pencil.

with "together"

　He goes to the library with his friends.

5 Prepositions that Frequently Occur in the Same Sentence

Some prepositions frequently occur in the same sentence. If you have one, you should expect to use the other. Space has been left for you to add others that you already know or new ones that you discover.

1. *from . . . to*

　He walked from his house to the store.

　We were in class from 3:00 to 5:00.

　The final grades ranged from 65 to 95.

2. *from . . . until*

　We worked from 8:00 until 5:00.

3. *out of . . . into*

　We walked out of the building into the rain.

　He moved out of a house into an apartment.

4. _____

　_____

5. _____

_____

6 Deletion of Prepositions

Sometimes a preposition is optional—you have a choice about using it. You know that in giving short answers to questions in conversation that prepositions are frequently not repeated:

Instructor: When can you go to the library?

Student: (At) 2:00 this afternoon.

Here are two other optional uses of prepositions:

1. *for* to mean "a span of time"

   We have been here (for) two years.

2. *on* with days of the week

   We went to the library (on) Saturday.

   We go to chemistry lab (on) Wednesday afternoons.

7 Prepositions that Are Synonyms

In the early stages of learning English, your instructors usually chose to tell you only the most commonly used words. But, as an advanced student, you know that you have different choices that have more or less the same meaning. Space is left to add any others that you know or learn.

1. *by/near* for location

   He lives near/by the railroad station.

2. *around/about* for approximate time/degree

   The party will start around/about 7:30.

   We expect around/about 30 guests.

3. *of/to* and *after/past* for telling time

   It is quarter to/of 10:00.

   It is 12 past/after 10:00.

4. *on/along* for location on a line

   There are many chemical factories on/along the Mississippi River.

5. *to/until* for time

   He studies to/until 5:00.

6. *in/during* for time

   He studied in New York in/during 1987.

7. *below/beneath/under* for location

   He put his book bag below/beneath/under his chair.

8. *above/over* for location

   She hung the photograph above/over her desk.

9. _____

   _____

10. _____

    _____

8 Prepositions and Indirect Objects

The *indirect object* is the receiver of the *direct object* (check the Index for other information on the direct and indirect object):

            DO   IO
He gave the book to his roommate.

                 IO   DO
He gave his roommate the book.

            DO   IO
He got the book for his roommate.

            DO   IO
He asked a favor of his instructor.

Indirect objects can cause these problems:

—What verbs take which prepositions?

—When is it possible to remove the preposition?

—What passive sentences can be formed using indirect objects as the subject?

The indirect object can be tied to the sentence with a preposition—frequently *to*, but sometimes *for* or *of*. Indirect objects are used for three major meanings: (1) They tell the "direction" something goes: *He sent the book to John.* (2) They mean that someone helps another person by doing something for him or her: *He bought the house for his family.* (3) They are used to ask or request: *He asked the question of the student.* The most common meaning is "directional" and the least common is "asking."

to = "directional"

for = "helping"

of = "asking"

With many verbs, it is possible to remove the direct object preposition if the word order is changed. When the preposition is removed, then the indirect object switches positions with the direct object. (See Appendix K for a list of the verbs that allow this change.)

He sent John the book.

He bought his family the house.

He asked the student the question.

Very often the indirect object is given immediately after the verb if the direct object is long and complicated.

He gave his roommate the book that he bought at the sale.

She gave her mother the flowers that she picked in the garden.

He asked his advisor the question that he did not understand.

However, the preposition cannot usually be removed if the direct object is a pronoun: *He gave them to John* would not be changed to ▼*He gave John them.*

Also, some verbs do not allow the removal of the direct object preposition: *He opened the door for the old man* cannot be changed to ▼*He opened the old man the door.* (See Appendix K for a list of these verbs.)

English allows the use of the indirect object as the subject of a passive sentence (see Chapter 3, "Passive Sentences"):

Dr. Smith gave the book to John. = John was given the book by Dr. Smith.

9 Words that Can Be Either Conjunctions or Prepositions

Conjunctions or joining words combine words, phrases, or sentences. Some joining words can also function as prepositions:

I finished the paper before I went to class. (joining word)

I finished the paper before dinner. (preposition)

Other words that can have either function include *after, as, since, until.*

10 Prepositions at the End of Sentences

In spite of what you might have heard, it is quite common to end sentences with prepositions. Sometimes it would be impossible to have any other order, for example:

What does the instructor look like?

He is impossible to talk to.

In other situations where there are two choices, the more formal choice moves the preposition to be with its object. The more formal version is typical of academic writing.

The research project that you are thinking about will be very difficult. (less formal but still grammatical)

The research project about which you are thinking will be very difficult. (formal)

11 Problem Prepositions

Students of ESL have been observed to have special problems with some of the commonly used prepositions.

One such problem is that *in, on,* and *at* can be used for both space and time. Have you ever noticed that textbooks always list these prepositions in the same order—*in* first, *on* in the middle, and *at* last? Native speakers seem to think of them in that order. It makes sense for time meanings because the order is from most general to most specific:

He graduated in 1988. (*in* + year, month, season, period of the day—morning, evening)

He graduated on June 22, 1988. (*on* for dates and days of the week)

He graduated at 1:30 p.m. (*at* for times of the day)

He graduated at 1:30 p.m. on June 22, 1988.

For space meanings, the *in, on, at* order is not quite as easy to understand, but it seems to reflect spatial dimensions:

She is waiting in the lab. (three dimensions, *inside* a space)

The book is lying on the desk. (two dimensions, *on top of*)

The university is at the corner of Main and First. (one dimension, a point or intersection)

Another problem is that *since* and *for* are both used to account for the length of time something happened, but they represent different ways of giving the time. *Since* gives the starting point. *For* gives the total amount of time. (See Section 8a on p. 54 for information on their use with the present perfect verb form.)

He has taught here since 1970.

He has taught physics for over 20 years.

12 EXERCISES: Prepositions

A. Even advanced students can have three kinds of problems with prepositions: (1) They do not use them when they should: ▼*I will go class tomorrow.* (2) They use them when they are not needed: ▼*I will go to home after class.* (3) They use the wrong one: ▼*I will go from home at 3:00.* To find out what kinds of problems you have with prepositions, look at the first drafts of two papers you have written recently. Ask your instructor to mark all of the places where prepositions are not used or are misused. Then, fill in this chart to see the number of times you made each type of mistake. Also, list any verb + preposition mistake that you made for the same verb more than one time. When you know what kinds of problems you have with English, editing for those errors will be easier.

Type	*Number of Errors*
Preposition missing	_____
Preposition not needed	_____
Wrong preposition	_____

List of verbs + preposition that I still have trouble remembering:

1. _____

2. _____

3. _____

4. _____

5. _____

B. What's the difference in meaning between the underlined prepositions in these sentences?

The window was broken <u>by</u> Jack.

The window was broken <u>with</u> a rock.

Jack broke the window <u>with</u> a friend.

Jack broke the window <u>with</u> a rock.

I read the letter <u>to</u> my sister.

I read the letter <u>for</u> my sister.

I read the letter <u>from</u> my sister.

C. Look back at Section 4c on p. 254 on the use of prepositions to show relationships. Which type of relationship is indicated in each of these sentences?

The wheel has not yet been invented *by* some cultures.

She gets to school *by* car.

He carried the groceries into the house *for* his wife.

The chairman gave the final examination *for* the instructor.

He borrowed the maps *from* the library.

She returned the damaged book *to* the bookstore.

I prepared the report *with* my computer.

He went to the airport *with* his brother.

D. Write 10 sentences in which you give important historical information that includes dates. This information could be about your home country, your home city, your family, or some other topic. *But,* all 10 sentences need to be about the same topic. If necessary, go to the library to get accurate information from appropriate reference materials. For example, (1) The United States began its rebellion in the summer of 1776. (2) Tradition tells us that the Declaration of Independence was signed on July 4, 1776. (3) However, historians think that the date might have been July 5, 1776.

E. Fill in the blanks in the passages with appropriate prepositions.

The United States took its first census _____ 1790.

Few Americans lived _____ urban areas then. Most

Americans live _____ cities now. Seventy percent of

our people are living _____ about 1 percent of our

land. Life _____ the city can be extremely lonely. Many rural people live _____ poverty. The U.S. must solve these problems _____ the 21st century. We can reverse the flow of population _____ the metropolitan centers.

Adapted from *Communities of Tomorrow* (U.S. Department of Agriculture, undated)

The son of slaves who had escaped _____ Kentucky, Elijah McCoy was born _____ Canada and trained as a mechanical engineer _____ Edinburgh, Scotland. He moved _____ the United States _____ the end of the Civil War. McCoy created an "automatic locomotive lubricator" and received a patent for his invention _____ 1872.

Adapted from *Eureka!* (U.S. Small Business Administration, 1982)

What is it like to live _____ a community _____ polluted waters or _____ inadequate water supplies? If you live _____ such a community, it has probably been so long since you have even thought of swimming, fishing, or boating _____ nearby water that you have forgotten it was once possible.

Adapted from *Focus on Clean Water* (U.S. Department of Health, Education, and Welfare, 1964)

Agriculture uses over seven times as much water _____ irrigation now as it did _____ 1900. While it uses less water than industry, it "consumes" more because almost all the water used _____ industry is recoverable whereas about 60 percent of water used _____ irrigation is "lost." In addition, much of the irrigation water returned _____ various watercourses is laden with salts, other minerals, and agricultural chemicals which are difficult to remove _____ conventional waste treatment methods.

_____

Adapted from *Focus on Clean Water* (U.S. Department of Health, Education, and Welfare, 1964)

F. English has many prepositions in addition to the nine most common listed at the beginning of this chapter—for example, *during*. A helpful source of information about prepositions is an English-English dictionary that has definitions and examples. This is the definition of *during* from the *Merriam-Webster Dictionary*.

> **dur·ing** \,d(y)ŭr-iŋ *prep* **1** : throughout the course of ⟨there was rationing ~ the war⟩ **2** : at some point in the course of ⟨broke in ~ the night⟩

Here are some sentences that use *during*. Which meaning is being used?

1. During the past two decades, major advances have been made in our understanding of human language.

2. During the final examination, the instructor walked up and down the rows between the desks.

3. The politician made several factual errors during the news conference.

4. During the test flight, the pilot reported continuously on the performance of the plane.

G. Find the definition of each of these prepositions in an English-English dictionary. Then, write sentences to illustrate each of the meanings listed.

onto

into

H. Look back at the analysis of your problems with prepositions in exercise A. Select a preposition that you have trouble using correctly, and look up its definitions in an English-English dictionary. Write example sentences for each definition given.

I. Prepositions are all around you in the advertisements you see in magazines, on billboards, or on buses. They are easily heard in the popular music on the radio. Find 10 phrases or sentences that are interesting to you and that include prepositions. Share your favorites with the class.

J. Try writing definitions for the prepositions you selected for exercise I. Then, compare your definitions to those given by an English-English dictionary. Did they include your meanings?

K. Prepositions have meanings that range from the very definite to the very abstract. Some meanings are easy to demonstrate physically (*put the book in the briefcase*) while others are impossible to show physically (*they live in poverty*). Here is the definition for *in* from the *Merriam-Webster Dictionary*. Arrange the meanings into two groups: those that can be physically demonstrated and those that cannot be physically demonstrated. Work with another student if you find that helpful. Then, think of ways to demonstrate analysis and demonstrations with the rest of the class.

¹**in** \(ˈ)in, ən, ᵊn\ *prep*   **1** — used to indicate physical surroundings ⟨swim ~ the lake⟩   **2** : INTO 1 ⟨ran ~ the house⟩   **3** : DURING ⟨~the summer⟩   **4** : WITH ⟨written ~ pencil⟩   **5** — used to indicate one's situation or state of being ⟨~luck⟩ ⟨~love⟩ ⟨~trouble⟩   **6** — used to indicate manner ⟨~a hurry⟩ or purpose ⟨said ~ reply⟩   **7** : INTO 2 ⟨broke ~ pieces⟩

L. Section 8 on p. 257 describes two major types of indirect objects that can be illustrated by these two sentences: *I gave the book to John*, and *I got the book for John*. What is the difference in the meaning of these sentences? Decide in each of the following situations which preposition should be used.

1. A scientist is working on a project to design a new medicine. Therefore, he is designing a medicine _____ cancer patients.

2. The scientist gave a copy of a research report _____ his supervisor. His supervisor now has the copy of the report.

3. The scientist also teaches a class at the university. When he was out of town, his supervisor taught the class _____ him.

4. When the scientist returned home, he gave a test _____ the class.

M. Work with another student to write a set of four sentences like the ones in exercise L to illustrate the differences between *to* and *for*. After you check the sentences with your instructor, test the rest of the class to see if they can provide the correct answers.

N. Decide if the indirect object in each sentence can be moved to the position immediately after the verb—and the preposition removed.

1. John sent the book to his mother.

2. His mother bought a computer for John.

3. His mother bought a computer that had all the most modern features for John.

4. His mother bought it for John.

5. Because John had a broken arm, his sister opened the computer box for him.

6. When he could not get the computer to work, John told his troubles to his best friend.

7. His friend explained the problem to John.

O. The contrast between *to* and *from* is illustrated in these verbs: *sell* something to someone versus *buy* something from someone. Others that have this pattern include *give/take, lend/borrow, teach/learn, write/hear*. Work with another student to write examples that show the differences between these verbs. As a method of learning the words that you do not yet know, make these example sentences part of a funny, silly, or dramatic story.

CHAPTER 14

Negation

1 Introduction to Negation

English sentences can be made negative in a number of different ways:

He does not *know Pascal.* (not is the verb phrase)

Rarely *will you need to repair a computer.* (negative adverb)

No *one passed the test.* (no with a pronoun)

No *loud music can be played after 10:00 p.m.* (no as a determiner in a noun phrase)

She is unhappy *about her class schedule.* (negative prefix)

The instructor told me not to miss *the test.* (not with infinitive)

Neither *the instructor* nor *the students were happy about the results of the examination.* (neither/nor)

Many advanced students have problems with these aspects of using the negative:

—confusing *not* and *no*

—not using *some* and *any* correctly

—not recognizing that words like *rarely* are negatives (and cannot usually be used with *no* or *not*)

—not understanding when double negatives can be used

2 Differences Between *Not* and *No*

Not can be used in the verb phrase or to modify a noun phrase:

He does not *speak Arabic.*

Not *a single student missed the test.*

   No is never used in the verb phrase or to modify a complete noun phrase. *No* is part of the noun phrase and serves as a determiner (like *the, this, many*). *No* can modify comparative forms of adjectives. *No* is used in some idioms such as *no good* and *no different.*

No students missed the test. (*No* is grammatically parallel to *the*.)

He is no longer a student. (*No* modifies an adjective.)

This answer is no good. (*No* can be used with this phrase.)

3 *No* in Academic Writing

Compare these two sentences. The second one is commonly used in academic writing because it seems more formal and it seems more emphatic.

He doesn't have any money means *He has no money.*

   Research has shown that a very large percentage of the negative sentences in university textbooks use *no* + noun. For example,

No results are in fact results.

There seem to be no good answers for the problem.

The president obviously has no idea what to do next.

A manager often has no choice but to fire competent workers.

4 A Special Meaning for *No*

In some uses, *no* has a special meaning. Look at these two sentences:

She is not a teacher. (She must be something else.)

She is no teacher. (She has the job of teacher, but she does not do it very well.)

No is used in this kind of sentence to mean something like "the person appears to be something but does not do it very well."

He is no friend of mine.

He is no lawyer.

5 Negative Words that Do Not Look Negative

English has a small number of negative words that do not look negative. These include *barely, hardly, seldom, rarely, scarcely.* Also, *little* and *few* fit this category (in contrast to *a little* and *a few*). These words are problems for two reasons:

First, if you do not recognize that they are negative, you may (a) not understand their meaning, (b) create double negatives, and (c) use *some* rather than *any.*

▼ *He does not hardly ever miss class. (He hardly ever misses class.)*

▼ *She rarely takes some books home to study. (She rarely takes any books home to study.)*

Second, in formal usage, *little, rarely, scarcely,* and *seldom* can move to the beginning of the sentence. The verb auxiliary then changes places with the subject—just as in the formation of yes-no questions.

Rarely will he miss a class.

Seldom does she conduct serious research.

Little did he realize the results that would come from his decision.

Scarcely was he elected when he began changing the government.

6 Using *Some* and *Any* Correctly

Some and *any* alternate with each other as indefinite plural determiners in positive and negative sentences:

He has some money.

He does not have any money.

This change is potentially confusing when the sentence contains a negative word that does not look negative. The rule in formal English is that for a negative meaning only one negative is allowed.

He seldom has (any? some?) time to talk.

Since *seldom* is negative, the correct form is *any.*

He seldom has any time to talk.

This rule also involves words such as *anyone/someone* and *anything/something.*

He seldom has any time to talk with anyone.

7 Double Negatives

To give a negative meaning in formal English, you cannot have two negative words in the same sentence. Such use is called *double negative* (see the Index for more information). (You will certainly hear double negatives used by some Americans for emphatic meaning in everyday spoken English.)

▼ *He did not mean nothing disrespectful by his questions.*
He did not mean anything disrespectful by his questions.
He meant nothing disrespectful by his questions.

However, if you want a positive meaning that involves a double element, you can create sentences such as the following:

I will not not go to the party. (This is an emphatic way of saying that you will go to the party.)
I did not not study. (I studied.)
When you are ill, you must not not eat. (You must eat.)

In each of these examples, the second *not* is combined with the word immediately after it: *not go, not study, not eat.* The speaker in the first two examples is saying that he/she will not (not go) or did not (not study). The third example gives advice about (not eating).
This usage is acceptable emphatic formal English.

8 Giving Variety to Your Writing

Using negatives other than *not* can make your writing more varied and more sophisticated. Remember, *no* + noun is often used in academic writing. To add variety, you can try the following:

—Change the sentence to use *no* rather than *not.*
—Find a way to change from *not* to a negative adverb (*never, rarely*).
—Add a negative prefix.

Try giving versions of the first sentence that have the same meaning but do not use *not.*

1. The new policy is not making the students happy.

_____

2. Students are not permitted in the faculty lounge.

_____

3. We do not see any problems with this report.

_____

4. She is not studying computer science any longer.

_____

5. He will not have this problem ever again.

_____

9 EXERCISES: Negation

A. Turn to the editorial page of a recent issue of a newspaper. Find all the various negative statements. How many different kinds of negations did you find?

1. Number of *nots*: _____

2. Number of *nos*: _____

3. Number of *nevers*: _____

4. Number of negative adverbs that do not look negative (*rarely*):

_____

5. Number of negative prefixes (*un-, il-*): _____

B. Put the appropriate negative in the blanks in this passage.

WHO STUTTERS?

Stutterers represent the whole range of personality types, levels of

emotional adjustment, and intelligence. There are more than 15 million

stutterers in the world today and approximately 1 million in the United

States alone.

Most stuttering begins after a child has mastered the basics of speech and is starting to talk automatically. One out of 30 children will then undergo a brief period of stuttering, lasting six months or so. Boys are four times as likely as girls to be stutterers.

Occasionally stuttering arises in an older child or even in an adult. It may follow an illness or an emotionally shattering event, such as a death in the family. Stuttering may also occur following brain injury, either due to head injury or after a stroke. _____ matter how the problem begins, stutterers generally experience their worst moments under conditions of stress or emotional tension: ordering in a crowded restaurant, talking over the telephone, speaking in public, asking the boss for a raise.

Stuttering does _____ develop in a predictable pattern. In children, speech difficulties can disappear for weeks or months only to return in full force. About 80 percent of children with a stuttering problem are able to speak normally by the time they are adults—whether they've had therapy or _____. Adult stutterers have also been known to stop stuttering for _____ apparent reason.

Indeed, all stutterers can speak fluently some of the time. Most can also whisper smoothly, speak in unison, and sing with _____ hesitations. Most stutterers also speak easily when they are prevented from hearing their own voices, when talking to pets and small children, or when addressing themselves in the mirror. All these instances of fluency demonstrate that _____ is basically wrong with the stutterer's speech machinery.

If the problem is _____ in the mouth or the throat,

is it in the brain? Stuttering can arise from specific brain damage, but only

_____. In general, stuttering is _____

associated with any measurable brain abnormality and is _____

_____ related to intelligence.

Adapted from *Stuttering: Hope Through Research* (U.S. Department of Health and
Human Services, 1981)

C. Using the information given in exercise B, prepare a statement of the
things that stutterers cannot do. Try to use a different negative in each
statement. After writing the sentences, share them with another student
to be sure that your statements are accurate. Then, revise them for content. Finally, edit the sentences to be sure that you have used the negative
correctly.

D. Take a textbook that you are studying in a scientific or technical subject. Look through the first chapter to see what negative words are used.
Make a list of five examples using *no*, five examples using *not*, and five
examples of other types of negation. Share that list with the rest of the
class. Write this list in the space given here to use for models when you
are writing your own scientific or technical English.

Examples of No

_____

_____

_____

_____

_____

Examples of Not

_____

_____

_____

_____

Other Negatives

_____

_____

_____

_____

E. Look back over at least two different papers that you have written recently. Were there any problems with the negative? Did you use *no* when *not* was required? Was there any variety in your negative sentences? Did you use anything other than *not* or *no*? If you have problems with particular forms of the negative, be sure to include that information on your list of things that you always edit your papers for. Also, if you are not trying a variety of forms, try something different in the paper that you are currently writing.

CHAPTER 15

Question Formation and Embedded Questions

1 Introduction to Question Formation and Embedded Questions

While the asking of questions is more often a feature of speaking than of writing, you will sometimes use written questions. For example, writers sometimes present a topic sentence in the form of a question. Another use of questions is in quotations or in statements of purpose.

In this project, we wanted to discover what instructors can do to improve student motivation. (The question is What can instructors do to improve student motivation?)

2a Question Formation

Some advanced students continue to have trouble with the grammar of questions (1) when the auxiliary must be moved away from the rest of the verb phrase, or (2) when *do/does/did* must be used. These two problems are related to each other.

2b Moving the Auxiliary

The first auxiliary in the verb phrase is moved in front of the subject to form yes/no questions:

Is he studying business calculus?

Has she gone to the library?

Can I check out this journal?

The first auxiliary in the verb phrase is moved in front of the subject to form information questions when the *wh-* word (*why, when, what,* and others) is *not* the subject of the question. In the first example given below, the *wh-* word is the subject of the sentence, so the auxiliary is not moved. In all the other examples, the *wh-* word has some function other than subject of the sentence, so the auxiliary moves in front of the subject.

subject
Who is going to teach business calculus next term?

      subject
When will we go to the library?

     subject
What is he doing in the lab at this time of day?

2c Adding *Do/Does/Did*

When the verb is a simple present tense or a simple past tense, there is no auxiliary to move in front of the subject. The correct form of *do* must be added as the auxiliary.

Did she go to the library?

Does he know Pascal?

Do you plan to take business calculus?

When do you go to the lab?

Why does the university require health insurance?

Where did you get that calculator?

3a Embedded Questions

While some students continue to have problems with question formation, the most difficult part of written questions for advanced students has to do with the placement of a question inside another sentence. The rules that you so carefully learned for question formation do not apply; the auxiliary does not move; *do/does/did* are not needed.

embedded question

My advisor asked me where I got my data.

My advisor asked me if I spoke Arabic.

The questions are, of course, *Where did you get your data?* and *Do you speak Arabic?* but, when that question is placed inside a sentence, it is changed significantly. The next section of *The Handbook* discusses and illustrates these changes.

3b Formation of Embedded Information Questions

Embedded questions do not follow the usual order for regular questions shown in Sections 2b and 2c on p. 275. Look at these examples:

Question:

When did he begin his research project?

Question embedded in a statement:

His advisor asked him when he began his research project.

Question embedded in another question:

Can you tell me when he began his research project?

When a question is embedded in another sentence (statement or question), the word order does not change to the usual question order and *do, does, or did* is not added.

3c Formation of Embedded Yes-No Questions

As with information questions, embedded yes-no questions do not have the changed word order that you learned to do for questions. In addition, you must add a question word to indicate that a question has been embedded. You can add either *if* or *whether*. Please notice that this meaning of *if* is very different from its use in conditional and hypothetical sentences (see Chapter 5).

Question:

Do you speak Arabic?

Question embedded in a statement:

He asked if I spoke Arabic.

He asked whether I spoke Arabic.

3d Difference Between *If* and *Whether* in Embedded Questions

Some instructors think that *whether* is more formal than *if*. Other instructors think that both are equally formal. In this situation, as in some others, you must ask your instructors their preferences.

Whether can be used in questions for preferences, for example.

Question:

Do you or do you not like calculus?

Embedded question:

She asked whether or not I liked calculus.

In addition, *whether* must be used after prepositions and after *-ing* participles functioning as prepositions:

He inquired as to whether or not the university gave scholarships to foreign students.

I wrote to him regarding whether a scholarship would be possible.

3e Sequence-of-Tense Rules and Embedded Questions

The same rules apply to embedded questions as to indirect quotations. That is, in very formal usage, you might write

Question:

When will the project be finished?

Embedded question:

He asked when the project would be finished.

(If you have any questions about the rules for tense formation for embedded sentences, see Section 12 on p. 75.)

4 EXERCISES: Questions

A. *Brainstorming* is a process that is used by writers to think up ideas on a topic before writing about it. The idea is to think up as many different ideas as possible without judging them as good or bad. After the brainstorming session, then the ideas can be sorted to see which ones are most interesting and useful for the particular writing project.

Try writing as many questions as you can on one of the following topics. Write questions for five minutes without stopping. Try to fill a sheet of paper with questions. Do not edit during the five minutes. After the five minutes, then go over the list to check the grammar. Do the whole thing over again writing on a different topic for five minutes without stopping to edit. Edit the grammar only after you have brainstormed questions for five minutes.

Possible topics are world peace, cancer, AIDS, TOEFL, money, the importance of family life, the city you are living in, the city you came from, or anything else that you would like to have information about.

B. Analyze the errors that you made in writing the questions in exercise A. Do you have any problems? If not, great. If so, add questions to your personal editing list.

C. What is the difference in grammar between questions and embedded questions? Compare these versions of the same question.

1a. *Where did John get this information?*

1b. *The instructor asked where John got this information.*

2a. *Who has the department chosen to teach calculus?*

2b. *The students want to know whom the department has chosen to teach calculus.*

D. Put these questions into the object of the sentence that is begun in parenthesis after the question. Use the formal written tenses unless the meaning would be distorted.

1. Where is the library? (He asked. . . .)

2. When can I expect to hear from you? (The salesman wanted to know. . . .)

3. Why will we be required to complete the project in only six weeks? (The students inquired. . . .)

4. How much time has the research taken so far? (The advisor expected to learn. . . .)

5. Who teaches Business Calculus? *(Careful!)* (The student asked. . . .)

6. What is the name of the text for this course? (She told her friend to ask. . . .)

7. Do you know the teacher's name? (The secretary asked. . . .)

8. Do you prefer physics or astronomy? (The advisor inquired as to. . . .)

E. Turn the sentences that you wrote in exercise D into questions. For example,

1. Did he ask where the library is? *or* Did he ask where the library was?

2. _____

_____

3. _____

_____

4. _____

_____

5. _____

_____

6. _____

_____

7. _____

_____

8. _____

_____

F. Find the embedded questions in the following sentences. Change each embedded question to make it into a regular question. Remember that not all clauses are embedded questions; relative clauses also begin with *who* and *what* along with other relative pronouns.

1. There are approximately 19 million Americans who have serious drinking problems. Why some people have such obvious problems with alcohol and others do not is a question researchers are trying to answer.

2. To find out what is associated with stuttering, investigators are analyzing how speech sounds are normally produced and what goes wrong when a person stutters.

3. While research has yet to explain why stuttering occurs, some new findings have been applied to therapy.

4. A major question of women clericals is where they can get training in office computer skills.

5. To determine if asbestos-containing materials are present in a building, examine construction records and conduct a thorough inspection of building materials.

G. Embedded questions can make effective thesis statements for compositions. In fact, the examples given in exercise F are all thesis statements used by professional writers to establish the topics of their compositions. Listed here are some topics that have been used in essay tests to assess the writing skills of university students. Working with the other students in your class, plan thesis statements for each topic that include embedded questions. One approach to this assignment would be to brainstorm questions raised by each topic. Then, those questions could be embedded in a thesis statement.

1. Explain the reasons you chose to attend this university.

2. Discuss the circumstances in which an employer is justified in firing an employee.

3. Discuss the characteristics of a successful student.

4. Select a profession. Then, explain the responsibilities of members of that profession to society.

H. For any writing that you are currently doing (or planning), talk with your instructor about using an embedded question in the thesis statement. If you decide to use this grammatical form, edit the final version carefully for correct word order.

CHAPTER 16

Comparison

1 Introduction to Comparison

Technically, the word *comparison* refers to statements of similarity. However, in general academic usage, *comparison* is used to refer to both similarities and to differences. If you are instructed to write a paper that is a comparison, you will most likely be expected to address both similarities and differences. It would probably be a good idea to talk with your instructor to be sure of the meaning of the term in that particular context.

Comparison is one of the most common and most useful tools for students and scholars. It is a method that is helpful for both discovery and communication. Researchers use comparison for their investigations; they then use comparison to explain their discoveries.

Indeed, students should find that comparisons are among the easier types of compositions and reports to organize and to collect materials for. This chapter provides patterns and examples for the most common sentence-level comparatives used in English.

2a Similarity

Similarity patterns can be divided into two groups based on meaning and grammar: (1) complete similarity patterns and (2) partial similarity patterns.

2b Complete Similarity: Type 1

The basic sentence is

subject + verb + [*the same as* + noun phrase].

For example,

The final examination is the same as the mid-term.

Thus, the comparison phrase *the same as . . .* serves as the complement of the basic sentence. *The same as . . .* is followed by a noun phrase. Very often the subject and the noun phrase in the complement have possessive noun phrases preceding them in the determiner position.

Jose's book is the same as Nasrollah's book.

Frequently, the noun phrase in the complement is reduced to simply the determiner.

Jose's book is the same as Nasrollah's.

Notice that when a possessive pronoun is used to replace the entire noun phrase in the complement, the determiner form changes, for example *my* becomes *mine.* The forms used are *mine, his, hers, its, ours, yours, theirs.*

Your plans are the same as my plans means *Your plans are the same as mine.*

John's fears are the same as their fears means *John's fears are the same as theirs.*

2c Complete Similarity: Type 2

The basic sentence can be changed to put both of the noun phrases in the subject:

_____ and _____ are the same.

John's plans and my plans are the same.
John's plans and mine are the same.
Our plans are the same.

This can be made more specific by the addition of a noun that names the category that is the same:

Jose's and Sergio's computers are the same price/the same brand/the same power.
These flowers are the same color/the same shape.

2d Complete Similarity: Type 3

Another complete similarity sentence is

subject + verb + [the same _____ as _____].

For example,

Jose's computer is the same brand as Nasrollah's.

The same . . . is followed by a noun that names the category that is being compared. The purpose of this sentence is to focus on one characteristic that two items share.

2e Complete Similarity: Type 4

Another complete similarity sentence is

subject + verb + as _____ as _____.

For example,

This computer is as powerful as that one.

John's computer was as expensive as Jose's computer.

John's computer was as expensive as Jose's.

As . . . as . . . gives an adjective and then the noun phrase.

2f Partial Similarity

The most general type of partial similarity uses *alike* in the complement. The two items to be compared are in the subject position:

subject + verb + *alike.*

The verb is usually a form of *be;* however, other verbs are possible: *seem, taste, feel.*

Jose's and John's computers are alike.

These books are alike.

You and your mother seem alike.

The usual response to this very general statement is "How?" or "In what ways?" A reader will ask questions like these and will expect a writer to go beyond such generalities. An answer can be formed by adding *in +* noun to the basic sentence:

Jose's and John's computers are alike in price.

These books are alike in size.

You and your mother seem alike in temperament.

Or, the answer can change to a more specific verb:

These flowers smell alike.

These drinks taste alike.

Those students act alike.

3a Differences

The most general patterns use the verb *differ* or its adjective form *different* plus [*from +* noun phrase]:

Jose's computer differs from John's computer.

Jose's computer differs from John's.

Jose's computer is different from John's computer.

Jose's computer is different from John's.

When *different* is in the complement, the verb is usually a form of *be*, but it can be any verb that can have an adjective in its complement (*taste, smell, sound, seem, appear*).

Jose's computer seems different from mine.

Jose's computer looks different from mine.

Because these statements are so general, they are frequently supported with specifics. These specifics can be added to the basic sentence with [*in +* noun phrase]:

Jose's computer differs from mine in size, power, and cost.

A more common version of this sentence moves both of the things compared into the subject position:

Jose's computer and mine differ in size, power, and cost.

3b Making Differences More Specific

Differences can be drawn more specifically by using comparative forms of adjectives and adverbs in the complement:

subject + verb + comparative + *than* + noun phrase.

For example,

Jose's computer seems more powerful than my computer.
His computer is more expensive than mine.

3c Comparative Forms of Adjectives and Adverbs

The rules for forming the comparatives of adjectives and adverbs are as follows:

1. One-syllable adjectives and adverbs: _____ + *-er*.
    fast—faster
    slow—slower
    tall—taller
    short—shorter
    kind—kinder

2. Two-syllable adjectives ending in *-y* use *-er*; *y* becomes *i*.
    friendly—friendlier
    busy—busier

3. All other adjectives and adverbs use *more*. *More* + adjective forms a unit that precedes a noun—when it is used with a noun.
    Detroit is a more industrial city than Atlanta.
    Detroit is more industrial than Atlanta.
    beautiful—more beautiful
    clever—more clever

    The word *less* can be used with adjectives and adverbs in the comparative pattern with *than* to add the meaning "not more."

Computer A is less expensive than Computer B. Or, *Computer B is more expensive than Computer A.*

In all of the above comparisons only two items are compared. It is possible to compare three or more items. These difference comparisons use *-est* and *most* to form the comparison. The writer is establishing a set that runs from the *least* through the average up to the *most*.

John was the youngest student in the class while Jose was the oldest. (All of the other students are placed on a continuum between John and Jose.)

The formation rules parallel those for *-er/more*.

1. Single-syllable adjectives and adverbs take *-est*.

   fast—fastest

   slow—slowest

   tall—tallest

2. Two-syllable adjectives that end in *y* take *-est; y* becomes *i*.

   friendly—friendliest

   busy—busiest

3. All other forms use *most*.

   most quickly

   most intelligent

When *most* and *-est* forms are used in comparison, the article *the* is normally required. Look at the difference between these two sentences:

You are older than your brother. (You have only one brother.)

You are the oldest student in the class.

It is possible to use the *-est/most* forms for emphasis even where there are only two items, especially with the irregular *best* (*good, better, best*) and *worst* (*bad, worse, worst*).

We both gave good reports, but yours was best.

Americans like to be emphatic and will use *best* and *worst* even when they do not really have much evidence for the contrast.

This is the best car in the world.

You are my very best friend.

This is the worst hamburger in town.

In academic writing, it is not a very good idea to use this unrestrained style—professors like to see evidence for claims of distinction.

4 EXERCISES: Comparison

A. Section 2a through Section 3c of this chapter give the basic patterns that are needed to make comparisons in English. The general patterns make good topic sentences for paragraphs or for whole papers or reports. The more specific patterns are then used to explain the generalities. Use a highlighter to mark all of the comparison sentences in these passages. Which sentences are topic or thesis sentences? Which sentences are used to develop the topic or thesis?

TEMPERATURE DIFFERENCES AMONG THE GIANT PLANETS

The temperature differences among the giant planets are due to differences in solar heating and to the amount of energy coming independently from the interiors of the planets. At the level where the total pressure is equal to one atmosphere, the temperature of Jupiter is about 166 K (-160 degrees F.) and the temperature of Saturn is about 91 K (-295 degrees F.). Uranus and Neptune are both roughly 72 K (-330 degrees F.) at the same pressure level. The temperatures of both Jupiter and Saturn are known to change with position on the planet and with season. The surface temperature of Pluto is estimated at 55 K (-360 degrees F.), and its surface pressure is at least 0.0001 atmosphere.

Adapted from the "Solar System" (*New Encyclopaedia Britannica*, 1986)

A COMPARISON OF THE ATMOSPHERES OF VENUS AND MARS

The chemical composition of the atmospheres of Venus and Mars are similar. The atmosphere of Venus is 96 percent CO_2 and 3.5 percent N_2 (molecular nitrogen); Mars is 95 percent CO_2 and 2.7 percent N_2 with another 1.6 percent Ar (argon). In contrast, Earth's atmosphere is 77 percent N_2, 21 percent O_2 (molecular oxygen), 1 percent H_2O, and 0.93 percent Ar. The remainder of the composition of each atmosphere is shared by several species of chemicals. For Venus the most abundant of these are SO_2 (sulfur dioxide), H_2O, Ar, and CO (carbon monoxide); for Earth they are CO_2, Ne (neon), and He (helium); and for Mars they are O_2, CO, and H_2O.

Adapted from the "Solar System" (*New Encyclopaedia Britannica*, 1986)

Comparative Forms of Adjectives and Adverbs   **287**

A COMPARISON OF EARTH AND VENUS:
SIMILARITIES AND DIFFERENCES

The Earth and Venus have been described as sister planets because their sizes, masses, and densities are roughly the same. Both have extensive atmospheres, but the composition of these are not the same. Venus has no moon. It is difficult to take the comparison further owing to observational difficulties caused by the extensive cloud cover over Venus. Surface relief and the existence of various landforms such as mountains, volcanoes, craters, and rift valleys have been discovered by radar. Oceans cannot exist on Venus because of the high surface temperature of about 730 K.

Adapted from the "Solar System" (*New Encyclopaedia Britannica*, 1986)

SIMILARITIES BETWEEN MARS AND EARTH

Mars, though smaller than Earth, has some similarities, and more extensive photographic coverage in the 1970s revealed the presence of many features on Mars that may have similar origins to those of their counterparts on Earth. Results from space probes sent to Mars and from radar studies have allowed some direct comparisons between planetary details. Many Martian features indicate ancient fluvial erosion, widespread volcanism, and extensive tectonics. Large areas resembling groups of calderas and craters have been photographed. Further, rifts and cracks in long double and single nearly straight lines and areas of intersecting sets of parallel rift systems have been found on Mars. All these can be matched on Earth.

Adapted from the "Solar System" (*New Encyclopaedia Britannica*, 1986)

B. In the space provided below, write example sentences on a topic from your field of study to illustrate each of the types of comparison sentences.

Complete Similarity Sentences

1. _____

_____

2. _____

_____

3. _____

_____

4. _____

_____

Partial Similarity Sentence

5. _____

_____

Sentences about Differences

6. _____

_____

7. _____

_____

8. _____

_____

9. _____

_____

5 Adding Variety to Written Comparisons

There are many ways to modify or change the basic comparison sentence. The following is a list of ways you can make your comparisons more exact or can give them more variety.

Numerous single-word modifiers can be used in comparison sentences either to reduce the amount of similarity or difference or to make the similarity or difference stronger.

1. *Almost, nearly, about, approximately, somewhat,* and *a little* reduce the strength of the comparison.

   My report is approximately the same length as yours.

2. *Just* and *exactly* are used to make similarity statements stronger by saying that there are no differences between the items. They emphasize the completeness of the similarity.

   My report is exactly the same length as John's.

3. *Quite, rather,* and *very* can be used to make comparisons stronger by adding emphasis to adjectives such as *different* and *similar. Entirely, completely,* and *totally* are very strong; they mean there are no similarities or differences at all.

   My report is very different from yours.

   Our ideas are quite similar on this issue.

   Our reports are completely different in content and design.

   John's research and mine have entirely the same results.

4. *Similar* can be substituted for *alike.*

   Our reports are similar in length.

5. *Like* can be used in a sentence that means the same as the sentence with *alike.*

   Our reports are alike. = My report is like your report.

6. The sentence with *as . . . as . . .* can be changed to include an indefinite noun phrase that has *a* in the determiner position.

   My report is as good as your report. = It is as good a report as yours.

7. The comparative adjective can be inside the noun phrase.

   Jose's report is a better study than John's report.

8. The following sentences are used to say that one item has two characteristics. However, the item has more of one of them than of the other.

   He is wider than he is tall.

   He is more intelligent than practical.

   This experiment was more expensive than productive.

   That book is more attractive on the outside than interesting on the inside.

9. There is a cause-result sentence that uses *-er/more* forms of adjectives and adverbs. These sentences mean that an increase in the first causes an increase in the second. (It is possible to use *less* to alter the terms of the relationship.)

The more you work, the more you learn.

The bigger they are, the harder they fall.

The closer a comet comes to the sun, the longer its tail becomes.

6 EXERCISES: Comparison and Difference

A. Plan and write at least five sentences that describe the similarities and differences of oxygen and hydrogen. Use the following information and any additional information that you might have. After you have compared your sentences to those of other students in the class, select the best ones to put together to make a short comparison composition.

Oxygen
atomic weight = 15.9994
atomic number = 8
odorless
invisible
tasteless
gas
most abundant element in the earth's crust
boiling point = -182 degrees C
needed for combustion and respiration
not flammable

Hydrogen
atomic weight = 1.00797
atomic number = 1
odorless
invisible
tasteless
gas
lightest substance known
inflammable
most abundant element in the universe
boiling point = -252.87 degrees C

B. Write at least five sentences to explain the differences between photosynthesis and respiration. Use this list and any other information that you might have. Compare your sentences to those of other students in the class. As a group, select a set of these sentences to turn into a paragraph by the addition of a topic sentence and connecting words.

Photosynthesis

occurs only in light

stores energy in food

occurs only in green cells

reacting substances: water and carbon dioxide

products: glucose and oxygen

Respiration

occurs in light and in darkness

releases energy from foods

occurs in all living cells

reacting substances: glucose and oxygen

products: carbon dioxide and water

C. Select any of the following example sets or suggest a set that interests you. First make lists of the characteristics of each part individually; then, compare the two parts in sentences that give their similarities as well as their differences.

Possible Sets:

knife/fork

accounting/bookkeeping

Coke/Pepsi

high school/university

breakfast/lunch

urban life/rural life in your country

sun/moon

breakfast in your country/breakfast in the U.S.

D. Plan and write a composition in which you explain the function of a hook by comparing a hook to a human hand.

E. How is an airplane like a bird? Plan and write a paragraph that compares airplanes to birds.

F. How is something mechanical like something living? Work with another student to think of sets like the one in exercise E—computer/human brain, for example. Try to think of three clever ones to share with the class. From the class list, select your favorite to analyze as in exercises A and B. Then, write comparison and contrast sentences based on your analysis.

CHAPTER 17

Clauses

1 Introduction to Clauses

A clause is a group of words with a subject and a verb. Clauses can be divided into two major types—independent and dependent. An independent clause can be a complete sentence by itself. A dependent clause is a part of a sentence; it cannot be used by itself but must be combined with an independent clause. Dependent clauses include noun clauses, adverbial clauses, and relative clauses.

English has a variety of ways to make sentences of greater complexity. We can use compounding. We can add more and more words to noun phrases or verb phrases. One major device is to use one sentence as part of another sentence. This process is sometimes called *subordination* when words like *although* are used to make complex sentences.

Although he studied with great dedication, he was not able to pass the calculus test.

A very similar process is called *embedding*: One sentence is embedded in another. In this example, the embedded clause is called a *relative clause*. It is also sometimes called an *adjective clause* because it functions like an adjective—it modifies the meaning of a noun.

The project used data that was collected by the Census Bureau.

Sentence 1: *The project used data.*

Sentence 2: *The data was collected by the Census Bureau.*

Relative clause: *that was collected by the Census Bureau*

Noun that is modified: *data*

　　Another embedding method is to use a clause in place of a noun. Naturally enough, these clauses are called *noun clauses.*

subject　　　　　　　　　　verb　　　complement
That he was very unhappy was clear to everyone.

　subject　　　　　　　　　　　　verb　　　complement
What method to use in this project is a complicated question.

subject　　verb　　　　　　　　　　DO
We must find out when and where Ramses II lived.

2a Noun Clauses

English has many important verbs that can be followed by *that* plus a complete sentence. These verbs, then, can have complete sentences embedded as their direct objects. Clauses that function as nouns are called *noun clauses.* Since *that* is a connecting word and not a grammatical part of the embedded sentence, it does not have to be used.

The student newspaper reported that tuition will increase next fall.

The student newspaper reported tuition will increase next fall.

Verbs for Reporting Speech　These verbs have this grammar: *inform, report, say, tell (someone).*

Verbs that Refer to Mental Activities　These verbs also can be followed by *(that)* plus a sentence: *believe, complain, decide, dream, expect, find out, forget, hope, know, learn, notice, predict, pretend, realize, regret, remember, show, suppose, think, understand.*

Adjectives Followed by *that* Plus a Sentence　*That* is required in written English—although you may not hear it in spoken English. Notice in examples 3a and 4a that *it* is used in the subject to create a less personal statement.

1a. *I am unhappy that the report was not completed on time.*

2a. *He is confused that his check has not yet arrived from home.*

3a. *It is surprising that his check has not yet arrived from home.*

4a. *It is amusing that he cannot remember where he parked his car.*

Note: A different set of adjectives can require the subjunctive form in formal English. These are discussed in Chapter 4. For example,

It is important that the project be finished on schedule.

You will also very often see sentences using this form: *It is a . . . fact that . . .*

5a. *It is a well-known fact that the White House is a wonderful place to live.*

6a. *It is a disturbing fact that over 50 percent of marriages end in divorce.*

7a. *It is an amusing/unhappy/ironic/unfortunate/irritating fact that . . .*

***That* Clauses as Subject of a Sentence**   This use is very formal and not very common. In this use, *that* is required. Notice that these sentences usually have this grammar: subject + *be* + adjective. Another common pattern is: subject + *be* + *a fact*. Compare these examples to 3a and 4a above.

3b. *That his check has not yet arrived from home is surprising.*

4b. *That he cannot remember where he parked his car is amusing.*

2b EXERCISES: Noun Clauses

A. Find a copy of today's *New York Times, Washington Post,* or of the most recent *Christian Science Monitor.* Your school's library will have one. Write sentences about facts reported on the front page. Select appropriate adjectives to modify *fact—amusing, unhappy, infuriating, sobering, frightening.*

It is a well-known fact that The New York Times *claims to print all the news that is fit to print.*

B. Turn those sentences around, use the *that* clause as subject.

That The New York Times *claims to print all the news that is fit to print is a well-known fact.*

C. While reading the *Times,* look for examples of *that* clauses. What functions do they have? Subject? Object? Share your list with the rest of the class. Write the verbs that you find in the space provided on p. 297 to use when you are writing your own papers.

_____

_____

_____

_____

2c Noun Clauses with Question Words

Information questions (those using *who, what, when,* and other *wh-* words) can be embedded in sentences as subjects. More often they are used as objects of the verb. See Chapter 15 for exercises to practice writing embedded questions.

1a. *What is the purpose of this project?*

object of *understand*

1b. *We need to understand what the purpose of the project is.*

2a. *Who will teach Business Calculus next fall?*

subject

2b. *Who will teach Business Calculus next fall has not been decided.*

2d Noun Clauses with *Whether* or *If*

Yes-no questions can be embedded as subjects and objects of sentences by using *whether* or *if* as the subordinating word. (See Chapter 15 for more information and exercises for embedded questions.)

1a. *Is the report due on the last day of class?*

1b. *The students asked if the report was due on the last day of class.*

1c. *If the report was due on the last day of class was asked by the students.* (Notice that a passive sentence can be created.)

2a. *Does the university have modern computing services?*

2b. *I wonder whether or not the university has modern computing services.*

2c. *Whether or not the university has modern computing services is an extremely important question for researchers.*

3a Adverbial Clauses

A very useful type of clause adds information about time, manner, reason, place, purpose, and other adverbial meanings. (See Chapter 12 for more information on meanings and uses of adverbs and adverbials.)

Here are three examples of adverbial clauses:

adverbial clause
The library closed before I could finish my research.

adverbial clause
He is studying English because he wants to study engineering.

adverbial clause
Although he studied hard, he failed to make an "A."

Writers can have three problems with adverbial clauses:

—Punctuation when the adverbial clause comes at the beginning of a sentence

—Verb form when the verb in the independent clause is future time, especially with *will*

—Creation of fragments by using adverbial clauses as independent sentences

The category "adverbial clause" also includes other areas that are discussed elsewhere in *The Handbook*. For example, comparative clauses, conditional clauses, and hypothetical clauses can be considered subcategories of the adverbial. Check the Index for references to these subjects.

3b Punctuation of Adverbial Clauses

If the adverbial clause is attached to the end of an independent clause, no punctuation is added. Look at these examples:

He studies in the library after his last class is over.

He studies in the library although it is very noisy.

If the adverbial clause is moved to the beginning of the sentence as an *introductory clause,* then a comma must be added to separate it from the independent clause.

After his last class is over, he studies in the library.

Although it is very noisy, he studies in the library.

3c Verbs in Future Time
Adverbial Clauses

When the sentence is about future time, usually the verb in the adverbial clause is in simple present tense.

We will go *to the library when class* is *over.*

The new tuition will go *into effect when the fall quarter* begins.

However, there are special cases when the "determination/willfulness" or "promise" meanings of *will* are used in the adverbial clause, especially in conditional sentences:

I will talk *with the professor about changing the test date if* you will go *with me.* (This means "I promise if you promise" so the meaning is more than simply "future time.")

3d Adverbial Clauses
as Sentence Fragments

A third problem many students have with adverbial clauses is trying to use them as independent sentences. They are dependent clauses and must be combined with an independent clause to make a sentence. By themselves, they are only *fragments* as in this example:

▼ *Because he wants to study engineering in the U.S. He is studying English.*

Because he wants to study engineering in the U.S., he is studying English.

3e Commonly Used
Adverbial Connectors

You already know many of these. Work with your instructor and other students in the class to make the list more complete. Space has been left to write the words on the following chart.

1. Time: *after, as, as soon as, before*

2. Reason: *because*

3. Purpose: *in order that*

4. Place: *wherever*

5. Concession: *although*

6. Manner: *as though*

3f EXERCISES: Adverbial Clauses

A. Sentences frequently involve subordinate clauses that are added to give time. If you and your class have not completed the chart in Section 3e, do so at this point. Notice that many more connectors are available to write about time. Write 10 sentences on a topic of your choice using an adverbial clause of time in each sentence. Work with another student first to revise the sentences for meaning and then edit them for correct use of the adverbial clause. After you have revised and edited both sets of sentences, share them with the class.

B. Adverbial clauses are also used to give reasons, causes, and results. The conjunctions used include *because* and many others. Write five sentences on a topic of your choice using the adverbial clauses to express the reasons for something. Since not as many connectors are available, you may need to use the same connecting word more than once. Follow the process described in exercise A for writing, revising, editing, and sharing of your sentences.

C. Write a passage in which you explain an important event in the history of your major field of study. If necessary, look for information in the library to make your passage more exact. Use at least five adverbial clauses.

D. Look back at several long passages you have written recently. Do any errors with adverbial clauses occur? If you have any problems with this area, add it to your personal editing list.

4a Restrictive Relative Clauses

Relative clauses are divided into two major types. *Restrictive relative clauses* provide necessary information and are tightly tied to their sentences. *Nonrestrictive relative clauses* add extra information and are not essential to their sentences.

Since restrictive relative clauses are much more common and much more important than nonrestrictive relative clauses, *The Handbook* focuses primarily on restrictive relative clauses.

Many nouns in most functions can have a sentence attached as a restrictive relative clause—subjects, objects of verbs, objects of prepositions, and even possessives. Just about any noun in any function can be moved to the front of the embedded sentence to make the restrictive relative clause. This chapter will present relative clauses in this order: (1) relative clauses in the subject, (2) relative clauses in the object of the verb and preposition, and (3) other types of relative clauses.

To make a relative clause, you change a sentence by replacing some noun phrase with a relative pronoun: *who, which, whom, whose,* or *that.* You will remember that *who* or *whom* refer to human beings. *Which* can be used for nonhuman meanings—both animal and nonanimal. *That* can be used for all meanings. *Whom* is used in very formal English to replace an objective noun. *Whose* is used when the relative pronoun replaces a possessive noun phrase.

4b Relative Clauses in the Subjects of Sentences

Analyze these two sentences. Mark them for subject, verb, object.

1. *The book costs $27.*

2. *The book is required for Business Calculus.*

Obviously, *the book* is subject of both sentences. To combine these two sentences, the second sentence is changed into a relative clause. Since *the book* is nonhuman, you have the choice of *that* or *which* as the relative pronoun.

that

The book is required for Business Calculus.

that is required for Business Calculus (Sentence 2 is changed into a relative clause.)

The book that is required for Business Calculus *costs $27.* (The relative clause is placed inside sentence 1.)

Do this one yourself:

The computer seems too expensive for a student to buy.

The computer was recommended in the magazine.

Relative clause: _____

New sentence: _____

Analyze these two sentences:

The book costs $27.

I lost the book.

In this combination, the second sentence will once again become part of the subject of the first sentence—just as in the first example. But, the relative clause is different because *the book* is the direct object of the embedded sentence.

I lost the book.	Make this into a relative clause.
I lost that	Substitute *that* for *the book.*
that I lost	Move *that* to the front of the relative clause.
The book that I lost costs $27.	Put the relative clause in the subject of the first sentence.

Do this one yourself:

The paperwork took eight hours to complete.

The university requires the paperwork for admission.

Relative clause: _____

New sentence: _____

4c Relative Clauses in Objects of Verbs and Prepositions

It is also possible for the relative clause to be put into the direct object of the basic sentence.

I lost the book.

      that   costs $27
The book costs $27.

        DO
I lost the book that costs $27.

Do this one yourself:

I lost the book.
I need the book for class tomorrow.

Relative clauses can be used with nouns after prepositions:

I am looking for the book that I lost.

Do this one yourself:

This information is important for the report.
The report will determine 50 percent of the grade for this course.

Relative clauses can be used in indirect objects:

            IO
The janitor gave the book to the student who had lost it.

Do this one yourself:

The instructor gave a failing grade to the student.
The student did not complete the research project.

4d Relative Clauses and Possessive Nouns—*Whose*

Relative clauses can also involve possessive nouns.

The student thanked the janitor.

whose   book was returned
The student's book was returned.

The student whose book was returned thanked the janitor.

Do this one yourself:

The country will have better economic life.
The country's citizens have better physical health.

_____

_____

4e Relative Clauses Inside Relative Clauses

Since nearly every noun can have a relative clause and since relative clauses can contain nouns, very complex sentences can be built. You might have heard the children's rhyme about Jack's house:

> This is the farmer sowing the corn,
> That kept the cock that crowed in the morn,
> That waked the priest all shaven and shorn,
> That married the man all tattered and torn,
> That kissed the maiden all forlorn,
> That milked the cow with the crumpled horn,
> That tossed the dog,
> That worried the cat,
> That killed the rat,
> That ate the malt,
> That lay in the house that Jack built.

Serious sentences in serious academic writing can also have relative clauses inside of relative clauses:

Their fundamental argument was to the effect that* the social signifi-cance of many objective conditions could not be ascertained without taking into account their perceived meaning and importance to the people who were directly involved.

1. The social significance of many objective conditions could not be ascertained without taking into account their perceived meaning and importance to the people . . . .

2. The people were directly involved.

4f EXERCISES: Restrictive Relative Clauses

A. Combine these sets of sentences. The first five are simple but do them anyway as a review. Then combine the sentences from the passages that follow.

1. The research project cost $1,000,000.
   The research project led to these important results.

2. The research project was finished after two years of work.
   The government financed the research project.

3. I am working on a research project.
   The research project could improve health care in rural Africa.

4. I am working on a research project.
   I have been interested in the research project for many years.

5. I am working as assistant to a medical doctor.
   The doctor's speciality is infectious diseases.

WORKING WIVES

6. Some wives tend to have professional and managerial positions.
   These wives earn more than their husbands.

7. However, this group is a minority of couples.
   Both the husbands and wives in these couples work.

8. It is a fact.
   Husbands usually earn more than their working wives.

9. How many of the 4 million wives were permanently surpassing their husbands in earnings?
   These wives earned more than their husbands in 1981.

---

*This sentence uses a *that* clause built on the phrase *to the effect that.* . . .

10. That year about 1.95 million wives earned more than their husbands.
    These husbands were full-time, year-round workers.

11. This suggests that half of the wives might earn more on a sustained basis.
    These wives outperformed their husbands.

Adapted from *Wives Who Earn More Than Their Husbands* (Bianchi, 1983)

COMPLAINTS

12. Many people can remember a time when they knew nearly everyone.
    They did business with everyone.

13. If the butcher sold them meat, they complained.
    The meat smelled funny when they unwrapped it for dinner.

14. This booklet was written to help you understand and use the consumer rights and power.
    You have these rights and power at your disposal.

15. It explains major rights.
    The Federal Trade Commission has set down these rights for people.
    These people find it easier to buy from door-to-door or mail order sellers.

16. This booklet also suggests other action.
    You can take these actions to make sure something is done.
    Your rights are respected.

17. But before you can exercise the power, you first must realize something.
    The law gives you the power.
    You can complain if the product is faulty.

Adapted from *How to Write a Wrong: Complain Effectively and Get Results* (American Association of Retired Persons with the U.S. Federal Trade Commission, undated)

B. Analyze these sentences in the following passage. What relative clauses can you find? Not every sentence has a relative clause.

MORE ON COMPLAINTS

We owe it to ourselves to complain. We owe it to the seller who might improve the business. And we owe it to others who may benefit from our complaint. Knowing when to complain is largely a matter of common sense and knowing your rights. All big companies have professional buyers or purchasing agents whose only job is to get the very best buys for their companies. When you shop for yourself, you are your own purchasing agent. Your responsibility is to use methods that get you what you pay for. It is important to remember that you are the one who paid for this product or service, and you are the one who must live with its defects or shortcomings.

Adapted from *How to Write a Wrong: Complain Effectively and Get Results* (American Association of Retired Persons with the U.S. Federal Trade Commission, undated)

C. In today's newspaper, find a story that is interesting to you. Analyze it for examples of relative clauses. Share your discoveries with another student and with your instructor.

D. Look at the corrections you have made on a long composition that you have written recently. Do any of those corrections involve relative clauses? For example, have you used too many very short sentences that could be combined? Did you use the wrong word order? Did you use the wrong relative pronoun? If your analysis shows that you have problems with relative clauses, add them to your personal editing list.

5a Nonrestrictive Relative Clauses

Clauses can be used to give additional information that is not required for the meaning of the noun phrase.

President Eisenhower, who was in office in the 1950s, developed his managerial style while in the Army.

There has been only one President Eisenhower in the history of the United States. The phrase *who was in office in the 1950s* gives extra information but does not identify President Eisenhower. If the clause modifies a proper noun, it is always nonrestrictive.

However, you might see a sentence like the following:

The John Smith that I know is not the John Smith that you know.

In this sentence, the writer is actually changing the proper noun *John Smith* into a common noun—it is no longer the name of an individual. Since the name is used by two different people, the writer uses restrictive relative clauses to limit the meaning.

The more difficult type of nonrestrictive clause involves sentences such as these.

1. *The students who took the test passed the course.*

2. *The students, who took the test, passed the course.*

In sentence 1, the writer means that two types of students exist—those who took the test and those who did not take the test. Only the students who took the test passed the course. In sentence 2, all the students took the test; all the students passed the course.

Try these two. How are they different?

1. *The students who ran in the race were very tired.*

2. *The students, who ran in the race, were very tired.*

Nonrestrictive relative clauses are always marked with commas—be careful to use two commas if the clause comes in the middle of a sentence. (See Section 3a on p. 338 for more information on the use of commas.)

That cannot be used to refer to human beings in nonrestrictive relative clauses:

▼ *President Eisenhower, that was in office from . . .*

5b EXERCISES: Nonrestrictive Relative Clauses

A. For practice with proper names, select 10 famous people in your country or around the world. Think of two things that you know about each person. Then, write sentences about those people. Share your sentences with the rest of the class. You might find it helpful to work with other students from your country to remember important facts about important people.

Muhammad Ali: boxer, brain damage

Edgar Allan Poe: writer of stories, died poor

Muhammad Ali, who was a skillful boxer, seems to have suffered some brain damage.

Edgar Allan Poe, who was a famous writer of stories, was very poor when he died.

B. In the *Encyclopaedia Britannica* find the article about your home country. In the article, find nonrestrictive relative clauses. Bring the ones you find to class. (By the way, was the article accurate in its presentation of your country?)

6a Relative Clauses with *Why, When, Where*

Look at these examples:

We need to know the time at which the examination will begin.

We need to know the place in which the examination will be given.

We need to know the reason for which the examination will be given.

These relative clauses have to do with time, place, and reason. The combination of preposition + *which* can be replaced by *when, where,* or *why.*

We need to know the time when the examination will begin.

We need to know the place where the examination will be given.

We need to know the reason why the examination will be given.

These clauses with *when, where,* and *why* are acceptable in written English, but are usually considered less formal than the preposition + *which* versions.

Some authorities do not like *the time when, the place where,* or *the reason why* because they are redundant. That is, *time* and *when, place* and *where,* and *reason* and *why* mean the same thing. Therefore, these people prefer to leave out either one word or the other:

We need to know the time the examination will begin.

We need to know when the examination will begin.

We need to know the place the examination will be given.

We need to know where the examination will be given.

We need to know the reason the examination will be given.

We need to know why the examination will be given.

6b EXERCISE: Relative Clauses with *Why, When, Where*

Combine these sentences first with the preposition + *which.* Then, change them to use *when, where,* or *why.*

SET A

1. A good news article tells the time.
   Something happens at that time.

2. A good news article tells the place.
   Something occurs at that place.

3. However, even a good news article seldom reveals the true reasons. Something happens for those reasons.

SET B

1. This report has many purposes, but the most important of them is to report the reasons.

   These are the reasons that the accident at the nuclear power plant occurred.

2. However, before reporting the reasons, we must provide the reader with background information that makes these reasons easier to understand.

   The reasons are for the accident.

3. First, the report describes the place in the plant.

   The accident began in that place.

4. Second, the time factor is discussed by revealing the connections between the times.

   Different parts of the safety system broke down at those times.

7a Reduction of Relative Clauses

Writers of English frequently make relative clauses shorter by leaving out certain words. This reduction makes the clauses much more compact and leads to a writing style that is valued by educated writers.

7b Leaving Out the Relative Pronoun

If the relative pronoun substitutes for the subject of the embedded sentence, you *must* keep it. In all other cases, the relative pronoun can be left out.

The book that is required for Business Calculus costs $27. (*That* is the subject of embedded sentence—it must be kept.)

The book that I lost costs $27. (*That* is the direct object of the embedded sentence—it can be left out.)

The book I lost costs $27.

I am looking for the book that I lost. (Can *that* be left out? Explain.)

The janitor gave the book to the student who lost it. (Can *who* be left out? Explain.)

7c EXERCISES: Reduction of Relative Clauses

A. Look at the sentences that are combined in exercise A in Section 6b on p. 309. Can the relative pronoun be left out of any of these sentences?

B. Remove *that* and *who* where possible in the following passage.

A BLIND AMERICAN

Because the people *that* I met recently in China were so kind and generous, I had not one bit of apprehension.* When we were going through the Forbidden City, we had to climb many steps, and I cannot walk very well. We had a wheelchair as well as a cane, and my husband, Charlie, would take me up the steps and then go back down for the wheelchair. While waiting for Charlie at the top of the platform, I decided *that* I would try to walk some, but I found *that* walking was impossible because of the big traveling bag *that* I was carrying. A Chinese man came over to me and put out his hand to help me; without one moment's hesitation, I gave my bag to him to hold for me. He not only carried my bag, but he held my arm most of the way down. When I got down to the bottom, I got into the wheelchair, with many Chinese people watching with great interest. Charlie bent down to release the one brake *that* he usually uses and the fellow *who* had helped me touched Charlie on the shoulder to tell him *that* he had put on the second brake and it would have to be released as well. Now can you imagine my purse in the hands of a complete stranger? I had absolute confidence *that* I did not have to worry about it. Everyone was kind, especially the tour bus drivers, *who* helped Charlie figure out a simple way to fold up the wheelchair on the bus.

One time we were at the Great Wall, which I could not attempt to climb. I waited in the bus with the driver, *who* took out a book and said

---

*The writer is an elderly American woman who is almost completely blind and who usually has a lot of trouble walking. A "talking book" is a cassette tape on which someone reads a book.

to me, "How are you?" He was studying English, so we had a whole lesson during our wait. *That* was an interesting experience.

If you go to China, you can take a talking book along with you. I took my cassette player because I knew *that* there would be times when I would be too tired to go out and there would be places *that* I could not go because of problems involved in walking.

Adapted from "Rhea Melov" (The U.S. Library of Congress, 1982)

C. In each passage, the place where a relative pronoun has been left out is marked _____. Decide if the reduction was grammatical. If you find a mistake, add the correct word.

FARMING AND AMERICAN INDIANS

The ownership and control of land is the most important issue

_____ faces American Indians. Indians hold title to

vast tracts of agricultural land _____ is not being

farmed by Indians. The profit on the land _____ is

being farmed by native Americans is nearly half what it is for non-Indian

farmers.

Adapted from *Indian Tribes: A Continuing Quest for Survival* (U.S. Commission on Civil Rights, 1961)

FREE SAMPLES!

There are only two kinds of merchandise _____ legally

can be sent to you through the mail without your consent. They are free

samples _____ are clearly labeled as "free" and goods

_____ are mailed by charities seeking contributions—

such items as key rings or other small gifts. You can keep these items, and

it is illegal for any seller to try to bill you for something _____

_____ you did not order. Always ask the seller for

proof _____ you placed the order.

There are many ways to send things these days besides the U.S. Postal Service. United Parcel Service (UPS) is one of them. If you get something _____ is delivered by a private delivery service _____ you did not order, you must do two things before you can keep the item: (1) You must tell the sender _____ you received merchandise _____ you did not order, preferably in writing so you can prove it later if you are billed. (2) You must give the sender a reasonable amount of time, such as 30 days, to pick up the merchandise at the sender's expense. Tell the sender what you will do with the merchandise if it is not picked up—keep it, toss it out, whatever.

_____

Adapted from *How to Right a Wrong: Complain Effectively and Get Results* (American Association of Retired Persons with the U.S. Federal Trade Commission, undated)

7d Relative Clause Reduction When the Verb of the Embedded Sentence Is *Be* or *Be* Is the Auxiliary Verb

Analyze the embedded sentences in these two examples:

The book that is required for Business Calculus costs $27.
The student who is on the research team is majoring in finance.

The relative clauses both have *be* in the verb phrase. The first example is a passive verb, and the second has *be* as the main verb.

that is required for Business Calculus
who is on the research team

In both of these situations, the relative pronoun and the form of *be* can be left out to reduce the relative clause. This is true of passives in perfective, too.

required for Business Calculus
The book required for Business Calculus costs $27.

on the research team

The student on the research team is majoring in finance.

The text that has been required since 1975 needs significant revision.

The text required since 1975 needs significant revision.

Relative clauses that have progressive verbs can also be reduced by removing the relative pronoun and the auxiliary *be*.

The student who is majoring in finance will be on the research team.

The student majoring in finance will be on the research team.

7e EXERCISES: Relative Clause Reduction When the Verb Is *Be*

A. Combine the sentences in this introduction to a report on health issues. The writer is telling the kinds of charts that will be given in the report. Do the full form first. Then, decide if a reduction is possible—if so, write the reduced sentence.

---

1. The charts show major trends.
   The charts are in this book.

2. The first charts describe the increase in longevity.
   The longevity has been realized by Americans since 1960.

3. These charts are followed by a section of charts.
   These charts describe the health status of infants, children, and young adults.

4. The next section shows trends.
   These trends are in the availability and utilization of health resources.

5. It is followed by a section of charts.
   These charts are on selected dangers to human health.

Adapted from *Charting the Nation's Health: Trends Since 1960* (U.S. Department of Health and Human Services, 1985)

B. Combine the sentences in this passage about changes in smoking habits in the U.S. Make any reductions that are possible.

---

1. The number of cigarette smokers has shown a major decline since the first Surgeon General's Report on Smoking and Health.

   The report was released in 1964.

2. Even the relatively sharp rise in smoking among teenage females has since been curbed.

   The relatively sharp rise in smoking among teenage females occurred in the mid-to-late 1970s.

3. A major pattern in smoking behavior is a convergence of the proportion of smokers for males and females.

   The behavior pattern has emerged over the past two decades.

   The pattern is primarily attributable to the marked decline in the number of males.

   These males smoke cigarettes.

4. While in 1965 there were proportionately 1.5 times as many male cigarette smokers (52 percent compared with 34 percent), in 1983 the percent of males and the percent of females were just about equal.

   These males and females smoked.

5. Among persons, however, the percent has been increasing.

   These persons smoke.

   The percent smoke 25 or more cigarettes per day.

Adapted from *Charting the Nation's Health: Trends Since 1960* (U.S. Department of Health and Human Services, 1985)

7f Reduction of Nonrestrictive Relative Clauses to Make Appositives

A relative pronoun that is followed by *be* (as auxiliary or as verb) can be reduced in nonrestrictive clauses, too. This is the source of the phrase that is traditionally called an *appositive*.

Dwight David Eisenhower, who was U.S. President from 1953 through 1960, learned his management style in the Army.

Dwight David Eisenhower, U.S. President from 1953 through 1960, learned his management style in the Army.

7g EXERCISE: Appositives

Find an article in the *Encyclopaedia Britannica* on a famous person you are interested in. If the person is not included in that reference book, ask a reference librarian for help in finding the information. Copy out any sentences that have appositives in them and share those sentences with your instructor and the rest of the class. Work with another student to expand the appositives to the complete nonrestrictive relative clause.

8a Reasons for Using Relative Clauses

Why, as a writer of English, would you use a relative clause? There seem to be two major reasons for using these structures: (1) to put ideas into relationships and (2) to have a more mature writing style.

Relative clauses allow the writer to show which information is more important. The relative clause material is put into a subordinate relationship to the basic sentence. Which of this information is the most important if you want to emphasize financial loss and unhappiness about the cost of the book?

book = $27   I/lose/book

Most writers would think that the cost of the book was the important information and so would write:

The book that I lost cost $27.

If you were writing about mistakes that you have made, foolish and costly things that you have done, you might write:

I lost a book that cost $27.

Relative clauses also allow the writer to have a more mature and sophisticated writing style. While we think of children as writing with a lot of short sentences, educated adults put ideas and information into compound and complex sentences. Simple sentences can be used effectively if they are placed in deliberate contrast to the more complex sentences around them.

8b EXERCISES: Using Relative Clauses

A. Most revision of sentence structure will use many different methods for combining sentences—not just relative clauses. Work with two or three other students to make a list of the methods that can be used to combine sentences. How many different ways can your group think of? List them here.

Ways to Get Rid of Too Many Short, Simple Sentences

1. *use and*

2. _____

3. _____

4. _____

5. _____

6. _____

7. _____

8. _____

B. This passage has too many short, simple sentences. Decide on combinations that would improve the style. You can use any of the methods English has for combining sentences—from compounding to relative clauses. Sentences that could be combined are numbered in sets.

WORLD COOPERATION IN RESEARCH

1. The United Nations is the focal point for collecting information.
   This information is on new research developments.
   It is also on changes in social conditions.

2. The United States cooperates with the U.N. to prepare materials.
   These materials are on new trends in U.S. society.

3. The U.N. combines these reports with reports from around the world.
   The combined report includes factual data.
   The data is used to measure worldwide progress.
   The data is used to formulate principles and standards.
   These principles and standards are applicable around the world as countries work to improve social services.

C. The following passage is from a U.S. government handbook on physical fitness. While the information is accurate, the writing is too abrupt because of the excessive number of simple sentences. Make a draft revision with fewer simple sentences. Compare your ideas on making the changes to the suggestions of other students. Add any methods that you now remember to the list in exercise A above. The sentences are written out as a list after the passage to make them easier to work with.

STRESS MANAGEMENT

Stress is not all bad. Fundamentally it is any demand placed on the body. These demands can be mental or physical. However, it is generally thought of in a negative sense. We respond to stress in many different ways. These include increased pulse rate, increased blood pressure, and increased blood sugar. These responses are due to our mind's perceiving stress. This perception leads to an outpouring of adrenalin into the bloodstream.

Adapted from *Drug Enforcement Administration: Physical Fitness Handbook* (U.S. Drug Enforcement Administration, undated)

---

1. Stress is not all bad.

2. Fundamentally it is any demand placed on the body.

3. These demands can be mental or physical.

4. However, it is generally thought of in a negative sense.

5. We respond to stress in many different ways.

6. These include increased pulse rate, increased blood pressure, and increased blood sugar.

7. These responses are due to our mind's perceiving stress.

8. This perception leads to an outpouring of adrenalin into the bloodstream.

D. Analyze a paper that you are currently revising. How many really short, simple sentences have you included? If more than two occur in each paragraph, then you probably have too many. Look over the paper with your instructor to talk about the need for combining or expanding sentences. Then, make the revisions that you discussed.

CHAPTER 18

Conciseness

1 Introduction to Conciseness

Very often teachers will give strict word or page lengths for written assignments. For example, "Write a passage of no more than 200 words" or "Write a research paper of no more than 20 pages." Usually these restrictions are to be followed very carefully.

When required to limit the number of words that you write, your purpose is not to make your writing simplistic, but rather to increase its conciseness. Sentences can be combined. Unnecessary words can be left out. Written English achieves its conciseness through the use of subordination and embedding: fewer words are used, and more complex meaning relationships are indicated.

If after using all the grammatical and word choice tricks that you know, you are still over the length requirements, you will have to consider reducing the content in some way. (See Chapter 19 for more information on summarizing.) Teachers make these limits because they know that such requirements will force students to give priorities to information. The limits, that is, will force students to make decisions about what is important enough to leave in the paper. Thus, in leaving out information you will have to rethink the entire paper to establish essential and nonessential information. Such changes will, of course, require revisions of the entire paper to be sure that the introduction, thesis statement, and conclusion are still accurate for the body of the paper. Also, the connections and transitions from one section of the paper to another will need reconsideration. After that revision process, another thorough editing of the paper will be needed.

A Warning
When reducing the wordiness and length of a passage, do *not* leave out important connecting words so that you end up with a passage of short, choppy sentences. The idea is to create sophisticated, educated, adult writing through the use of combinations and reduction of nonessentials.

2 Conciseness and Parallel Structure

Look at this sentence illustrating parallel structure:

He likes to eat breakfast, to exercise, and to take a shower before he goes to class.

It is possible to leave out *to* from the second and third parts of the parallel set. The reader understands that *to* is meant, so it is not necessary to repeat the words. Because the reader understands that you mean *to eat*, *to exercise*, and *to take*, this is still an example of parallel structure.

He likes to eat breakfast, exercise, and take a shower before he goes to class.

The basic principle is: words that are repetitions are not always necessary and can be left out when they are not needed. However, you must be consistent. In parallel structure, the first word must remain and then all other repetitions must be left out. For example, the following version of the sentence is incorrect because of the inconsistency in dropping *to* before *exercise* and then adding *to* before *take*.

▼ *He likes to eat breakfast, exercise, and to take a shower before he goes to class.*

3 Leaving Out *That*

Another common type of reduction is to leave out *that* when it is not required. This can occur in two grammatically different contexts: (1) in relative clauses when *that* is not the subject of the embedded sentence (see Section 4a, "Restrictive Relative Clauses," on p. 301) and (2) when *that* is used with verbs like *say* to tie a whole clause into a sentence (see Section 2a on p. 295).

The text that I bought for Chemistry 101 cost $40.

The text I bought for Chemistry 101 cost $40.

The schedule says that Chemistry 101 will be taught at 11:00.

The schedule says Chemistry 101 will be taught at 11:00.

4 Using Various Combination Strategies

The various methods of combining sentences can be used to tighten sentences and thereby to reduce the length of a passage. For example, phrases can be created from whole sentences using *-ing* forms of the verb. (See Section 9 on p. 230 on participle phrases and Chapter 17 on various types of clauses.)

John entered the library. He took the elevator to the fourth floor.

Entering the library, John took the elevator to the fourth floor.

5 Using Shorter Synonyms

Another method is to use a shorter version of the same phrase, for example, *to* rather than *in order to.*

In order to use the library, you must have an ID card.

To use the library, you must have an ID card.

6 Leaving Out Empty Words

Writing can be made more concise by leaving out two types of empty words.

First, edit your writing carefully to delete unnecessary qualifying terms that have little if any meaning. Such words include *very, significant, really, quite,* and others. Use these words sparingly. If they are used often, they take up space without adding meaning.

Second, edit your writing to remove nonreferential *it* and *there* when possible. You cannot, of course, just leave the pronoun out; use the "real" subject of the sentence in the subject position. (See Section 4 on p. 204.) The first sentence is too wordy; the idea is better expressed in the second example.

There were three major events that led me to choose engineering for my major.

Three major events led me to choose engineering for my major.

Be careful, however; *it* cannot be removed from sentences such as

It was already 32 degrees outside when the Boston Marathon began.

7 EXERCISES: Conciseness

A. What can be left out? What can be combined? Reduce this passage by at least 10 words.

COMPLAINTS

When Benjamin Franklin was seven years old, he learned a very important lesson about complaining that he remembered for 70 years. There was a whistle that he wanted very much, and he saved for it for a very long time. He took all of his savings to the store, he spilled his coins on the counter, and he demanded the whistle without ever asking its price.

He was very pleased with his purchase until he found out that he paid far more than the whistle was worth. Decades later in a letter to a friend, Franklin remembered that he had paid too much for his whistle. He said that the whistle caused him "more chagrin than it ever gave pleasure." Ben Franklin should have complained.

It has been estimated that buyers are dissatisfied with 75 million purchases a year. Yet most dissatisfied customers do not complain. In fact, it is believed that the average business hears from as few as 4 out of 100 unhappy customers.

Adapted from *How to Write a Wrong: Complain Effectively and Get Results* (American Association of Retired Persons with the U.S. Federal Trade Commission, undated)

B. Many universities require a written statement of purpose when you apply for admission. Write a one-page description of your reasons for wanting to get a degree from an American university.

C. Reduce that one-page description to one-half of a page. What can be left out? What can be combined? Show the edited version to your instructor.

CHAPTER 19

Using Grammatical Information in Paraphrasing and Summarizing

1 Introduction to Paraphrasing and Summarizing

University students often need ways to use information found through research in articles, books, and other reference sources without using the exact words of the source. Obviously, if the exact words are used, you will have to use quotation marks to indicate that the words are someone else's. Paraphrasing and summarizing are techniques used by academic writers to use the ideas and information from their sources without using exact quotation.

It is important to understand that the source must be listed even when you are not using the exact words. As a scholar, you are required to credit the sources of ideas and information even if you are not using their exact words.

2a Paraphrasing

Paraphrasing is taking a sentence written by someone else and changing it in a way that keeps the meaning but changes the words. In paraphrasing, you "use your own words" to express someone else's meaning. You add nothing. You do not change the tone. You leave nothing out. The major purpose of paraphrasing is to avoid exact quotation. It is also a way of making the information you have found fit the style of your own writing. In addition, paraphrasing is a good test of your understanding of what you have read.

You can use the following methods to paraphrase:

Change the Word Order   Move modifiers to different positions, change from active to passive (or passive to active), and so forth.

"A group of interested citizens founded the school in 1853."

Paraphrase: *In 1853, the school was founded by a group of interested citizens.*

Change a Word from One Part of Speech to Another

"The recipe calls for tequila from Mexico."

Paraphrase: *The recipe uses Mexican tequila.*

Use Synonyms   Use phrases for single words or single words for phrases as well as word-for-word substitution.

"Originally, the school offered only undergraduate degrees."

Paraphrase: *In the beginning, the institution gave only B.A. and B.S. degrees.*

Use a Negative Form   Use a negative or some other reversal that does not change the meaning.

"Originally, the school offered only undergraduate degrees."

Paraphrase: *The institution did not offer graduate degrees at first.*

Combine Sentences   Although paraphrasing is thought of as something that you do to single sentences, it can involve combining a few sentences, especially if they were short in the original.

"In the 1850s, the U.S. bought a number of products from China. These included tea and ginger."

Paraphrase: *Tea and ginger were among the things purchased from China by the U.S. in the 1850s.*

Another possibility: *Tea and ginger were among the Chinese products imported into the U.S. in the 1850s.*

Do Not Change Proper Names or Terms That Have Only One Form
However, different versions of names can be used.

"President Lincoln was assassinated in 1864."

Paraphrase: *In 1864, Abraham Lincoln was killed.*

Another possibility: *In 1864, Lincoln was killed by an assassin.*

Note, however, that the following is not a good paraphrase because *die* is not an accurate synonym for *assassinate*:

In 1864, Lincoln died.

Use Pronouns to Replace Names
In the context of your writing, you can use pronouns to replace proper nouns. For example,

In 1864, he was killed by an assassin.

2b EXERCISES: Paraphrasing

A. Here are some quotations followed by paraphrases. In each paraphrased version, find the underlined words from the original quotation. How are the paraphrases different from the originals? *Q* means quotation; *P* means paraphrase.

1. Q: "Since 1945, the U.S. has changed dramatically."
   P: The United States has altered in a number of significant ways in the past 40 to 45 years.

2. Q: "It is difficult to explain the reasons for the government's decision."
   P: The reasons for the decision by the government are difficult to explain.

3. Q: "The university has rapidly expanded its engineering program to fill two needs."
   P: The rapid expansion of the university's engineering program has been for the purpose of filling two needs.

4. Q: "There were six definitions for *space* in the dictionary."
   P: Six definitions for *space* were in the dictionary.
   P: The dictionary had six definitions for *space*.

                       1   2   3   4
5. Q: "The university serves the state in a number of ways.
                     5   6
        These include research in agriculture and medicine."

   P: Agricultural and medical research are among the benefits of the
      university to the state.

                          1   2   3   4
6. Q: "Before World War II, only men were admitted to the university."

   P: Women could not attend the university prior to the mid-1940s.

   P: Since World War II, the university has been coeducational.

B. Use an English-English dictionary or a dictionary of synonyms to find
words that can be used in paraphrases of these sentences. Then, write the
paraphrases using the synonyms and changing word order where possible.

1. He perfected his idea over a period of many years.

2. Your statement precludes my giving you any help.

3. Abraham Lincoln was born in Kentucky, but he grew up in Illinois.

4. Eventually, the students will receive an answer to their questions.

5. Beginning in 1984, all of the models contained improved safety
   devices.

6. Annually, the manager must report to the owner on the financial
   condition of the store.

C. Write paraphrases of these sentences.

1. It is necessary for this peach variety to have 300 hours of temperature below 45 F to produce fruit.

2. It is advised that all tourists use traveler's checks rather than cash.

3. There are only a few cars with gas mileage at over 25 miles per
   gallon.

4. James Naismith invented the game of basketball in 1891 in Springfield, Mass.

5. The Warner Brothers movie production company introduced sound
   movies in 1926.

6. In the United States, there is a great variety in climate.

7. In 1944, Franklin D. Roosevelt was re-elected President of the U.S.
   for the fourth time.

8. Snakes do not hibernate in the winter in Florida.

9. He would go for long walks every morning when the weather
   was good.

D. Write paraphrases of these quotations from encyclopedias commonly available in libraries in the U.S. If you used these paraphrases in a composition, you would have to include a reference to indicate the source for your information.

1. There is a long record of observations and experiments on regeneration. ("Regeneration." 1987. *McGraw-Hill Encyclopedia of Science and Technology.* New York: McGraw-Hill Book Company. Vol. 15, p. 264)

2. In the eighteenth and early nineteenth centuries, natural ice cut from lakes and ponds in winter was stored underground for use in summer. ("Refrigeration." 1987. *McGraw-Hill Encyclopedia of Science and Technology.* New York: McGraw-Hill Book Company. Vol. 15, p. 257)

3. There are three types of harbors: land locked, natural harbors protected from the sea by a narrow inlet; unprotected harbors at which ships may dock even though unprotected from the hazards of changing tides, ocean waves, fogs, and ice; and artificial harbors carved out at sites where the natural features are not favorable. ("Harbor." 1987. *McGraw-Hill Encyclopedia of Science and Technology.* New York: McGraw-Hill Book Company. Vol. 8, p. 314)

4. As a public official—legislator, diplomat, and executive—he served the province and commonwealth of Virginia and the young American republic almost 40 years. ("Jefferson, Thomas." *The Encyclopedia Americana, International Edition.* Danbury, Conn.: Grolier, Inc., Vol. 16, p. 1)

5. In 1949, Button received the Sullivan trophy, the Amateur Athletic Union's award for the nation's outstanding amateur athlete; he turned professional in 1952. ("Button, Dick." *The Encyclopedia Americana, International Edition.* Danbury, Conn.: Grolier, Inc., Vol. 5, p. 77)

6. After his father's death in 1704, Byrd went back to Virginia, and in 1706, he married Lucy Parke, daughter of Daniel Parke, a Virginia planter and governor of the Leeward Islands. ("Byrd, William." *The Encyclopedia Americana, International Edition.* Danbury, Conn.: Grolier, Inc., Vol. 5, p. 86)

7. As human beings, we habitually divide the chemical senses into a *sense of taste* (gustatory) and a *sense of smell* (olfactory). (*Grzimek's Encyclopedia of Ethology.* 1977. New York: Van Nostrand Reinhold Company. Chapter 6, p. 98)

8. On the whole, the olfactory sense plays a secondary role in humans. (*Grzimek's Encyclopedia of Ethology.* 1977. New York: Van Nostrand Reinhold Company. Chapter 6, p. 98)

9. The results lead us to conclude that there are two significant molecular traits: dispersive power and dipolar momentum. (*Grzimek's Encyclopedia of Ethology.* 1977. New York: Van Nostrand Reinhold Company. Chapter 6, p. 104)

10. One of the most remarkable phenomena in nature is the migration of animals, especially that of birds. (*Grzimek's Encyclopedia of Ethology.* 1977. New York: Van Nostrand Reinhold Company. Chapter 13, p. 199)

11. Year after year we can observe how the migratory birds in our part of the world fly away to their winter quarters in autumn and return in the spring. (*Grzimek's Encyclopedia of Ethology.* 1977. New York: Van Nostrand Reinhold Company. Chapter 13, p. 199)

12. Everybody knows that migratory birds fly south in the fall. (*Grzimek's Encyclopedia of Ethology.* 1977. New York: Van Nostrand Reinhold Company. Chapter 13, p. 199)

E. Write a paragraph on some aspect of walking as exercise. Include the following statement in the paragraph in a paraphrased form. You must include a reference to show the source of your information. Your instructor will show you the correct form for indicating the reference to the author and book.

In a second study, deVries* discovered that a 15-minute walk reduced neuromuscular tension more effectively than did a standard dosage of tranquilizers.

---

*Earlier in the book, deVries was identified as a medical doctor.

Charles T. Kuntzlemand and the Editors of Consumer Guide, *The Complete Book of Walking.* N.Y.: Simon & Schuster, 1979, p. 63

F. Write a paragraph in which you make some prediction about the future. Include a paraphrase of the following sentence. You must include a reference to show the source of your information. Your instructor will show you the correct form for indicating the reference to the author and book.

The inability to speak with precision and certainty about the future, however, is no excuse for silence.

Alvin Toffler, *Future Shock*, p. 5

3a Summarizing

A *summary* is a shortened form of something. It is possible to summarize a sentence—if the sentence is very long and you make it shorter. But, summarizing usually refers to the reducing of paragraphs, chapters, and even whole books.

Summarizing uses the skills of paraphrasing: you must once again find ways to change structure, substitute synonyms, and combine sentences. Summarizing is more difficult because you must also make decisions about what to leave out and about what not to say. Obviously, you must have a thorough understanding of the materials before you can decide what is important enough to include and trivial enough to leave out.

To summarize accurately, you must analyze accurately. Most things that you read can be analyzed into these general divisions: (1) content, including generalizations and evidence, and (2) organizational guides. *Organizational guides* are those things writers say to help you understand the organization of compositions. They are not part of the information. They exist to help you follow the writing and to understand the relationships among the sentences, the paragraphs, and even the chapters—for example, words and phrases like *first, next,* and *in this chapter.*

Look at this paragraph from the beginning of the chapter called "Matter and Minerals" in a textbook titled *Introduction to Geology: Physical and Historical.* The last two sentences are organizational guides rather than content; the writers are not talking about the nature of matter but are explaining the organization of the chapter. These are the first words that can be dropped when you are writing a summary of a passage. With a highlighter, mark all of the words that you think can be dropped from the paragraph. Talk over your ideas with the rest of the class.

The fundamental building blocks of the rocks of the earth's crust are chemical elements and chemical compounds called *minerals.* Because geologic history is recorded in the rocks, we need to know something about the minerals that compose rocks. But if we look further, we find that the minerals themselves contain smaller units—*atoms*—and these in turn are made up of still smaller units, of which protons, neutrons, and electrons are the most important to us here. So before we begin our study of minerals, we must review briefly the nature of matter, specifically as it applies to minerals. Later in this chapter we will find out what constitutes a mineral and will examine a handful of the most important minerals.

Stokes, et al., 1978, p. 56

A summary is a shortened statement in your words of the general meaning of some longer piece of writing. Thus, one step to take in summarizing is to look for the thesis and topic sentences provided by the author; these can, then, be paraphrased. When you are writing your own compositions, a major task is to include appropriate examples to explain your generalizations. When writing summaries, you can usually drop the examples and focus on the generalizations.

If you are summarizing a longer passage, look for the topic sentences and paraphrase them if you think the topic sentences contain the full meaning of the passages. In some cases, the topic sentences will indeed give the content of the paragraph with all the other sentences providing evidence but not further development of the central idea. In other cases, the topic sentence only starts the discussion, and the rest of the paragraph provides important development of the idea. In such cases, the summary must include information beyond that in the topic sentence. Here are examples of both types.

Modern, well-designed buildings of steel-frame construction can withstand the shaking of even the most severe earthquakes. In the Tokyo earthquake of 1923, the Mitsubishi Bank Building was surrounded by many badly damaged structures of an older type of construction, but it escaped comparatively unharmed. In the July 28, 1957 earthquake, the 43-story Latino-Americano Tower in Mexico City rode the shock waves undamaged, while surrounding buildings suffered greatly.

Stokes, et al., 1978, p. 170

The first sentence in the paragraph gives the generalization. All of the other sentences are examples to show that the general statement is true. A possible summary for the paragraph would be

The strongest earthquakes cannot destroy correctly planned buildings constructed with steel frames.

In the following passage, however, a paraphrase of the first sentence would not be an adequate summary of the meaning of the whole paragraph:

Students of living plants and animals had their problems, too. They found surprising contrasts and comparisons among the life forms of different continents, particularly between the western and eastern hemispheres; no hummingbirds, cacti, or sloths in the Old World; no elephants, hippopotami, or apes in the New World. Yet there were also curious similarities: large flightless birds in Africa, South America, and Australia; lungfish with the same distribution; and sea cows in both America and Africa. Consider Madagascar, only 450 km from Africa, but with no monkeys, apes, lions, leopards, hyenas, zebras, elephants, giraffes, or antelopes! Some of these distribution problems are illustrated by Figures 2-3. Thousands of other curious almost inexplicable cases of distribution were being accumulated and discussed in the late nineteenth and early twentieth centuries. At this particular time the fashionable thing to do was to call upon "land bridges," imaginary or otherwise, to get organisms from place to place.

Stokes, et al., 1978, p. 29

The following generalizations must be included in any summary of the passage:

—"Students of living plants and animals had their problems, too."
—"They found surprising contrasts and comparisons among the life forms of different continents. . . ."
—"At this particular time* the fashionable thing to do was to call upon 'land bridges,' imaginary or otherwise, to get organisms from place to place."

A possible one-sentence summary is

The difficult-to-explain contrasts and similarities between living plants and animals in different continents led scientists in the late 19th and early 20th centuries to develop a theory that land bridges must have existed for the plants and animals to travel over.

---

*"At this particular time" means the late 19th and early 20th centuries.

Two sentences would probably be easier to read.

The contrasts and similarities between living plants and animals on the different continents were difficult for scientists of the late 19th and early 20th centuries to explain. One theory was that land bridges must have existed for the plants and animals to travel over.

Another technique in summarizing is useful when you are writing a summary of a longer composition, such as an article in a journal or a chapter in a text. Look first to see if the writer has included a summary. Many professional journals include summaries called *abstracts* at the beginning of the article. You need to compare the abstract to the article to be sure the abstract is complete and accurate. Then, you can paraphrase the abstract.

Some abstracts only provide an outline for the article, so the content of the abstract will not be useful for the summary. This outline can, however, be useful in the sentence outline process suggested next.

If the article or chapter does not have an abstract, then you must have an orderly way to separate the general meaning from the evidence and the guides. One way to do this is to outline the composition. You can expect most academic materials to have this outline:

  I. Introduction

 II. Body

III. Conclusion

Outlines can be made either with words or with complete sentences. Be careful in writing sentence outlines not to use the exact words of the writer unless you add quotation marks to remind yourself that they are not your words. One advantage of the word type of outline is that it helps you avoid direct quotation by giving you keywords on which to build your own sentences. In using single words, try to keep parallel grammatical structure because such structure can be fairly easily turned into your own sentences.

3b EXERCISES: Summarizing

A. Give a one-sentence summary of the following passage.

The greatest technological achievement of man to date was to leave the Earth and reach the Moon. One of the results of this exploit was a better view of the Earth. Many photographs were returned, including spectacular views of the entire globe. To the ordinary citizen this view of his home may have had more significance than the moon walks and moon rocks. It is no coincidence that the comprehensive views of Earth from space came when we also began to see clearly the nature and limitations of our earthbound mineral and energy resources.

Stokes, et al., p. 1

B. Outline the following passage using single words rather than complete sentences. Then, close *The Handbook,* and write a one-paragraph summary based on your memory and your notes. Compare your summary to those written by other students. Revise yours if you left out any important information. Revise yours if you used a sentence that has the exact words of the original. Be sure to include a reference to your source. Your instructor will provide information on the style the reference should have.

HISTORY OF THE ROAD SYSTEM IN THE U.S.

When the United States came into existence, it had a primitive transportation system that evolved during colonial days. The rivers and the sheltered coastal waters, such as Long Island Sound, Chesapeake Bay, and Albemarle Sound, were the principal arteries for travel and commerce, and most early settlements centered around them. Extending back from and between these waterways were roads in various stages of development. A very few of these, near the largest cities, were "engineered," ditched, and sometimes hardsurfaced with gravel or with "pounded stone."

The first engineered and planned "intercity" road built in the United States was the privately constructed toll turnpike from Philadelphia to Lancaster, Pennsylvania. Built between 1793–94 at a cost of $465,000, it was 62 miles long and was surfaced with broken stone and gravel.

Similar roads were constructed during the next half century, including the Cumberland Road (National Pike), which opened in 1818 between Cumberland, Maryland, and Wheeling, West Virginia. It was extended in 1838 to Springfield, Ohio, and part of the way to Vandalia, Illinois. The total cost of this project was $6,825,000.

With the advent of the railroad era, roadbuilding in the United States practically came to a halt for several decades. A renewed stimulus for improved roads began in the 1880s and 1890s when bicycle riders and farmers launched a concerted movement for better roads. But, the major impetus came with development of the automobile.

In 1892–93, Charles E. and J. Frank Duryea created the first American gasoline-powered automobile, and by 1898, there were more than 50 automobile clubs in existence. A three-horsepower Oldsmobile was the first commercially successful automobile although only 5,000 of them were sold in 1904. The real breakthrough occurred four years later, when Henry Ford produced an inexpensive Model T, which immediately converted the automobile from a luxury and a plaything into a practical necessity.

The automobile provided mankind with a type of personal mobility and freedom that it had never even dared to dream of in all the centuries past. Previously, lack of transportation had largely preordained that most people would live, work, and die in the locality of their birth, with very little opportunity to personally experience anything outside of their own immediate environs.

The automobile changed all that. It became possible to travel hundreds of miles a day, and allowed individuals to go when and where they desired. Employment patterns changed; no longer was a worker necessarily destined to live in the shadow of the factory or office; no longer were factories tied to rail and water transportation services.

Of course, to take advantage of the automobile's potential, existing roads needed improvement along with construction of new ones. So development of highway systems occurred along with increasing use of automobiles.

Highways and the automobile accelerated the development of the suburbs for those who wished to leave city-living and who yearned for a share of the open spaces. Together, they led to the creation of major new industries, such as shopping centers, technology parks, fast food franchises, and motels. They also brought with them new problems: urban sprawl, deterioration of the central city, increased demands on community services, and a decline in public transportation, and air and noise pollution.

Highways and the automotive age also drastically changed the face of industry. Produce and goods could now be trucked hundreds of miles with relative ease. Daily deliveries became possible. The farmers were able to get their crops to market with much greater frequency. Conversely, highways and the automobile ended the isolation of rural living, permitting the farm families to enjoy the amenities of urban living.

Adapted from *Americans on the Move* (U.S. Department of Transportation, 1984)

C. With another student select an article of interest to you both from the student newspaper. Decide together on the material that is not essential to the meaning of the article; mark that material out with your pens. After you have finished, you should have left only a few words, phrases, and sentences that give the basic information in the article.

D. By yourself, summarize that article in no more than five sentences. Edit the sentences carefully. Share the summary with the student who worked with you in exercise C to see how he or she used the information to write the summary in his or her own words. Be sure to include a reference to your source. Your instructor will provide information on the style the reference should have.

E. Select a current article from a journal in your field of study. Make a Xerox copy of the article so that you can write on it. Read the article carefully. Mark out any material that is not essential to its meaning. Mark with a highlighter any material that is basic. Show the marked article to another student to see if other materials can be marked as not essential to the meaning of the article.

F. Summarize the article in exercise E in no more than one page. Edit the summary carefully before giving it to your instructor along with the marked copy of the article. Be sure to include a reference to your source. Your instructor will provide information on the style the reference should have.

CHAPTER 20

Punctuation

1 Introduction to Punctuation

An important part of the process of editing your academic writing is the proper use of conventional symbols. Punctuation is important because it influences meaning and aids the reader in moving efficiently through the materials. This chapter presents rules that you should use to produce more effective writing by correct use of punctuation symbols. No attempt is made to explain all of the rules of punctuation; however, the following pages review those conventions that are most important for formal writing—and that give advanced students the most difficulty.

Advanced students frequently make these mistakes:

—Use of a comma rather than a period at the end of a sentence

—Lack of any punctuation at the end of a sentence when a period should be used

—Use of incomplete sentences where complete sentences are required

In addition, even advanced students do not include semicolons (;) or colons (:) in their writing often. These punctuation marks can be very useful in adding variety to academic writing.

The rest of this chapter provides an overview of the punctuation of written academic English. The comma is dealt with first because it is the source of most of the errors made by advanced students.

2 Types of Marks Used in Written English

Here is a summary of the types of marks that are used in written English.

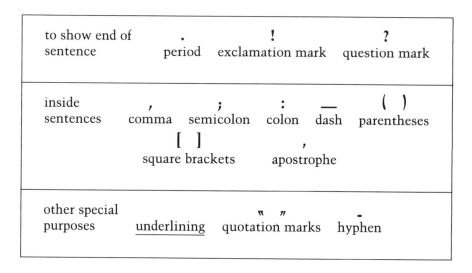

to show end of sentence	. period	! exclamation mark	? question mark		
inside sentences	, comma	; semicolon	: colon	— dash	( ) parentheses
	[ ] square brackets		, apostrophe		
other special purposes	underlining	" " quotation marks	- hyphen		

3a Uses of Commas

Commas are very weak punctuation marks; they are used only within a sentence. They cannot be used to indicate the end of a sentence. *Only a period, a question mark, or an exclamation mark can be used to mark the end of a sentence.*

Commas have the following uses:

To Combine Sentences   Commas are used with joining words such as *and, but, for, or, nor, so,* and *yet.*

I am taking calculus, but I would have preferred physics.

Calculus is a required course, for it is necessary for all areas of engineering.

To Mark the End of Introductory Elements   Commas mark the end of elements such as adverbial clauses and introductory phrases.

When he entered the library, he went straight to the reference department.

Opening the textbook, he began to do his homework.

To Separate Items in a Series Commas separate series items, including the name of a town and its state or country.

He is from Cairo, Egypt, but he now lives in Atlanta, Georgia.

I am taking calculus, world history, and English 111.

      1,   2,   3

Eating, drinking, and sleeping are his hobbies.

The comma is not always required after the second item in the series. In fact, in journalism and some other fields the second comma is never used. Check with your instructor to be sure that you use the correct method for your field of study.

I am taking calculus, world history and English 111.

Eating, drinking and sleeping are his hobbies.

To Mark Nonrestrictive Relative Clauses and Appositives

My advisor, who is usually very helpful, did not allow me to take the physics course that I preferred this term.

Dr. Johns, my advisor, did not allow me to take physics this term.

To Mark Words and Phrases that Interrupt the Sentence Structure Commas mark interrupting words: *for example, such as, especially, unlike,* and transitional expressions.

The university needs a better system for advising. For example, my advisor, unlike my professors, is seldom available during the term.

I wanted to take physics this term; my advisor, however, made me wait until next term.

To Separate Parts in Dates and Addresses

He left Cairo, Egypt, on July 19, 1954, and has never returned.

3b The Comma Splice

The biggest problem for advanced students is not the correct use of commas but the *incorrect* use of the comma to replace a period. This mistake is called a *comma splice* and is considered a major error by ESL and English instructors because of the confusion that the comma splice causes the reader. The reader depends on the writer to indicate the end of sentences. Sentences such as the following are very confusing and irritating for the reader because it is difficult to know which clauses and phrases go together. The reader is forced to do work that the writer should have done.

▼ *My advisor did not allow me to take the physics course that I preferred this term, after he told me his reasons, I understood his actions better, however, I still disagreed with him, thinking that I might be able to change his mind, I went to his office to talk again.*

My advisor did not allow me to take the physics course that I preferred this term. After he told me his reasons, I understood his actions better. However, I still disagreed with him. Thinking that I might be able to change his mind, I went to his office to talk again.

3c Misusing a Comma to Separate Basic Parts of the Sentence

Never use a comma to separate the subject from the verb, the verb from the object, the object from an adverb. You may pause in these places when you speak, but you must not use a comma. Here are some examples of this error:

▼ *The important work of Einstein, will not be forgotten soon.*

▼ *The important work of Einstein will not be forgotten, soon.*

▼ *The book that is required for calculus, costs too much.* (Remember that the comma is required for nonrestrictive relative clauses—not for restrictive relative clauses. See Section 4 on p. 301.)

4a Run-on Sentences

Another related punctuation error is called the *run-on sentence* or the *fused sentence*. In this error, two different sentences are put together without any punctuation at all. This combination is even more difficult for the reader to sort out.

▼ *I explained to my advisor that I wanted to take physics calculus is taught in high school in my country.*

I explained to my advisor that I wanted to take physics. Calculus is taught in high school in my country.

4b Fragments

One major problem that some writers have with English grammar is the use of incomplete sentences. These are called *fragments*. A fragment is frequently a subordinate clause that is written alone rather than as part of an independent clause. The following is incorrect—the second part is *not* a complete sentence. The two parts must be combined to make one sentence.

The process must be designed carefully. ▼*Because a mistake in a nuclear power plant can be deadly.*

The correct version is as follows:

The process must be designed carefully because a mistake in a nuclear power plant can be deadly.

English instructors in the U.S. usually take this kind of mistake very seriously for two reasons: first, the fragment indicates that you do not understand basic English sentence structure; second, fragments can be very difficult to read and so are a sign of poor writing skills. You will sometimes find fragments in the writing of very skilled writers. In these cases, the writers have used the fragment deliberately for special emphasis. The problem that English instructors are concerned about is the accidental use of fragments by writers who think that they have written complete sentences.

A common way of indicating a fragment is to underline or circle the fragment and to write *frag* in the margin. In other systems, the instructor will indicate the fragment by writing a number in the margin that is keyed to a chart of symbols. The number 1 written in the margin could, for example, mean that you have written a fragment and need to edit the sentence.

One cause of fragments might be the difference between the way we speak and the way we write. Conversation is full of short answers—of fragments. In written English, a fragment is usually a mistake. (Check the Index for the information on fragments in other chapters.)

5a Semicolons and Colons

A writer of English cannot avoid using commas and periods because they are the basic punctuation of English. While the semicolon and the colon are not so basic, they are useful devices for the writer of academic English. Correct use indicates an advanced level of skill in writing English.

5b Semicolons

This punctuation mark is used to combine whole sentences when they are closely related in meaning and the writer does not want to use a period or a comma plus conjunction. The semicolon is stronger than a comma in that it can combine whole sentences. It is weaker than a period in that it cannot be used at the end of a sentence.

I talked with my advisor; he would not change his mind.

Semicolons are also a choice when a series is combined that has commas inside the parts of the series. To combine these three actions into one sentence, you could end up with a confusing series of commas.

To deal with the problem, I talked with my advisor, the chairman, and the dean.

To deal with the problem, I wrote a petition.

To deal with the problem, I met with the advisory committee.

To deal with the problem, I talked with my advisor, the chairman, and the dean; wrote a petition; and met with the advisory committee.

Semicolons are frequently used in sentences like the following. Notice that words like *however, for example, also, indeed,* and *therefore* are added at the beginning of the second sentence. They are followed by a comma.

I wanted to take physics this term; however, my advisor would not agree.

The university does not provide enough services during the break between terms; for example, the library is not open on weekends.

5c Colons

The colon (:) is an uncommon punctuation mark that can be very useful in academic writing. It is used for these purposes: (1) to add an explanation to a statement, (2) to introduce a list of items or examples, (3) to follow a salutation in a business letter, (4) to separate a main title from a subtitle (for articles as well as chapters and books), (5) to introduce a formal quotation, and (6) to separate divisions of time.

1. *Jose was not given a choice: he had to take the calculus course.*

2a. *To deal with the problem, I did three things: talked with my advisor, wrote a petition, and met with the advisory committee.*

2b. *Please submit the following:*

    a completed application form

    a $10 nonrefundable application fee

    three letters of recommendation

    a completed financial statement

3. *Dear Professor Smith:*

4. *William Faulkner: Symbolism in the Later Novels*

5. *The politician said: "People are the common denominator of progress."*

6. *Class begins at 1:55 p.m.*

When used to precede an explanation, the colon could be replaced by a semicolon or a comma plus conjunction. In less formal writing, a dash could be used.

I was not given a choice; I had to take the calculus course.

I was not given a choice, for I had to take the calculus course.

I was not given a choice—I had to take the calculus course.

When a colon is used in the title of an article, usually the first phrase is more general and the subtitle clarifies the purpose of the article. Sometimes the main title is so clever that without the subtitle the reader would not know what the article was about.

Rites of Passage: Ph.D. Curricula in the United States

6a Marking Quotations

Anytime that you use the exact words of another writer or speaker, you must use marks to indicate that the words are not your own. To do otherwise is to commit a major academic offense called *plagiarism*. (In fact, even if you change the wording to words of your own, you are expected to give a reference to indicate the source of the ideas or information.) You have two choices to indicate a quotation.

For a short quotation of less than four or five sentences, enclose the words in quotation marks and give appropriate references for the material. Any commas or periods are enclosed inside the quotation marks.

Most Americans know General MacArthur's words "I shall return."

Be sure to have both the beginning and the end sets of the quotation marks. A typical error is to give the first set and to forget the second so that the reader has trouble knowing where the quotation ends. Where does the quotation end in this passage?

President Franklin Delano Roosevelt made the following statement in a speech at Oxford University in 1941, "We, too, born to freedom, and believing in freedom, are willing to fight to maintain freedom. We, and all others who believe as deeply as we do, would rather die on our feet than live on our knees. Surely we must admire a man who can use these words when he had been paralyzed from the waist down for some twenty years.

For a longer quotation of more than four or five sentences, you separate the words by double-spacing at the beginning and end and by indenting 10 spaces from the left (the margin is five spaces from the left). Some instructors expect these longer quotations to be single-spaced while the main body of your paper is double-spaced; other instructors like for everything in your paper to be double-spaced. Ask your instructor for the rules that he/she prefers. For example, the writer of this passage includes a long quotation by a famous U.S. economist:

Engineers must learn that human resources of a country are as vital to its success as computers, heavy equipment, roads, and other objects of engineering. In fact, ill-trained human beings cannot properly use and maintain the products of modern engineering. As John Kenneth Galbraith commented in *Economic Development* (1964):

People are the common denominator of progress. So . . . no improvement is possible with unimproved people, and advance is certain when people are liberated and educated. It would be wrong to dismiss the importance of roads, railroads, power plants, mills, and the other familiar furniture of economic development. . . . But we are coming to realize . . . that there is a certain sterility in economic monuments that stand alone in a sea of illiteracy. Conquest of illiteracy comes first.

6b Using Punctuation Marks to Show Changes in Quotations

In the quotation given above from John Kenneth Galbraith, the writer chose to leave out some parts of the actual passage. When you leave out words inside a sentence, use three periods (. . .) to indicate that something is missing. These spaced periods are called *ellipsis* marks. When you leave out words at the end of a sentence, indicate the missing part with three periods and the end of the sentence with a fourth period (. . . .).

Usually, sections are left out of quotations when the quoter thinks those particular words are not relevant to the point being made.

You must never leave out words if the meaning of the quotation is changed. For example, the full quotation says,

The president of the university believes that students are not lazy.

You cannot have the following ellipsis:

▼ *The president of the university believes that students are . . . lazy.*

Sometimes you must add words to a quotation to clarify its meaning. For example, pronouns that are meaningful in the original context might need to be explained when the passage is quoted. To add your own words to the quotation, use square brackets as in this example:

In the fall of 1987, many Americans were upset when an Indian leader protested that Thanksgiving is not a happy day for the American Indian. Celebrating successful settlement of the U.S. by Europeans probably does not seem appropriate for most modern Indians because of their loss of traditional homelands and because of their extreme poverty. This same point had been made by the Indian leader Tecumseh in 1810 when he said "Once they [the Indians] were a happy race. Now they are made miserable by the white people, who are never contented but are always encroaching [to take land away from the Indians]."

---

7 Indicating Titles

In printed materials, italic forms of letters are used to indicate the titles of whole works—books, movies, plays, record albums, newspapers, magazines, and ballets. When you type a paper, these titles are indicated by underlining them. Technically, the underlining is a signal to a printer that the materials should be printed in italics.

Never underline the title of your own paper.

Underlining and italics are not used when naming sacred writings such as the Bible, the Koran, and the Talmud.

At the orientation session, we saw a videotape about U.S. English entitled <u>American Tongues</u>.

We went to see <u>Death of a Salesman</u>.

In contrast, titles for works that are part of larger publications are indicated with quotation marks, for example, titles of poems, songs, articles in magazines/journals, chapters in books, and short stories.

We are studying a poem called "The Road Not Taken."

The most important chapter in the book is the last one, which is titled "Looking for Solutions."

Educated Americans do not agree about how to punctuate the title of a television show. Some prefer to underline the title (to indicate italics) while others insist on quotation marks. Ask your instructor which form to use.

The secretary of state was interviewed on <u>Meet the Press</u>.

The secretary of state was interviewed on "Meet the Press."

8 Commas, Dashes, and Parentheses— Adding Extra Material to a Sentence

Parenthetic elements are additional words or phrases that are added to a sentence. They add extra but nonessential information. These elements can be punctuated in three different ways—with commas, with parentheses, or with dashes.

As shown in Section 3a on p. 339, commas are used to set off appositives or other breaks in the flow of the sentence.

My advisor, Dr. Johns, is seldom on campus.

All agricultural workers, migrant and nonmigrant, are covered by the new legislation.

Parentheses are used to add information and comments to a sentence or passage. They are especially important as part of the system for giving references to sources in research papers and other academic writing.

In short, students (unlike instructors) pay to use the computer center.

The pronunciation of Ontario English, according to Joos (1942: 141), is nearly identical to that of General American. (This information refers the reader to a publication listed in a reference section at the end of the article. You know the publication is by a writer named Joos and was published in 1942. The reference is to information given on page 141 of the Joos publication.)

Be careful of the punctuation of material in parentheses. If the material is inside a sentence, then no additional punctuation is used. Notice the location of the final period in these examples.

Joos maintains that the pronunciation of Ontario English is nearly identical to that of General American (1942: 141).

Hoover became president in January, 1929 (only some nine months before the Stock Market Crash).

A parenthetical statement can be a complete sentence that stands by itself. In this situation, the period is placed inside the parentheses.

Regular membership in the association costs $40 per year. (Full-time students pay only $15 per year.)

Dashes are used to make a more dramatic break in the sentence. The writer stops abruptly to add information before continuing with the sentence. Because they are used for stylistic effect, dashes should not be used often. Be sure that in typing a paper you use two hyphen marks to make a dash. That is, be sure that you make a difference between a dash (—) and a hyphen (-).

In his dream, he saw his mother—who had been dead for 25 years— walking toward him on a narrow path.

Many still believe that access and quality are mutually exclusive in education. I deny that. We can have both—we must have both.

Sometimes dashes are used to replace commas to set off a list because the list itself contains commas:

Breakfast—which consisted of cheese, bread, olives, and tea—was served in the kitchen at 7:00 a.m.

9 Apostrophes in Contractions and for Possessives

In informal writing, contractions are used to suggest the typical pronunciations of words such as *can't, won't,* and all the others. Generally in formal written English it is better to use the full form rather than the contraction: *cannot* and *will not,* for example. You will notice that contractions are seldom used in academic journals or in textbooks except in quotations.

The apostrophe is used to mark contractions involving verbs and the negative.

Contractions with Forms of Be
He is = He's
We are = We're
I am = I'm
who is = who's
who are = who're

Contractions with Auxiliary Have
I have studied = I've studied
He has studied = He's studied
She had studied = She'd studied

Contractions with Will
They will = They'll

Contractions with Not
She is not = She isn't
They are not = They aren't
They were not = They weren't
He cannot = He can't
You will not = You won't
We do not = We don't
He does not = He doesn't

The apostrophe is also used with nouns to indicate the possessive. There is no difference in pronunciation between *boys* and *boy's*. When you speak, the context reveals the meaning. In writing, you use the apostrophe to show the difference:

The university has 110 departments.

The department's *computer is constantly in use.*

If a plural noun ends in *-s,* the apostrophe is put outside the final *-s.*

The student's dictionary was found on the bus. (One student is involved.)

The students' dictionaries were placed on the floor under their desks during the final examination. (More than one student is involved.)

If the plural noun is irregular, then it is followed by apostrophe and then -s:

The children's books were scattered all over the house.

A problem for some writers is the difference between *its* and *it's*. The first is the possessive form of *it*; the second is the contraction of *it* and *is*.

▼ *The department traded* it's *old computer for a more modern one.*

The department traded its *old computer for a more modern one.*

It's very important to keep good business records.

Apostrophes are sometimes used to indicate the plural forms of words, numbers, and individual letters of the alphabet. This is optional. It is not used in *The Handbook* because it can sometimes be confused with the possessive.

The exercise requires you to find all of the not's *in the passage.*

The exercise requires you to find all of the nots *in the passage.*

His novels were popular in the 1860's.

His novels were popular in the 1860s.

Some words, especially those expressing units of time and measurement, require the apostrophe.

He won a year's salary in the lottery.

10 Hyphens

The hyphen (-) is used in various ways to form combined words:

a noun + adverb: *runner-up*

an adjective created from a noun phrase: *cold-blooded, blue-eyed*

a compound when the first part is a single capital letter: *U-Haul, H-bomb, X-rated*

two nouns are coordinated to make a modifier: *an English-English dictionary, a Spanish-English dictionary*

In addition, hyphens are commonly used for multiword numbers and fractions: *thirty-six, three-fourths.*

Hyphens are frequently used when a multiword modifier occurs before a noun (see Section 5a on p. 164):

an up-to-date report

a 100-item test

a face-to-face confrontation

a twenty-five-dollar check

The hyphens are not used when the modifier is moved to an object or complement position:

This report is up to date.

The test has 100 items.

They need to talk face to face.

The check is for twenty-five dollars.

11 Capitalization

Most capitalized words in English fall into three categories: proper names, first word of a sentence, and key words in titles.

Capital letters are used to indicate proper nouns (names of persons, places, geographical regions, countries, languages, historical periods, days of the week, months, organizations, religions, and names of ships).

William S. Johnson	Thailand	Christmas
Atlanta	Lutheran	Ramadan
California	Moslem	General Motors
Lake Michigan	Spanish	the Koran
Mount McKinley	American	the Bible
the Empire State Building	Arabic	the Talmud
Memorial Drive	World War II	the Constitution of the United States
Fifth Avenue	the French Revolution	the Declaration of Independence
Georgia State University	Kleenex	the *Mayflower*
the Midwest	Monday	
	April	

Dictionary entries for words that are usually capitalized begin with capital letters.

Capital letters are also used to mark the beginning of a sentence.

Capital letters indicate major words in the titles of books, plays, magazines, articles, chapters, poems, short stories, other published works of art, and your own compositions.

Deciding to use a capital letter can be somewhat more complex than the list suggests. For example, what are the answers to these questions?

Do you capitalize the adjective form of a proper noun? (Japan = japanese? or Japanese?)

Do you capitalize the names of the seasons of the year? (Fall or fall? spring or Spring? summer or Summer? winter or Winter?)

Do you capitalize a title if it is added to a name? (aunt Mary or Aunt Mary? General Smith or general Smith?)

How do you decide which words are *major* words in a title of a book or work of art? Look at these titles to decide which words are not capitalized.

Places in the Sun

The Book of Great Desserts

The Psychology of Mathematics for Instruction

The Poetry and Prose of John Milton

For Whom the Bell Tolls

A Portrait of the Artist as a Young Man

The rule seems to be that articles, prepositions, and conjunctions are not capitalized. However, if the conjunction or preposition has five or more letters it is usually capitalized.

Teaching Across Cultures in the U.S. ESL Program

Gardening Without Effort

12 EXERCISES: Punctuation

A. What are the differences in the following sets of sentences?

1a. He went to high school in Atlanta.

1b. He went to Midtown High School in Atlanta.

2a. She is a university graduate.

2b. She is an Emory University graduate.

3a. I took a history course last year.

3b. I took History 101 last year.

3c. I took an English course last year.

3d. I took English 101 last year.

4a. According to the map, the college is about 50 miles north of here.

4b. I always wanted to go to school in the East.

B. Write the full forms of the following:

1. She'd rather study = _____

2. She'd studied = _____

3. She's studying = _____

4. She's studied = _____

5. She'd better study = _____

C. Read this information about the invention of the telephone. All periods, semicolons, and colons have been changed to commas. Also, the capital letters at the beginning of sentences have been changed to small case (not capital) letters. The result is difficult to read; revise the passage by putting in the correct punctuation.

TELEPHONE

Alexander Graham Bell was a Scotsman whose father and grandfather had been specialists in speech, in 1871, at the age of 24, Bell moved to Boston to teach his father's method of Visable Speech to deaf children, he opened his own school and became Professor of Vocal Physiology at Boston University, in his spare time, Bell experimented with finding a way to transmit several telegraph messages over a single wire simultaneously, the fathers of two of his pupils gave him financial backing, and a young man named Thomas A. Watson was hired to help Bell build the electrical parts that he needed, on June 2, 1875, Bell was in one room of his laboratory, Watson in another, both were tuning the reeds of a "harmonic telegraph" that Bell had designed, Watson had screwed his reed so tightly that it stuck to the pole of its electromagnet, he plucked the reed to get it loose, in the next room, Bell heard a distinctive twang coming over the wire, quite unlike the sound of a telegraph, the next day, Bell transmitted the sound of his voice, although not distinct words, over his new "telephone," after months of further experimentation, he filed for a patent and was awarded his first one in March, 1876, that same month, Bell and Watson were about to try out a new liquid transmitter one evening after work, accidently spilling some acid on his leg, Bell said into the transmitter, "Mr. Watson, come here, I need you," Watson, down the hall in another room, heard Bell's voice distinctly over his receiving telephone and rushed to help, in 1877 the first Bell Telephone Company was established in Boston, at that time, only 778 telephones were in operation, with great salesmanship and enthusiasm, Bell officers convinced the public that the telephone was an essential means of communication, by 1881, a telephone company report stated that ". . . only nine cities of more than 10,000 inhabitants in the United States . . . are without a telephone exchange," after his original telephone work, Bell himself retired from active association with the company, and spent the rest of his life in Washington, D.C., and Nova Scotia, working with deaf children and developing innovations in communications, aeronautics, and other areas.

Adapted from *Eureka!* (U.S. Small Business Administration, 1982)

D. Only commas are used in the passage below so that a number of comma splices have been created. Where appropriate, change the commas to periods or semicolons. Or, you might wish to add a conjunction.

NUTRITION

The body utilizes food to supply the nutrients for energy and for the growth and maintenance of body tissue, a prudent nutritional program consists of a balanced and varied diet, a balance between the calories we consume in the form of food and the calories we burn through exercise must be maintained. Many nutrients have been identified as necessary for optimal life, foods supply these nutrients, these nutrients have been categorized into six groups:

1. carbohydrates
2. proteins
3. fats
4. vitamins
5. minerals
6. water

A large proportion of the foods we eat are processed foods, canned and processed foods are often high in sugar, fat, salt, and have nonnutritional additives, these additions may be directly related to obesity and other diseases such as coronary heart disease and diabetes, choose fresh foods whenever possible.

The trend to eat more meat and fat and less carbohydrates has resulted in decreased intake of starch and fiber as well as some necessary vitamins and minerals, about thirty to forty percent of our average daily caloric intake is comprised of empty calories such as sugars and alcohol.

No single food or any food group contains all the required nutrients, it is also difficult to isolate the health effect of one dietary change from another because all nutrients are interrelated, thus, it is necessary to maintain a varied and balanced diet.

Adapted from *Drug Enforcement Administration: Physical Fitness Handbook* (U.S. Drug Enforcement Administration, undated)

E. All of the punctuation has been left out of the following explanation of the invention of xerography, making the passage even more difficult to read than the one in exercise A. Find the separate sentences. Decide on the best punctuation to use.

XEROGRAPHY

While working in a corporate patent department in new york city during the depression chester carlson was alarmed by the amount of time and money it took to reproduce business documents manuscripts for example had to be completely typed and patent drawings had to be sent out to be photographed carlson who had majored in physics in college decided to experiment with possible techniques for copying such documents he set up a laboratory first at home and later in a rented room behind a beauty parlor in queens new york one day after three years of part-time research carlson wrote the date and place—"10-22-38, astoria"— on a glass slide and successfully transferred that image to a piece of waxed paper which he then heated over a hotplate to fix the image permanently his technique bypassed conventional photography using electricity to make images in a powder that was then heat-fused into a permanent record on paper carlson patented the process but lacked the resources to develop a workable copying machine in 1944 he entered into an agreement with battelle memorial institute a nonprofit research organization in return for a majority of any ensuing royalties in 1947 the tiny haloid company of rochester new york acquired a license from battelle giving it the right to develop produce and market any resulting machine "xerography" was coined from the greek words for "dry writing" to describe the copying method in 1950 haloid marketed its first xerographic product ten years later it marketed the first automatic dry-process copier the pioneering xerox 914 copier in the following decade carlson's concept revolutionized the way in which american business operated chester carlson earned hundreds of millions from his invention according to his wife but had given most of his fortune to charities before he died in 1968 most of his gifts were anonymous but he did not manage to achieve his stated wish: "I would like to die a poor man."

Adapted from *Eureka!* (U.S. Small Business Administration, 1982)

F. Look back at three long passages or papers that you have written. Analyze the mistakes that you made with punctuation into these categories:

Type	Number of Errors
Comma splices	_____
Run-on sentences	_____
Fragments	_____

If you find many of these errors, be sure to add the area to your personal editing list.

G. Look through a text used in your major field of study. Find any examples of the use of the colon (:). What types of uses did you find? Write examples here to use as models in your own writing.

_____

_____

_____

_____

_____

_____

_____

_____

_____

_____

H. Select an article of interest to you from a journal in your major field of study. Find any uses of parentheses. How are they used by writers in your field? Bring a copy of the article to class to share with the rest of the students. Write examples here to use as models in your own writing.

_____

_____

_____

_____

_____

_____

_____

_____

Ready Reference

This section of *The Handbook* pulls together lists that you might find useful for quick reference as you are editing your writing. Ready Reference contains these materials in alphabetized lists:

A Irregular Verbs

B Verbs + Adjective + Preposition

C Verbs that Take Infinitives as Direct Object

D Verbs that Take Gerunds as Direct Object

E Verbs that Can Take Either Infinitives or Gerunds as Direct Object with Same Meaning

F Verbs that Can Take Either Infinitives or Gerunds as Direct Object with Different Meanings

G Phrasal Verbs Divided into Groups Based on Grammar

H Irregular Nouns

I English Noncount Nouns that Are Count Nouns in Other Languages

J Phrases Used with Nouns for Measuring and Counting

K Verbs and Indirect Objects

L Stative Verbs

APPENDIX A

Irregular Verbs

The 133 verbs listed in Section 13a, "Irregular Verb Classes," on p. 79 are given here in alphabetical order. An advanced student should know how to spell all of these verbs. It would seem wise for you to take time to test yourself to find out which of these forms you do not yet know. Then, use whatever method of memorization you prefer to add these words to your written vocabulary.

awake	awoke	awoken
bear	bore	born
begin	began	begun
bend	bent	bent
bet		
bid		
bind	bound	
bite	bit	bitten
bleed	bled	
blow	blew	blown
break	broke	broken
breed	bred	

bring	brought	
build	built	built
burn	burned/burnt	burned/burnt
buy	bought	
cast		
catch	caught	
choose	chose	chosen
cling	clung	
come	came	come
cost		
creep	crept	
deal	dealt	
dig	dug	
dive	dived/dove	dived
do	did	done
draw	drew	drawn
drink	drank	drunk
drive	drove	driven
eat	ate	eaten
fall	fell	fallen
feed	fed	
feel	felt	
fight	fought	
find	found	
fit		
flee	fled	
fling	flung	
fly	flew	flown
forget	forgot	forgotten
forsake	forsook	forsaken
freeze	froze	frozen
get	got	
give	gave	given
go	went	gone
grind	ground	

grow	grew	grown
hang	hung	
have	had	had
hear	heard	
hide	hid	hidden
hit		
hold	held	
hurt		
keep	kept	
kneel	knelt	
knit		
know	knew	known
lead	led	
leap	leapt	
leave	left	
lend	lent	lent
let		
lie	lay	lain
light	lit	
lose	lost	
make	made	made
mean	meant	
meet	met	
mow	mowed	mowed/mown
prove	proved	proved/proven
put		
quit		
read	read	
rid		
ride	rode	ridden
ring	rang	rung
rise	rose	risen
run	ran	run
saw	sawed	sawed/sawn
say	said	
see	saw	seen
seek	sought	

sell	sold	
send	sent	sent
set		
sew	sewed	sewed/sewn
shake	shook	shaken
shave	shaved	shaved/shaven
shear	sheared	sheared/shorn
shoot	shot	
show	showed	showed/shown
shrink	shrank	shrunk
shut		
sing	sang	sung
sink	sank	sunk
sit	sat	
sleep	slept	
slide	slid	
sow	sowed	sowed/sown
speak	spoke	spoken
speed	sped	
spend	spent	spent
spin	spun	
split		
spread		
spring	sprang	sprung
stand	stood	
steal	stole	stolen
stick	stuck	
string	strung	
swear	swore	sworn
sweep	swept	
swell	swelled	swelled/swollen
swim	swam	swum
swing	swung	
take	took	taken
teach	taught	
tear	tore	torn
tell	told	

think	thought	
thrive	thrived/throve	thrived
throw	threw	thrown
thrust		
wake	woke	woken
wear	wore	worn
weave	wove	woven
weep	wept	
win	won	
wring	wrung	
write	wrote	written

Verb + Adjective + Preposition

Many students have found it useful to have an alphabetized list of verb + adjective + preposition. While this list has many of the most frequently used of these combinations, it does not attempt to be complete.

(be)	absent from	(have)	confidence in
(have)	access to	(be)	content with
(be)	accustomed to	(be)	dedicated to
(be)	acquainted with	(be)	delighted at, with
(be)	afraid of	(be)	devoted to
(be)	angry with, at	(be)	different from
(be)	appropriate for	(be)	disappointed with, in, by
(be)	ashamed of	(be)	divorced from
(be)	aware of	(be)	done with
(be)	capable of	(be)	dressed in
(be)	certain of	(be)	engaged to
(be)	committed to	(be)	enthusiastic about
(be)	composed of	(be)	envious of
(be)	concerned about	(be)	essential to

(be)	excited about	(be)	opposed to
(be)	faithful to	(be)	out of date
(be)	familiar with	(be)	out of order
(be)	famous for	(have)	patience with
(be)	fed up with	(be)	patient with
(be)	finished with	(be)	polite to
(be)	fond of	(take)	pride in
(be)	friendly to, with	(be)	proud of
(be)	frightened by	(be)	relevant to
(be)	frightened of	(be)	responsible to, for
(be)	generous about	(be)	satisfied with
(be)	good at	(be)	scared of, by
(be)	grateful for, to	(be)	sensitive to
(be)	guilty of	(be)	sorry about, for
(be)	happy with, about, for	(be)	suitable for
(be)	incapable of	(be)	sure of, about
(be)	in charge of	(be)	surprised by, at
(be)	in favor of	(have)	a talent for
(be)	innocent of	(be)	terrified of
(be)	interested in	(be)	thankful for
(be)	in touch with	(be)	tired of, from
(be)	jealous of	(be)	used to
(be)	known for	(get)	used to
(be)	lazy about	(be)	uneasy about
(be)	made of, from	(be)	worried about
(be)	married to, by		

APPENDIX C

Verbs that Take Infinitives as Direct Object

See Chapter 11 for information, examples, and exercises focused on infinitives.

Group I These verbs can be followed immediately by the infinitive: *I hope to participate in the research project.*

agree	expect	refuse
appear	hope	seem
ask	offer	swear
decide	pretend	wish
deserve	promise	

Group II These verbs can be followed immediately by the infinitive or by a noun or a pronoun then by the infinitive. The ones marked ** have different meanings in the different patterns: *He asked to go* is different from *He asked me to go.*

ask (someone)**

expect (someone)**

get (someone)**

promise (someone)

Group III For these verbs a noun or pronoun must come before the infinitive.

advise (someone)

allow (someone)

command (someone)

compel (someone)

encourage (someone)

force (someone)

instruct (someone)

invite (someone)

order (someone)

permit (someone)

persuade (someone)

remind (someone)

require (someone)

tell (someone)

warn (someone)

Verbs that Take Gerunds as Direct Object

Gerunds are explained in Chapter 11.

admit	discuss	imagine
appreciate	endure	keep
avoid	enjoy	mind
consider	escape	postpone
delay	fear	put off
deny	finish	risk

Verbs that Can Take Either Infinitives or Gerunds as Direct Object with Same Meaning

For some English speakers the gerund has a general meaning as the name of a type of activity—the way *swimming* can be the name of a sport like *tennis. I like swimming* is about liking that sport while *I like to swim* is about liking to do the thing yourself. It is possible to write *I like swimming, but I don't like to swim*—the speaker likes to watch other people doing the sport. This difference is subtle and not always maintained.

Infinitives and gerunds are discussed, illustrated, and practiced in Chapter 11. See the index for additional information.

begin	intend	stand ("endure")
continue	like	start
hate	prefer	try

Verbs that Can Take Either Infinitives or Gerunds as Direct Object with Different Meanings

The infinitive refers to something that has not yet been done while the gerund refers to a previous, completed, real action. *He stopped smoking* means he no longer smokes while *He stopped to smoke* means that first he stopped and then he smoked. These sentences are very different in meaning for all native speakers of English.

Infinitives and gerunds are discussed, illustrated, and practiced in Chapter 11. See the index for additional information.

forget	remember
quit	stop

Phrasal Verbs Divided into Groups Based on Grammar

This list gives common phrasal verbs divided into four categories: (1) separable transitive, (2) inseparable transitive, (3) intransitive, and (4) phrasal verbs that require prepositions. Within each category, the verbs are alphabetized.

A synonym is given in parentheses after each phrasal verb. These synonyms are usually not exact equivalents of the phrasal verb, so you must be careful to learn these words from observing American use of them.

For more information on phrasal verbs, see Section 16a on p. 99.

1. Transitive Phrasal Verbs Separation of these verbs is optional if direct object is a noun and required if direct object is a pronoun.

ask out (invite on date)

bring about (cause)

bring on (cause)

bring up (rear, mention)

call back (return a telephone call)

call in (require an official visit)

call off (cancel)

call up (telephone, find on computer system)

check out (take a book from the library, investigate)

cheer up (make someone feel happier)

clean up (make cleaner)

cross out (put a line through)

cut out (stop)

do over (repeat)

drop off (leave)

figure out (find the answer)

fill out (complete)

find out (discover)

give back (return)

give up (surrender something)

hand in (give, submit)

hang up (hang, put in place—as a telephone receiver)

have on (wear)

leave out (omit)

look over (examine)

look up (seek, search for)

make up (invent, do past work)

name after (give same name as another person, place, or event)

name for (give same name as another person, place, event)

pass out (distribute)

pick out (select)

pick up (learn informally, go get someone/something)

point out (call attention to)

put away (replace, store)

put back (return)

put off (delay)

put on (put clothes on body)

put out (extinguish)

shut off (stop)

take back (return)

take off (remove)

take out (take a person on a date, remove)

take over (control)

take up (begin, discuss)

tear down (demolish, destroy)

tear up (tear into pieces)

think over (consider)

throw away (discard)

throw out (discard)

throw up (vomit)

try on (see if something fits)

turn down (decrease, refuse)

turn on (light)

turn out (extinguish)

turn up (increase)

2. Transitive Phrasal Verbs These verbs cannot be separated.

call on (ask to recite or answer, visit)

check into (investigate)

come across (find, discover)

get into, get in (enter a vehicle, begin)

get off (leave a bus or airplane)

get over (recover)

go over (review)

look into (investigate)

look after (care for)

run into (meet accidently)

take after (resemble)

3. Intransitive Phrasal Verbs

blow up (explode)

break down (stop working, confess)

catch on (understand, become popular)

clean up (make a lot of money, be very successful)

come in (enter)

drop by (visit informally, visit without invitation)

get by (survive, be all right)

get up (arise in morning, leave chair)

give in (surrender, agree)

give up (surrender, quit)

go astray (not arrive, not act properly)

pass out (faint)

pass away (die)

play around (not be serious)

show off (show to get attention)

show up (appear, come)

take off (leave the ground)

touch down (land)

turn up (arrive, arrive unexpectedly)

4. Transitive Phrasal Verbs that Require Prepositions These verbs
need prepositions to connect the direct object.

break up with (end a relationship)

catch up with (reach the same position)

check out of (leave)

check up on (investigate)

close in on (get closer to)

come up with (find, discover)

cut down on (reduce)

drop in on (visit informally or without invitation)

drop out of (quit)

end up with (get)

get along with (be agreeable, like)

get away with (not be punished)

get back to (return)

get down to (begin)

get out of (leave a car, avoid)

give in to (surrender, quit)

go in for (do)

keep up with (stay even, level, in same position)

look down on (feel superior to)

look in on (visit)

make away with (steal)

pick up on (understand)

put up with (tolerate, endure)

run out of (finish a supply, use completely)

stand up for (defend)

APPENDIX H

Irregular Nouns

This list provides irregular nouns in alphabetical order with the singular form given first. See Section 2d on p. 150.

analysis	analyses
antenna	antennae/antennas
appendix	appendices
axis	axes
bacterium	bacteria
basis	bases
child	children
corpus	corpora/corpuses
crisis	crises
criterion	criteria
datum	data
deer	deer
diagnosis	diagnoses
ellipsis	ellipses
fish	fish
focus	foci/focuses

foot	feet
formula	formulae/formulas
fungus	fungi/funguses
genus	genera
goose	geese
hypothesis	hypotheses
index	indices
louse	lice
man	men
matrix	matrices
means	means
medium	media
mouse	mice
nucleus	nuclei
oasis	oases
ox	oxen
paralysis	paralyses
parenthesis	parentheses
phenomenon	phenomena
radius	radii
series	series
sheep	sheep
species	species
stimulus	stimuli
synthesis	syntheses
synopsis	synopses
thesis	theses
tooth	teeth
vertebra	vertebrae
vita	vitae
woman	women

English Noncount Nouns that Are Count Nouns in Other Languages

Noncount nouns are discussed in Section 2c, p. 149. Check the index for additional information on the use of noncount nouns.

anger	fun	publicity
behavior	furniture	refuse
cash	harm	research
chalk	homework	resistance
chaos	hospitality	safety
chess	leisure	scenery
conduct	moonlight	shopping
courage	music	smoking
dancing	news	sunshine
education	parking	traffic
equipment	photography	violence

Phrases Used with Nouns for Measuring and Counting

See Section 6 on p. 191 for information on the grammar and meanings of these phrases.

a few

a great deal of

a little

a lot of/lots of

a number of/numbers of

few

little

many

much

quite a few

several

a bottle of [water]

a bowl of [soup]

a box of/boxes of [computer paper]

a carful of [children]

a carton of [milk]

a cup of [soup]

a head of/heads of [lettuce]

a loaf of [bread]

a piece of/pieces of [paper]

a pound of/pounds of [nails]

a quart of [orange juice]

a roomful of [students]

a stick of [butter]

a gallon of [gas]

a tablespoon of [sugar]

a glass of [water]

a teaspoon of [salt]

a handful of [peanuts]

a tube of [toothpaste]

And many, many more. Use this space to add to the list of these phrases.

_____

_____

_____

_____

_____

_____

_____

APPENDIX K

Verbs and Indirect Objects

Check the index for references to indirect objects.

1 Verbs that can have either preposition + indirect object or can have the indirect object between the verb and the direct object: *I gave the paper to the teacher* means *I gave the teacher the paper.* These are mostly one-syllable words.

ask (of)

find (for)

give (for, to)

hand (to)

leave (to)

lend (to)

make (for)

offer (to)

order (for)

owe (to)

pay (to)

promise (to)

read (to)

reserve (for)

save (for)

send (to)

serve (to)

show (to)

teach (to)

tell (to)

throw (to)

2 Verbs that can have only preposition + indirect object: *I explained the problem to the teacher.* These words usually have two or more syllables.

address (to)	mention (to)
describe (for, to)	open (for)
explain (for, to)	say (to)

3 Verbs that cannot have preposition + indirect object: *The book cost me $49.95.*

bill	refuse
charge	wish
cost	

APPENDIX L

Stative Verbs

Stative verbs are discussed in Section 9c on p. 60.

appear	have ("ownership")	recognize
appreciate	hear	remember
believe	imagine	see
belong	know	seem
contain	like	smell
cost	look	suppose
desire	love	taste
dislike	mean	think
doubt	measure	understand
entail	need	want
equal	own	weigh
feel	prefer	wonder
hate		

References/ Acknowledgments

We wish to acknowledge the following authors and publishers whose material appears in this book:

Altner, H. "The Chemical Sense." In *Grzimek's Encyclopedia of Ethology*, pp. 98–106. New York: Van Nostrand Reinhold, 1977.

Arakaki, Emily A. "A Study of the U.S. Competitive Position in Biotechnology." In *Biotechnology*, 39–217. U.S. Department of Commerce, International Trade Administration, July 1984.

Asimov, Isaac. *The Gods Themselves.* Garden City, N.Y.: Doubleday, 1972.

Bradley, Omar. *In the Military Review*, September 1951, quoted in *Familiar Quotations: A Collection of Passages, Phrases and Proverbs Traced to Their Sources in Ancient and Modern Literature*, edited by Emily Morison Beck, p. 815. Boston: Little, Brown, 1980.

Bronfenbrenner, Martin, Werner Sichel, and Wayland Gardner. *Economics.* 2nd ed. Boston: Houghton, Mifflin, 1987. Used by permission of the publisher.

Buchholtz, Fredric. *Home Delivered Meals for Older Americans: Final Report and Guidelines.* St. Petersburg, Fla: The Neighborly Center, Inc., September 1971. Used by permission of the author.

Eisenhower, Dwight D. From *Infantry School Quarterly*, April 1953, quoted in *Familiar Quotations: A Collection of Passages, Phrases and Proverbs Traced to Their Sources in Ancient and Modern Literature*, edited by Emily Morison Beck, p. 815. Boston: Little, Brown, 1980.

The Encyclopedia Americana, international ed., s.v. "Dick Button," "William Byrd," "Thomas Jefferson."

Kuntzlemand, Charles, and the editors of *Consumers Guide. Complete Book of Walking*. New York: Simon and Schuster, 1979, p. 3.

McGraw-Hill Encyclopedia of Science and Technology, 6th ed., s.v. "Glands," "Harbor," "Refrigeration," "Regeneration."

The Merriam-Webster Dictionary. New York: Pocket Books, 1974.

Reisler, Mark. "Colleges Need Aggressive, Inspiring Leadership If They Are to Achieve Genuine Integration." *Chronicle of Higher Education*. January 20, 1988, p. A52. Copyright 1988. *The Chronicle of Higher Education*. Used by permission of the author and publisher.

Serway, Raymond A. and Jerry S. Faughn. "Introduction to Classical Mechanics," *College Physics*. Philadelphia: Saunders, 1985. Copyright © 1984 by Raymond A. Serway. Used by permission of Saunders College Publishing, a division of Holt, Rinehart and Winston, Inc.

"The Solar System." *The New Encyclopaedia Britannica*. Chicago: Encyclopaedia Britannica, 1986. Vol. 27. Used by permission of the publisher.

Stokes, William Lee, Sheldon Judson, and M. Dane Picard. *Introduction to Geology: Physical and Historical*. 2nd ed. Englewood Cliffs, N.J.: Prentice-Hall, 1978. Used by permission of the publisher.

Toffler, Alvin. *Future Shock*. New York: Random House, 1970.

Special thanks are due to the usually anonymous writers who prepared the materials published in the following U.S. government documents. While these materials are not copyrighted, we want to acknowledge the contribution of these writers of passages of expository prose appearing in *The Handbook*. Where the name of the writer was available, it is listed below; otherwise, no writer was named in the publication. Unless a different publisher is cited, the following were published by the U.S. Government Printing Office, Washington, D.C.

Americans on the Move. Federal Highway Administration, U.S. Department of Transportation, 1984.

A Basic Guide to Exporting. Bureau of International Commerce, Domestic and International Business Administration, U.S. Department of Commerce, 1976.

Bianchi, Suzanne M. *Wives Who Earn More Than Their Husbands.* Bureau of the Census, U.S. Department of Commerce, 1983.

Bianchi, Suzanne M. and Daphne Spain. *American Women: Three Decades of Change.* Bureau of the Census, U.S. Department of Commerce, 1983.

Bicycling for Everyone. U.S. Department of Transportation, 1974.

Biotechnology. High Technology Industries: Profiles and Outlooks. International Trade Administration, U.S. Department of Commerce, 1984.

Charting the Nation's Health: Trends Since 1960. Public Health Service, National Center for Health Statistics, U.S. Department of Health and Human Services, 1985.

Communities of Tomorrow. U.S. Department of Agriculture, undated.

Dewson, James H., III. "Toward an Animal Model of Auditory Cognitive Function." *The Neurological Bases of Language Disorders in Children: Methods and Directions for Research.* A symposium held at the National Institutes of Health, January 16–17, 1978. Eds. Christy L. Ludlow and Mary Ellen Doran-Quine. U.S. Department of Health, Education, and Welfare, 1979, pp. 19–28.

Disaster Medical Assistance Team Organization Guide. Department of Health and Human Services, Federal Emergency Management Agency, Veterans' Administration, U.S. Department of Defense, 1986.

Drake, Larry. "The Outlook for Computer Professions: 1985 Rewrites the Program." *Occupational Outlook Quarterly.* Ed. Melvin Fountain. Bureau of Labor Statistics, U.S. Department of Labor. Winter 1986, pp. 2–11.

Drug Enforcement Administration: Physical Fitness Handbook. Prepared by the Institute for Aerobics Research for the U.S. Drug Enforcement Administration, undated.

Eimas, Peter D. "On the Processing of Speech: Some Implications for Language Development," *The Neurological Bases of Language Disorders in Children: Methods and Directions for Research.* NINCDS Monograph Number 22. Washington, D.C.: U.S. Department of Health, Education, and Welfare, August 1979.

Eureka! A Celebration of American Innovation. U.S. Small Business Administration, 1982.

First Aid Book. Mine Safety and Health Administration, U.S. Department of Labor, 1980.

Focus on Clean Water: An Action Program for Community Organizations. Public Health Service, U.S. Department of Health, Education, and Welfare, 1964.

How to Write a Wrong: Complain Effectively and Get Results. American Association of Retired Persons with the U.S. Federal Trade Commission, undated.

The Human Collision—How Injuries Occur . . . How Seat Belts Prevent Them. U.S. Department of Transportation reprint of a research report originally published by the government of Canada, 1976.

Indian Tribes: A Continuing Quest for Survival. A Report of the United States Commission on Civil Rights. U.S. Commission on Civil Rights, 1961.

International Cooperation: The Contribution of the Welfare Administration. U.S. Department of Health, Education, and Welfare, undated.

Kay, Evelyn R. *Occupational Education: Enrollments and Programs in Noncollegiate Postsecondary Schools.* National Center for Education Statistics, U.S. Department of Health, Education, and Welfare, 1976.

Larson, Alice. "Last and Still Least: Migrant and Seasonal Farmworkers in U.S. Agriculture." *Perspectives on the Structure of American Agriculture. Volume I: The View from the Farm.* Ed. Kenneth M. Coughlin. Prepared by Rural America with a grant from the Community Services Administration, as part of a U.S. Department of Agriculture inquiry into the "Structure of American Agriculture." 1980, pp. 21–33.

Let's End Isolation. U.S. Department of Health, Education, and Welfare, 1971.

Long, Larry H. and Donald C. Dahmann. *The City-Suburb Income Gap: Is It Being Narrowed by a Back-to-the-City Movement?* Bureau of the Census, U.S. Department of Commerce, 1980.

Meeting America's Transportation Needs. U.S. Department of Transportation, 1979.

"Mutagens in Cooked Food." *E & TR: Energy and Technology Review.* Lawrence Livermore National Laboratory. Springfield, Va.: U.S. Department of Commerce, January 1986, pp. 1–15.

National Survey of Stroke. U.S. Department of Health, Education, and Welfare, 1980.

The Neurological Bases of Language Disorders in Children: Methods and Directions for Research. A symposium held at the National Institutes of Health, January 16–17, 1978. Eds. Christy L. Ludlow and Mary Ellen Doran-Quine. U.S. Department of Health, Education, and Welfare, 1979.

"Optical Coatings by the Sol-Gel Process." *E & TR: Energy and Technology Review.* Lawrence Livermore National Laboratory. Springfield, Va.: U.S. Department of Commerce, October 1985, pp. 8–14.

Planetary Exploration Through Year 2000: An Augmented Program. Part Two of a report by the Solar System Exploration Committee of the NASA Advisory Council. U.S. National Aeronautics and Space Administration, 1986.

Protect Someone You Love from Burns. Project Burn Prevention, U.S. Consumer Product Safety Commission, undated.

"Rhea Melov." *Speaking Out: Personal and Professional Views on Library Service for Blind and Physically Handicapped Individuals.* Ed. Leslie Eldridge. National Library Service for the Blind and Physically Handicapped. Washington, D.C.: The U.S. Library of Congress, 1982, pp. 54–56.

Stroke: Hope Through Research. Public Health Service, National Institutes of Health. U.S. Department of Health and Human Services, 1983.

Stuttering: Hope Through Research. Public Health Service, National Institutes of Health, U.S. Department of Health and Human Services, 1981.

Summary of State Occupational Safety and Health Legislation. U.S. Department of Labor, 1968.

Transportation Noise and Its Control. U.S. Department of Transportation, 1972.

Travel Barriers. U.S. Department of Transportation, 1970.

Verzariu, Pompiliu. *International Countertrade: A Guide for Managers and Executives.* International Trade Administration, U.S. Department of Commerce, 1984.

Young, Billie Jean. "Naheola, Alabama: A Remembrance of a Black Farming Community," *Perspectives on the Structure of American Agriculture. Volume I: The View from the Farm.* Ed. Kenneth M. Coughlin. Prepared by Rural America with a grant from the Community Services Administration, as part of a U.S. Department of Agriculture inquiry into the "Structure of American Agriculture." 1980, pp. 13–16.

Index

Perfect verb form (*continued*)
present perfect verb form, 25, 43, 53–59, 66, 76, 104, 123. *See also* Verb
editing for, 26–27, 29–30
for vs. *since* with, 54, 260
Period, 337, 338, 339, 341, 342, 343, 345, 347, 352, 353. *See also* Punctuation
Periphrastic modal, 52–53. *See also* Modal verb auxiliary; Verb
Personal editing list, 246, 278, 300, 307, 355. *See also* Editing
Personal pronoun, 8, 92, 157, 161, 186, 201, 202, 203, 205, 209, 224. *See also* Pronoun
Phrasal verb, 99–102, 371–374. *See also* Verb
Plural noun, 91–93, 151–153, 178, 181, 186, 195, 348, 349. *See also* Irregular noun; Noun
nouns that have only plural form, 153
spelling, 151–153
Possessive, 157, 161, 166–170, 185–186, 201, 203, 224, 282, 301, 304, 347–349.
apostrophe for punctuation, 347–348
its vs. *it's*, 349
of vs. the possessive noun, 166–167
possessive nouns and pronouns as determiners, 157, 161
possessive nouns and pronouns as subjects for gerunds, 224
possessive nouns and pronouns in comparison sentences, 282
possessive nouns and pronouns with names of

parts of the body, 185–186
possessive pronoun, 8, 157, 201, 203, 282
restrictive relative clauses with possessive nouns, 301
whose, 301, 304
Preposition, 2, 7, 8, 9, 15, 91, 99, 101, 156, 162, 167–168, 171–172, 174, 203, 215, 218–219, 224, 252–265, 277, 301, 303, 309, 351, 357, 364–365, 380–381
adjectives followed by, 357, 364–365
at end of sentence, 203
capitalization in titles, 351
deletion of, 256
editing for, 260
frequently used together, 255
indirect objects and, 257–258
meaning
relationships, 254–255
space and time, 253–254
objects of, 156, 171, 204
gerunds as, 215, 219
relative clauses in objects of, 301, 303
in phrasal verbs, 101, 380–381
problems with, 259–260
synonyms, 256–257
to as preposition, 218, 219
Prepositional phrase, 73, 93, 104, 240, 165–166, 252–265
as adverb, 240
by phrase in passive sentences, 104
causing subject-verb agreement problems, 93
as complement of *be*, 73
noun phrases modified by prepositional phrases, 165–166

Present participle, 73, 214, 226, 230, 234. *See also* Participle
Present perfect, 25, 26–27, 29–30, 43, 53–59, 66, 76, 104, 123, 260
Present progressive, 26, 27, 35, 39, 40, 54
Present tense, 21, 23–29, 35–42, 54, 57, 59, 60–66, 73, 76, 88–89, 95–99, 122–123, 129, 149, 247, 248, 249, 275, 299
in conditional and hypothetical sentences, 122, 123, 129
editing for, 24–29
in future time clauses, 35–39, 299
influence on subject-verb agreement, 21
passive form, 104
problems with term *present tense*, 23
sequence of tense, 76
stative verbs, 60–61
subject-verb agreement, 88–89, 95–99
vs. present progressive verb form, 61–65
Problems of advanced ESL students, 2–3, 22–24, 43, 54, 61, 73, 88, 100, 108, 150, 164, 177, 201, 202, 205, 215, 230, 257, 259, 260, 266, 268, 274, 276, 298, 299, 339, 341, 349
with adverbial clauses, 298
with *be*, 73
with embedded questions, 276
with fragments, 299, 341
with indirect objects, 257
with infinitives, gerunds, and participles, 215
with negation, 266
with negative words that do not look negative, 268

Summarizing, 319, 324, 330, 331, 333. *See also* Paraphrasing

Tense, 8, 21, 23–29, 35–39, 42–43, 52, 54–55, 57, 59–67, 73, 76, 78–89, 94–99, 104, 116, 122–123, 126–131, 248, 275, 299. *See also* Future time
 defined, 24
 past tense verb form, 24–29, 42–43, 52, 54–55, 57, 59, 66–67, 73, 76, 78–84, 85–87, 88, 94, 104, 116, 122, 126–131, 248, 275
 conditional and hypothetical meanings, 122, 126–131
 editing for, 24–29, 57
 passive form, 104
 sequence of tense in indirect speech and quotations, 76, 78
 subjunctive, 116
 used to, 52
 vs. present perfect verb form, 54–55
 present tense verb form, 21, 23–29, 35–39, 42, 54, 57, 59–65, 66, 73, 76, 88–89, 95–99, 104, 122–123, 129, 149, 247, 248, 249, 275, 299
 in conditional and hypothetical sentences, 122, 123, 129
 editing for, 24–29
 in future time clauses, 35–39, 299
 passive form, 104
 problems with term *present tense*, 23
 sequence of tense, 76
 stative verbs, 60–61
 subject-verb agreement, 21, 88–89, 95–99

vs. present progressive verb form, 61–65
Terminology of grammar, 7–8, 23
There is vs. *there are* as nonreferential subject, 204–205
To as preposition, 218, 219
Too with infinitives, 221–222. *See also* Infinitive
Two-word verb. *See* Phrasal verb

Underlining, 338, 346. *See also* Punctuation

Verb, 1–3, 8, 21–115, 123, 126–128, 149, 154, 203, 205, 215, 357, 359–363, 371–374, 382
 be, 72–74
 editing for, 24–34
 forms, 23–24
 future time choices, 34–39
 in quotations, 75–79
 sequence of tense, 75–79
 shall in academic writing, 47–49
 spelling, 85, 87, 215
 subject-verb agreement, 22, 40, 52, 73, 88–99, 126, 142, 149, 154, 203, 205
 system, 21–23
 tense. *See* Tense
 types of
  continuous. *See* Progressive
  irregular, 8, 22, 23, 24, 42, 79–85, 357, 359–363
  alphabetized list, 359–363
 classes based on pronunciation and form, 79–85
 modal, 22, 26, 28, 35, 43–53, 65–72, 104, 105, 107–108, 115, 123, 126, 127
 passive, 103–115, 141, 142, 254, 257, 258

past perfect, 25, 26–27, 28, 29–30, 43, 53, 54, 55, 57, 66, 105, 127–128, 226, 260. *See also* Perfect verb form
past progressive, 28. *See also* Progressive verb form
phrasal, 99–102, 371–374
present perfect, 25, 26–27, 29–30, 43, 53–59, 66, 76, 104, 123, 160. *See also* Perfect verb form
present perfect vs. simple present tense, 61–65
present progressive, 26, 27, 35, 39, 40, 54. *See also* Progressive verb form
regular, 8, 22, 23, 24, 42, 85. *See also* Irregular verb; Past tense
simple past tense vs. present perfect verb form, 54–59
stative, 26, 27, 45, 60–62, 382
two-word verb. *See* Phrasal verb

Were in hypothetical sentences, 126. *See also* Hypothetical; Subjunctive
Whether vs. *if* in embedded questions, 277, 297
Who and *whom*, 203–204, 301
Whose, 301, 304
Word choice problems, 246, 252, 364, 371
Word form problems, 8, 23, 64, 201, 214, 240, 246, 285, 366, 368, 369, 370
Word order problems, 1–7, 128, 157, 240, 246, 248, 250, 268, 274–275, 276